PHILOSOPHY, SCIENCE AND IDEOLOGY IN POLITICAL THOUGHT

Philosophy, Science and Ideology in Political Thought

David Morrice
Principal Lecturer in Politics
Staffordshire University

First published in Great Britain 1996 by
MACMILLAN PRESS LTD
Houndmills, Basingstoke, Hampshire RG21 6XS
and London
Companies and representatives
throughout the world

A catalogue record for this book is available
from the British Library.

ISBN 0-333-67424-3

First published in the United States of America 1996 by
ST. MARTIN'S PRESS, INC.,
Scholarly and Reference Division,
175 Fifth Avenue,
New York, N.Y. 10010

ISBN 0-312-16348-7

Library of Congress Cataloging-in-Publication Data
Morrice, David, 1951–
Philosophy, science, and ideology in political thought / David
Morrice.
p. cm.
Includes bibliographical references (p.) and index.
ISBN 0-312-16348-7 (cloth)
1. Political science—Philosophy. 2. Ideology. I. Title.
JA71.M67 1996
320'.01—dc20 96-26117
CIP

---

10 9 8 7 6 5 4 3 2 1
05 04 03 02 01 00 99 98 97 96

Printed in Great Britain by
The Ipswich Book Company Ltd
Ipswich, Suffolk

To the memory of my mother

Contents

Preface

This book is concerned with the nature and relationship of philosophy, science and ideology as modes of political thought. It is now common for all political thought to be seen as unavoidably ideological, or, at least, for political philosophy to be seen as mere political ideology. Political ideology is commonly seen as thought which is partisan rather than objective; action-related rather than reflective; dogmatic rather than self-reflective; and distorted rather than truthful. Political philosophy, precisely because it is normative, is thought to be ideological. Political science, if it is value-free, and so avoids the sources of distortion, and if it concerns itself only with explanations based on evidence of political behaviour, may, for some, be non-ideological or even the corrective of ideology. For others, even science, as human thought, may be ideological. Against such views I present an unfashionable, but not irrelevant or outdated, argument which distinguishes normative political philosophy as the rational antidote of political ideology, and sees political philosophy and political science as complementary disciplines. It is the task of political philosophy to search for the truth of the objective normative reality which acts as the foundation of politics. In this way political philosophy can do what political ideology fails to do, that is, distinguish proper from improper values. Normative political philosophy and empirical political science may be distinguished only in so far as this represents a convenient division of labour in the objective analysis of politics. However, in so far as modern political science presents itself as value-free, normative political philosophy is distinguished from, and critical of it.

The nature and relationship of philosophy, science and ideology as modes of political thought are not just academic issues, of theoretical interest only. They are practical issues, of political significance, concerned with, among other things, the justification and evaluation of political principles and practice. If all thought is ideological, there is no possibility of objective assessment of ideas and policies, and so no objective basis for political action. Only if there can be a non-ideological political philosophy, which can distinguish proper and improper political values, can there be both a proper study of, and a proper foundation for, politics.

This book is rather polemical in style. Political thought exists as the work of individual thinkers, and in order to move towards the truth it is necessary to engage in debate with those important and influential thinkers who may be in error. Thus I offer exposition of various writers together with criticism and original argument.

The organisation of the book, and the presentation of the argument is as follows. Chapter 1 introduces the nature and relationship of political philosophy, political science and political ideology by considering a number of important arguments about political thought in the latter half of the twentieth century. In the 1950s and 1960s, under the influence of historicism, positivism and linguistic analysis, many political theorists came to accept that normative political philosophy is exposed as being without rational justification and so intellectually impossible; that all normative political thought is ideological; that political philosophy, in so far as it persists, is reduced to an analysis of political concepts and arguments; and that science is the only proper basis for a substantive study of politics. Thus are distinguished empirical, explanatory political science; normative political ideology; and analytic political philosophy. Concurrent with this, the so-called behavioural revolution in political science proclaims the application of scientific methods in the study of politics, and the end-of-ideology theorists claim that normative political thought is redundant in the economically developed and politically stable Western liberal democracies. Thus, normative political philosophy is eclipsed by science in the academic world and by consensus in the political world. Despite the acknowledged revival of normative political philosophy in the 1970s, there remains the suspicion that the discipline entails ideological assumptions and arguments. Thus, there remains the problem of ideology, identified initially as normative thought which lacks objective foundation and rational justification; which distorts the appearance of reality; which rests on unquestioned and unprovable assumptions; which is subjective or relative to interests of particular social groups; and which lacks universal applicability.

In order to substantiate what I take to be the problem of ideology I consider, in Chapters 2 and 3, a range of conceptions of ideology, both Marxist and non-Marxist. Chapter 2 notes that the first serious conception of ideology, that of Karl Marx, emerges from the breakdown of traditional notions of an objective world which can be known objectively by human reason able to transcend particular interests and historically limited categories of thought. Marx offers a negative and restrictive theory of ideology, according to which only a limited range of distorted thought is ideological. Marx seeks to show that his own scientific thought is not to be identified as, and is corrective of, ideology. I argue that Marx and twentieth-century Marxists such as Georg Lukács and Louis Althusser fail to sustain this negative and restricted conception. Chapter 3 examines the conceptions of ideology of four non-Marxists. Two of these theorists, Emile Durkheim and Vilfredo Pareto, make failed attempts to sustain negative and restrictive conceptions of ideology. The other two, Karl Mannheim and Michael Oakeshott, make no such attempt. This survey of various conceptions of ideology confirms the problems of distortion, non-rationalism and subjectivism. Above all, it is apparent that the main problem of ideology is relativism: all thought is relative to particular interests or perspectives, and no thought transcends these limits so as to grasp objective reality.

To avoid and correct the distortions of ideology, some modern students of politics adopt the methods of science. Chapter 4 examines the work of four modern, post-positivist philosophers of science which might be expected to provide a foundation for a science of politics. Karl Popper and Imre Lakatos claim to offer a method to demarcate science and ideology, but both fail to sustain their claims. Popper fails to justify the moral decision for rationality which is the defining characteristic of his scientific method. Lakatos confirms the need for decisions in science and fails to justify these by failing to demonstrate any clear measure of scientific progress. Thomas Kuhn extends the conventionalism of Popper and Lakatos and concludes that science is no more than a social convention, and that different conventions are incommensurable. Paul Feyerabend makes explicit the relativism implicit in the work of Kuhn and concludes that science is just another ideology. These four contemporary philosophers of science fail to provide the resources for a demarcation of science and ideology, and fail to provide a model for an adequate science of politics capable of dealing with human values.

Not all students of politics accept that the methods of the natural sciences are applicable in their field, and not all naturalist political scientists accept the positivist and post-positivist philosophies of science. Chapter 5 considers the the non-naturalism of Peter Winch, and the realist naturalism of Roy Bhaskar. Winch argues that the methods of the natural sciences are inappropriate for a study of human and social behaviour, which is subject not to external, objective laws of nature, but to social rules understood by human agents. In place of a scientific analysis of causes and effects, Winch proposes a philosophical analysis of agents' conceptual understanding of social rules. Winch is rightly critical of the naturalist failure to deal with the meaningfulness of human and social behaviour, but the serious problem of his own thought is its conceptual relativism, which renders all human values relative to different social contexts. Bhaskar's realism, which maintains that there exists an objective reality beyond the empirical appearances recorded by the conventions of scientists, offers some hope of dealing with the distortion and relativism of ideology. However, Bhaskar's normative analysis offers an inadequate account of objective human nature and values and so fails to deal adequately with the problem of ideology.

Much, though not all, naturalist political science seeks to be value-free, in the belief that values can be given no scientific justification and that values distort analysis and so are best avoided. Chapter 6 presents a set of arguments which show that a value-free science of politics is both impossible and undesirable. The study of politics must be normative. The distinction between political science and political philosophy represents only a convenient modern division of labour. They are complementary approaches and ideally are united as moral political science, or rational political philosophy, which I take to be one and the same. The solution to the problem of ideology is not the avoidance of values, but, rather, the adoption of a normative study of politics which can avoid relativism and can distinguish proper from improper values. Chapter 7 examines the work of some contemporary political theorists who do not deny that political theory is normative, but who fail to make an adequate distinction between normative political philosophy and political ideology, or who simply identify the two modes of thought. Quentin Skinner and Richard Ashcraft both argue for the historical and contextual understanding of political thought. The communitarian Michael Walzer argues that political philosophy is concerned only to interpret the shared beliefs of distinct communities. Richard Rorty, in common with other postmodernists, denies the possibility of, and need for, an objective philosophical foundation for politics. The main problem with all four thinkers considered here is their relativism, which renders problematic or impossible any distinction between political ideology and political philosophy.

Chapter 8 presents a set of arguments against relativism, which show that it is morally and philosophically pernicious; incoherent; unsupported by evidence or argument; and inadequate for the study of politics. To avoid the problem of relativism it is necessary to distinguish political ideology, on the one hand, from political philosophy and political science, on the other, and Chapter 9 considers both the problems and possibilities of doing this. If such a distinction is to succeed, political philosophy must be given a rational and objective foundation. I argue in Chapter 10 that this foundation is human nature, as understood in the tradition of natural law theory, and that the task of political philosophy is the articulation and justification of the political arrangements required for the flourishing of human nature. I conclude that moral realism is the only sound alternative to moral relativism.

Over the many years of the writing of this book parts of it, in various forms, have been read and commented on by friends, colleagues and students. I am grateful to them.

1 The State of Political Theory and the Problem of Ideology

INTRODUCTION

The nature and relationship of philosophy, science and ideology as modes of political thought is the subject of a number of important debates in the latter half of the twentieth century. For most of the history of political thought little or no distinction is made between political philosophy and political science, and the term political ideology does not exist (although what is now termed ideology may have existed). For at least 2500 years, from the ancient Greeks to the great thinkers of the nineteenth century, such as Marx and Mill, there has been a recognisable and recognised tradition of political philosophy. Certainly the discipline has undergone great changes in this time, but there remains a tradition of normative political thought, concerned with the standards and goals of political life, and with the justification and criticism of political behaviour and institutions. In the second half of the twentieth century, however, political philosophy has experienced dramatic changes of fortune amid great debates on the nature and status of the discipline. In the post-Second World War period political philosophy has been declared dead; dismissed as non-scientific and non-philosophic ideology; reduced to the role of underlabourer to political science; supposedly rendered redundant by political consensus; and eventually revived. The consideration, in this first chapter, of the debates on the death of political philosophy, the behavioural revolution in political science, the end of ideology, and the revival of political philosophy, provides an introduction to important modern views on the nature and relationship of political philosophy, political science and political ideology. It provides no more than an introduction, though, and for a more adequate understanding it is necessary to pursue various arguments in other chapters.

THE DEATH OF POLITICAL PHILOSOPHY DEBATE

In his introduction to the first series of collected articles, entitled *Philosophy, Politics and Society*, published in 1956, Peter Laslett offers his now infamous claim: 'For the moment, anyway, political philosophy is dead.'[1] The death of political philosophy is marked by the absence of publications in the field, and itself marks the end of a long tradition. Laslett is clear that the discipline that has died is traditional normative political philosophy, which 'is, or was, an extension of ethics'.[2] Laslett is prepared to believe, and is perhaps hopeful, that a rebirth of the discipline is possible, but any born-again political philosophy will be distinct from the earlier tradition and is likely to be a more modest affair.[3] Laslett's obituary of the discipline is one of the the most noted, though he was not alone in recognising the death, or at least serious decline of political philosophy in the 1950s. In 1953 both Alfred Cobban, a noted historian of political thought, and David Easton, in a major survey of the state of political science, wrote of 'the decline of political theory'.[4] In 1955 even Leo Strauss, one of the great champions of traditional political philosophy, was obliged to note that 'political philosophy is in a state of decay and perhaps putrefaction, if it has not vanished altogether'.[5]

Given the death of any previously living thing, one may ask whether it died of natural causes, whether it committed suicide, or whether it was killed. What, then, were the circumstances of the so-called death of political philosophy? Did it fail because of some internal contradiction or some inability to adjust to new political conditions? Did it take its own life by refusing to have itself taught and published, and if so why? Or was it murdered or eclipsed by some other intellectual movement or body of thought? Most of the obituarists of political philosophy agree that some other theoretical development adversely affected the discipline, such that normative analysis of politics became very difficult or impossible in a changed intellectual climate. Laslett has no difficulty in identifying the theoretical culprit that killed political philosophy. 'The logical positivists did it', he accuses, and he includes the linguistic analysts in his accusation.[6] Strauss also blames positivism and adds historicism to the list of defendants. Cobban does not mention positivism, but, like Strauss, holds the influence of science and history on the modern mind responsible for the decline of political theory. Easton concentrates on historicism. I consider first the influence of positivism, and later the influence of historicism, on the so-called death of political philosophy.

Logical positivism may be seen as the formulation of positivism which is most influential in the twentieth century. Positivism, a nineteenth-century term, may be located in the general empiricist tradition, which reaches back perhaps to Francis Bacon in the early seventeenth century and certainly to the mainstream British empiricist thinkers of the late seventeenth and eighteenth centuries: John Locke, George Berkeley and David Hume. Empiricism holds that all factual human knowledge is based on experience and that the truth of factual statements can be established only by the evidence of the human senses. When Auguste Comte employs the term 'positivism' in the nineteenth century he seeks to distinguish scientific knowledge, based on positive facts as given in the world and known by sense experience, from theology, which is speculation on fictitious supernatural beings, and from metaphysics, which is speculation on abstract entities. Positivism, then, holds science, which formulates empirical propositions and tests them against our evidence of the world, to be the highest form of human enquiry. Logical positivism seeks to develop such empiricism by integrating it with developments in logical theory.

Logical positivism is associated with the Vienna Circle, a group of philosophers, mathematicians and scientists working and meeting in the city in the 1920s and 1930s. Perhaps the most influential vehicle for the ideas of logical positivism in Britain and the English-speaking world is A.J. Ayer's *Language, Truth and Logic*, first published in 1936: a youthful work by someone only loosely associated with the original circle. Ayer acknowledges the Vienna Circle as the group of philosophers with whom he is in closest agreement and claims that the views he expresses are the logical outcome of the views of empiricist thinkers like Hume. Ayer says:

> Like Hume, I divide all genuine propositions into two classes: those which, in his terminology, concern 'relations of ideas', and those which concern 'matters of fact'. The

> former class comprises the *a priori* propositions of logic and pure mathematics, and these I allow to be necessary and certain only because they are analytic. That is, I maintain that the reason why these propositions cannot be confuted in experience is that they do not make any assertion about the empirical world, but simply record our determination to use symbols in a certain way. Propositions concerning empirical matters of fact, on the other hand, I hold to be hypotheses, which can be probable but never certain.[7]

Having distinguished the two forms of human knowledge, analytic *a priori* propositions and synthetic empirical propositions, Ayer then introduces the verification principle, according to which the truth of propositions is determined. As noted in the quote above, analytic *a priori* propositions are true or false not in terms of evidence but in terms of the definition and use of symbols. Such propositions are tautologies, in that they do not offer any new factual information about the world. Synthetic empirical propositions, on the other hand, are verifiable by evidence. Ayer recognises that not all the necessary evidence may be available to verify any given proposition, and so he requires of an empirical hypothesis only that possible evidence be relevant to its verification, or that the relevant evidence be available in principle, if not in practice.

According to the verification principle, the meaning of a proposition is the means of its verification. Thus, propositions are meaningful only if they are empirically verifiable or are tautologous. Any other sort of proposition is meaningless, being neither true nor false. In particular, all substantive ethical propositions, which offer ethical judgements or prescriptions and are not merely propositions about ethical terms and concepts, are meaningless because not verifiable. Ayer states:

> There cannot be such a thing as ethical science, if by ethical science one means the elaboration of a 'true' system of morals . . . [A]s ethical judgements are mere expressions of feeling, there can be no way of determining the validity of any ethical system, and indeed, no sense in asking whether any such system is true.[8]

The serious threat posed to normative political philosophy by the influence of logical positivism should now be apparent. Traditional political philosophy deals with substantive normative propositions, about the proper standards of political conduct and about the nature of the good society, which are neither tautologies nor merely empirical, and so are, according to logical positivism, meaningless. If logical positivism becomes the dominant, or a very influential, school of philosophy, then the very possibility of a normative political philosophy will be questioned or denied. When Laslett identifies logical positivism as the culprit which killed political philosophy he assumes and implies its strong, and perhaps dominant, influence over mid-twentieth-century political thought.

What becomes of philosophy in general and political philosophy in particular if the basic tenets of logical positivism are accepted? Philosophy is seen not as an empirical discipline, like the various sciences, but, rather, as an analytic one, in which the philosopher has a 'useful function to perform in analysing and clarifying the concepts which figure in the everyday, and also in the scientific use of language'.[9] Philosophy functions primarily as the philosophy of language and of science. From the influence of logical positivism develops the tradition of linguistic analysis. When applied to the study of politics such an analytic approach establishes the distinction between empirical political science, analytic political philosophy, and normative political ideology: a distinction which is influential still in contemporary political thought. Such an application is to be found in Anthony Quinton's introduction to a collection of articles on political philosophy published in 1967. In analytic fashion, Quinton distinguishes first order substantive disciplines, which provide knowledge of the real world, and the (supposedly second order) discipline of philosophy, which has 'the task of classifying and analysing the terms, statements and arguments of the substantive, first order disciplines'.[10] Applying this distinction to politics, Quinton says: 'The first task of an analytic philosophy of politics is to distinguish the two main varieties of substantive political discourse: the factual statements of political science and the evaluative affirmations of ideology.'[11] Thereafter, the task of political philosophy may be no more than the 'negative business of revealing the conceptual errors and methodological misunderstandings of those who have addressed themselves in a very general way to political issues'.[12] Normative propositions are neither scientific, because not empirically verifiable, nor philosophic, because not merely analytic. They are ideological. Political ideology is thus defined as the non-scientific and non-philosophical body of value judgements of politics. Normative political philosophy dies because it is no longer recognised as a respectable academic discipline, and where its traditional subject matter remains, as perhaps it must, given the nature of politics, it is labelled political ideology.

Quinton provides perhaps the most succinct illustration of the application of linguistic analysis in political thought, but certainly the most noted is the work of T.D. Weldon. In a book appropriately entitled *The Vocabulary of Politics*, published in 1953, and in an essay entitled 'Political Principles', published three years later in the first series of *Philosophy, Politics and Society*, Weldon presents the classic analytic distinction between primary empirical study and secondary linguistic analysis. He argues that political philosophy should confine itself to the task of the analysis and clarification of the language and concepts of political study, which is primarily empirical. As for traditional, normative political philosophy, it is all a mistake. He claims that 'when verbal confusions are tidied up most of the questions of traditional political philosophy are not unanswerable. All of them are confused formulations of purely empirical disciplines.'[13] The most fundamental mistake of traditional political philosophy is the assumption that words and concepts have real, essential meanings, which can be discovered. The enquiry of traditional political philosophy is 'doomed to sterility because words do not have meanings in the required sense at all; they simply have uses'.[14]

In addition to positivism, historicism is a further enemy of normative political philosophy. Positivism attacks political philosophy by separating facts and values and by arguing that the latter are not susceptible of scientific proof. Historicism attacks political philosophy by arguing that all human thought and practice is historically relative and so not susceptible of objective evaluation. Strauss says: 'Historicism rejects the question of the good society, that is to say, of *the* good society, because of the essentially historical character of society and of human thought.'[15]

Strauss clarifies the differences and the relationship between positivism and historicism. Historicism abandons the distinction between facts and values because it holds that all human understanding, however theoretical, involves evaluation. Historicism denies that modern science is the highest form of human knowledge, and sees it, rather, as just another historically relative form. Also, historicism does not accept the historical process as progressive or reasonable.[16] Although historicism and positivism are distinguishable, they are also closely related. Strauss claims that '[p]ositivism necessarily transforms itself into historicism'. His argument, briefly, is that modern science can attempt to justify itself against other forms of knowledge only by appealing to basic values; modern, positivist science holds that values are not objective, but subjective and historically relative; and so 'modern science comes to be viewed as one historically relative way of understanding things which is not in principle superior to alternative ways of understanding'.[17] This line of argument suggests one of Strauss's criticisms of historicism: 'if the historicist thesis is correct, we cannot escape the consequence that that thesis itself is "historical" or valid, because meaningful, for a specific historical situation only.'[18]

The historicism with which Strauss is concerned is clearly historical relativism. The term 'historicism' is sometimes used in a different way to describe the belief that human history has both a pattern and an end-point which is the fulfilment of humanity. Thus the progressive theories of G.W.F. Hegel and Karl Marx are sometimes termed historicist. Strauss suggests a clear and handy way of distinguishing these related beliefs. 'The belief in progress stands midway between the non-historical view of the philosophic tradition and historicism.'[19]

A third sense of historicism which is relevant for political philosophy refers to the collapse of the normative discipline into the study of the history of political thought. David Easton sees the decline of political theory as the eschewal of value judgements and the pursuit of an antiquarian and irrelevant historical study of the master thinkers and their arguments.

In adopting the historical approach to their subject matter, political philosophers, says Easton, 'concentrate, first, on the relations of values to the milieu in which they appear; second, on a description of the historical process through which such ideas have emerged; and third . . . on the meaning and consistency of the ideas expressed'. Easton concludes: 'They have in effect assimilated political theory into empirical and causal social science and have thereby abandoned its genuinely moral aspect.'[20]

Although concerned about the decline of normative political theory, Easton does not advocate the resurrection of a traditional philosophy of political values, for he does not think values are susceptible of rational proof. For Easton, as for Ayer the logical positivist, 'values can ultimately be reduced to emotional responses conditioned by the individual's total life experiences'.[21] Of any proposition, only that part which refers to facts can be true or false; the part referring to value is meaningless, being neither true nor false. Because the logical separation of facts and values does not guarantee their actual separation in our thought and discourse, Easton alerts us to the problem that 'in actual research our moral frame plays an influential and inextricable part in conditioning our observation and conclusions'.[22] Easton does not go so far as to recommend a value-free science of politics, for he thinks this is an impossible goal. Rather, he advocates moral clarity, whereby a researcher makes clear from the start the nature and consequences of his or her moral convictions in order that both the researcher and his or her readers are made as aware as is possible how values may affect factual evidence and analysis. Moral clarity requires a constructive approach to value theory, such that the political consequences of basic value positions are worked out. Such an approach is not possible if political theory remains within the grip of historicism. Easton never explains how or why one should strive to be clear about values which are not susceptible of any clarity on their truth or falsity. If all research is to some extent biased by non-rational values, then no amount of clarity about bias will eradicate it and make the research more rational, and no piece of research can be said to be more rational than any other.

The role of historicism in the development of theories of ideology is considered in the next chapter. A further consideration of the damage historicism does to contemporary political thought is offered in Chapter 7.

The death of political philosophy thesis can be criticised in a number of ways. Criticism of the supposedly value-free political science which the thesis supports is the subject of Chapter 6. The empirical evidence offered for the thesis can be challenged. Later in this chapter, when I consider the so-called revival of political philosophy, I will note that the supposed absence of publications in the discipline in the early and mid-twentieth century may be no more than a neglect of relevant published works. The intellectual climate which was so hostile to political philosophy did not so much end the life of the discipline as prevent a widespread recognition of its continued existence. The main problem of the historicism which underpins the death of political philosophy thesis is its relativism. A critique of relativism is offered in Chapter 8.

Criticism of the positivism which underpins the thesis is not confined to those who were always opposed to it. Some of the most damning criticism comes from within the movement as positivists come to doubt the validity of their doctrine. Few are now prepared to defend it. Ayer, when asked to identify the main defects of logical positivism, admits that 'the most important of the defects was that nearly all of it was false'.[23] In particular, Ayer recognises that the verification principle was never properly formulated so as to include and exclude just those claims to knowledge which deserve to be so treated; that the reduction of even simple statements, far less abstract scientific ones, to statements about sense data is improper; and that the analytic–synthetic distinction is problematic and cannot be maintained easily, as originally thought. However, Ayer still maintains that his 'theory of ethics was along the right lines'.[24] It was, of course, the detrimental impact of logical positivism on ethics that led to the death of political philosophy thesis, and it is in this area that the after-effects of positivism remain greatest.

Against linguistic analysis and its application in political thought by Weldon, it may be argued that the problems of traditional political philosophy are not all mistakes which can be clarified and solved as purely empirical matters. By its very nature, politics presents problems which are normative. Furthermore, when applied to political thought, linguistic analysis will have a conservative bias, which, of course, will contradict its claims to moral neutrality. Such an argument is offered by a trenchant critic of linguistic analysis, Ernest Gellner, when he says that the approach will refuse to undermine accepted habits and will concentrate on showing that the reasons underlying criticisms of accepted habits are in general mistaken.[25] Linguistic analysis will accept uncritically the prevalent and dominant language, discourse and ideology of its day.

THE BEHAVIOURAL REVOLUTION IN POLITICAL SCIENCE

The influence of positivism on political studies is evident not only in the attack on normative political philosophy but also in the impetus it gives to the demands for an authentic science of politics. The decline of political philosophy may be seen, in part, as its eclipse by empirical political science. The quest for a political science, or the application of scientific method to the study of politics, is nothing new. Indeed it is as old as the recorded study of politics and is apparent in the writings of the ancient Greeks, for whom the distinction between political science and political philosophy would have made little sense. The quest which is relevant to contemporary political thought involves the attempted application of a conception of science which is quite distinct from political philosophy. This modern quest is a wide and diverse intellectual movement. In the 1950s in the United States of America there arose behaviouralism and there occurred the so-called behavioural revolution in political science. Behaviouralism, understood as the scientific study of various aspects of human behaviour, is to be distinguished from behaviourism, a rather narrow psychological doctrine, which holds that overt human behaviour is the response to some overt stimulus, and which thus neglects consideration of covert, subjective conditions of behaviour. Evron Kirkpatrick remarks that the 'term "political behaviour" was a sort of umbrella, capacious enough to provide shelter for a heterogeneous group united by dissatisfaction with various aspects of the discipline as they saw it'.[26] Robert Dahl also argues that the behavioural approach in political science was a protest movement, and a successful one at that.[27]

To understand the nature of behaviouralism and the behavioural revolution in political science it is necessary to appreciate the perceived inadequacies of traditional political studies. A critique of a traditional mode of study may stem from two sorts of consideration. First, a traditional mode of study may fail to take account of developments in the subject matter and so become inadequate and irrelevant. Second, whether or not there are changes in the subject matter, intellectual developments elsewhere may have the effect of convincing scholars that their mode of study requires development so as to take advantage of improved methods and theories now made available. Both sorts of consideration are relevant to the behavioural revolution in political science. Dennis Kavanagh argues that the traditional political studies which the behavioural approach reacted against consisted of political theory and political institutions.[28]

I have already noted how normative political philosophy is challenged by positivism and historicism, and characterised as ideology, and how the history of political thought is dismissed as antiquarian and irrelevant. Because values are seen as ideological and likely to distort scientific enquiry, behaviouralists tend to argue for a value-free political science, or at least a separation of facts and values. They seek a scientific method which will allow them to demarcate empirical science from value-laden ideology.

The second form of traditional political studies, the study of political institutions, was felt to be too formal and legalistic: concerned almost exclusively with the operation of the formal institutions and procedures of the constitution. Omitted from such a study was the whole range of important, informal political behaviour, including, for example, voting behaviour, pressure group activity, much of the activity of political parties, the operation of elites and other powerful bodies and persons, and the significance of political culture and beliefs. In short, the very stuff of politics was perhaps neglected. Such informal political behaviour became important because of increasing popular interest and involvement in politics, and increasing involvement of government in the everyday lives of people, through the operation of the welfare state, for example. A new behavioural political science, designed to facilitate the study of all sorts of political behaviour, both formal and informal, including attitudes and actions, was required.

The traditional study of political institutions was thought to be not only formal and legalistic but also largely descriptive and historical. A new political science, if it was truly scientific, could provide not only descriptions of the world of politics, but also explanations and, perhaps, predictions. Explanation would require the formulation and testing of empirical generalisations of a law-like nature. The introduction of explanatory theory would help overcome the problem of what Easton termed 'hyperfactualism'.[29] The increasing stock of facts and information about politics could be ordered and put to explanatory use only with the help of testable theories. Such theories could also be employed to direct the collection of further, relevant evidence.

In seeking to become an authentic science, political science should, argued the behaviouralists, adopt the methods of the natural sciences, which had made obvious progress. Political science should also integrate itself with the other social sciences, borrowing from them insights, theories and methods which are common to the behavioural sciences, as they were termed. The positivist hope for a unity not only of the social or behavioural sciences, but also of the natural and social sciences was maintained by some behaviouralists. Also, political science should avail itself of the new developments in methods of gathering and analysing data. In particular, the use of the increasingly sophisticated survey method for data gathering, the use of rapidly developing computers for data storage and handling, and the use of developments in statistical techniques for measurement and data analysis were recommended.

Against this background of the criticisms of the traditional study of politics, behavioural political science may now be characterised. Political science seeks to offer explanations and perhaps predictions of political behaviour and processes of all sorts; empirical generalisations with explanatory and perhaps predictive power are formulated and tested on the basis of evidence of political behaviour; reliable techniques and methods (preferably quantitative) for data gathering and analysis are used and developed; political science seeks to integrate itself with the other social sciences, and perhaps even the natural sciences; political science seeks to be value-free, or at least to keep separate facts and values, recognising the latter to be non-rational and non-scientific.[30] Such a political science would be very much in line with first order, empirical political science advocated by those logical positivists and linguistic analysts who applied their doctrines to the study of politics. This political science would stand in sharp contrast with non-rational, non-scientific, subjective, normative political ideology. To borrow and adapt a phrase of Adam Smith, political science would be the 'antidote' to the poison of political ideology.[31]

There are various criticisms of behaviouralism in particular and the general attempt to construct a science of politics. Chapters 4 and 5 consider the inadequacy of various philosophies of science as theoretical foundations for a science of politics, which might combat political ideology. Chapter 5 considers critically the argument that it is a mistake to attempt to build a science of society and human behaviour on any model of the natural sciences. Chapter 6 offers a set of arguments against value-free political science.

A criticism which may be shared by both original supporters and opponents of behaviouralism reflects the relative lack of success of the scientific approach to the study of politics. Four decades after the fervour of the behavioural revolution, it is now widely recognised that students of politics have not produced a significant body of tested and widely accepted empirical generalisations about political behaviour. The new political science seems not to have furnished the stock of political explanations expected of it. This relative lack of success produces different reactions, of course. Some may strive to perfect their scientific techniques and methods so as to achieve greater explanatory success; some may resign themselves to a more moderate science of politics, with more limited explanations; and some will seize on evidence which confirms their view that the scientific analysis of politics was always a mistaken enterprise.

Even from within the behavioural movement there emerged doubts that explanation alone might be the appropriate goal of political science. By 1969, Easton, who had earlier done so much to establish the basic principles of the behavioural revolution, writes of the 'post-behavioural revolution' in political science. The battle-cries of the new movement are 'relevance' to the pressing political problems of the age, and 'action' directed to the solution of these problems.[32] It may not be enough for the study of politics to concentrate on explanations of behaviour. Politics, by its very nature, may demand that some attention be given to normative issues of human conduct and the good political order.

Before leaving this section I wish to note, briefly, that behaviouralism was not the only effective challenge to traditional political studies. Another, perhaps less immediately obvious and influential, challenge came from Marxism. Not just the work of Marx, but the twentieth-century reinterpretations and developments of his work by such Western Marxists as Georg Lukács, Antonio Gramsci, Herbert Marcuse and Louis Althusser, have had an impact on the study of politics. The intentions and effects of Marxism are clearly not those of behaviouralism, for the two movements are mutually opposed, but the target of traditional political studies is similar. Marxism does not question the possibility of political philosophy, for Marxism would offer itself as the legitimate discipline, but it does seek to analyse non-Marxist political thought as ideological discourse. In this, Marxism shares little if anything with logical positivism and linguistic analysis, which it tends to dismiss as bourgeois ideology. For Marxism, political institutions and processes are located in a broader socio-economic and historical context and subjected to class analysis.[33] I offer further consideration of Marxism in Chapter 2.

THE END-OF-IDEOLOGY DEBATE

At about the time when the death of political philosophy was announced and the behavioural revolution was supposedly changing political science, there occurred another, and surely related, debate about the nature of politics and political thought: the end-of-ideology debate. Claims about the end of ideology are almost as old as the concept of ideology. Certainly such claims are implicit in Marx's thought on ideology, as will be noted in Chapter 2. The end-of-ideology debate of the 1950s and 1960s was sparked by the thesis that ideology has declined or ended in the West, having been rendered redundant by the end of fundamental political conflict and the development of political consensus. The thesis involves both empirical claims and normative assumptions about the changing nature of politics and political thought. An inspiration and focus for the thesis has been identified as the conference on 'The Future of Freedom', held in Milan in September 1955, under the auspices of the Congress for Cultural Freedom.[34] Two participants at this conference, Daniel Bell and Seymour Martin Lipset, later published chapters dealing with the end of ideology, which came to be regarded as classic statements of the thesis.[35]

Lipset and Bell argue that the postwar, Western industrial societies have enjoyed significant economic, social and political development, and that significant consensus has been nurtured by this. All groups or classes in society are now able to participate fully in the ordering of society and so able to articulate their demands and interests in a political system capable of processing such inputs. Moreover, such demands can be met because economic growth allows for the development and maintenance of a welfare state which distributes goods and redistributes wealth. The democratic left is satisfied with state intervention in a mixed economy and recognises that any further increase in state power will threaten freedom rather than solve economic problems. The conservatives, who might be expected to reject the increase of state activity for the purpose of achieving social justice, acquiesce in political, economic and social arrangements which are popular and which maintain general order.[36] In short: the fundamental problems of industrial society have been solved; the traditional cleavages have been closed and conflicts resolved; and consensus has been achieved.

The consequence of political consensus is the decline of ideology. Lipset claims: 'This very triumph of the democratic social revolution in the West ends domestic politics for the intellectuals who must have ideologies . . . to motivate them to political action.'[37] The intellectuals, who are the traditional producers of ideology and leaders of public opinion, now produce no radical critiques of society nor blueprints for a better world, for these excite no passions among those who are in agreement on the value of the general arrangements of society. Bell claims that the traditional, nineteenth-century-based ideologies, which drew their force from passion and were 'the conversion of ideas into social levers', are now 'exhausted'.[38] They lose their appeal and power because of consensus; because the twentieth century has witnessed the worst excesses of the extreme ideologies of communism and fascism; and because modern philosophy can no longer sustain 'simplistic, rationalistic beliefs'.[39]

Political consensus and the end of ideology do not mean the stagnation of politics and the end of all political conflict. For Lipset, the 'democratic class struggle will continue, but it will be a fight without ideologies'.[40] Democracy, upon which most are agreed, 'requires institutions which support conflict and disagreement as well as those which sustain legitimacy and consensus'.[41] The political conflicts which remain are subsumed under a more decisive agreement on how they should be resolved.

Lipset and Bell are in agreement that although ideology has ended, or is in decline, in the West, it remains a potent and necessary force elsewhere in the world. In those parts of the world, the Third World, where the problems of industrialisation remain, where full economic and so political development is yet to be attained, and where struggles for independence, national identity and justice remain, ideologies are produced by intellectuals and political leaders and appeal to the mass of the people.[42] Moreover, ideological struggle must continue in the world community so long as there is need to defend and promote the democratic consensus established in the West.[43]

When consensus rules and ideology ends, what will political thought be like? Lipset seems to envisage no need for traditional normative political philosophy, given that there is widespread agreement on the ultimate values of politics. He says of the book, of which the chapter on the end of ideology is a personal postscript, that its major premise is that 'democracy is not only or even primarily a means through which different groups can attain their ends or seek the good society: it is the good society itself in operation'.[44] Lipset sees a 'shift away from ideology towards sociology'.[45] Given political consensus, intellectuals will turn from a critique of politics to a critique of society. Bell says that the end of ideology is not the end of utopia as well. His distinction between ideology and utopia is one between simple passion and passion fused with intelligence. People will continue to need 'some vision of their potential', but this vision must be located securely in intelligent political, economic and social analysis. Bell says: 'the ladder to the City of Heaven can no longer be a "faith ladder", but an empirical one: a utopia has to specify *where* one wants to go, *how* to get there, the costs of the enterprise, and some realisation of, and justification for the determination of *who* is to pay'.[46] The end-of-ideology thesis assumes that consensus puts an end to value conflicts; that value-laden ideology is rendered redundant; and that empirical social science can replace ideology. These assumptions coincide with the positivist assumption that normative political philosophy is no more than ideology, and the behaviouralist assumption that the study of politics comes of age by becoming an empirical, value-free science. In the words of Barbara Goodwin: 'Ideology had been, in short, superseded by consensus politically and by the scientific method academically.'[47]

The end-of-ideology thesis may provide a fair snapshot of a limited postwar political consensus in the rich industrialised countries.[48] But the thesis was attacked almost as soon as it was articulated and the passing of time has seen falsifying evidence accumulate. Arguments against the thesis are of two sorts, theoretical and empirical, although it may not be possible to distinguish pure arguments of either sort.

Theoretical arguments are concerned with the definition of ideology involved in the end-of-ideology thesis, and with the ideological nature of the thesis itself. Bell proclaims the exhaustion of traditional ideologies and recognises the continuing need for some utopian visions capable of identifying and justifying the ends of political life. One can ask, therefore, why Bell restricts the term ideology to a characterisation of only certain older political ideas and why contemporary ideas are excluded. Similarly, for Lipset the term ideology applies only to the old, open class struggle and not to the contemporary, democratic class struggle. Again, one can ask why this restrictive definition of ideology is employed and how it can be justified. According to some critics, such a restrictive definition of ideology is not justified, and when used functions ideologically, or serves to conceal ideology. C. Wright Mills argues that the end-of-ideology theorists improperly restrict the term ideology to the particular ideology of socialism; thus mistake the decline of real commitment to socialism as the decline of all ideology; and talk about only one ideology while neglecting their own ideological assumptions.[49] He concludes that 'the end-of-ideology is of course itself an ideology' and, in particular, 'an ideology of political complacency which seems the only way now for many writers to acquiesce in or to justify the *status quo*'.[50]

Alasdair MacIntyre also argues that the end-of-ideology theorists improperly restrict the term ideology, in particular to a characterisation of Marxism, and that 'the end-of-ideology thesis, far from marking the end of ideology, was itself a key expression of the ideology of the time and place where it arose'.[51] He argues that Lipset's notion of democratic consensus involves certain ideological assumptions. Consensus is necessarily bound up with interests and the representation of interests. Any consensus will necessarily include some interests and exclude others. Thus, consensus politics will entail two possible types of politics: the politics of those included in the consensus and the politics of those excluded. The former will necessarily dominate the latter. MacIntyre argues that for Lipset democracy is the politics of rational, pragmatic individuals engaged in peaceful debate on their own terms. The passionate, partisan politics of those excluded from the consensus would be termed ideological by Lipset. Lipset's own ideological assumptions are betrayed by his commitment to democracy while acknowledging the low participation and unequal distribution of power in so-called democratic societies, which deny full and equal representation of interests. MacIntyre concludes that the end-of-ideology theorists fail to recognise 'that the costs of consensus are paid by those excluded from it'.[52]

The empirical criticisms of the end-of-ideology thesis may be stated simply. The thesis is valid only in the absence of serious political conflict. The reappearance of old conflicts, or the recognition that they never went away, and the emergence of new ones, constitutes evidence against the thesis. Some social scientists deny that the 1950s was a decade of growing affluence when greater social justice was secured by the redistribution of wealth. Poverty may never have gone away, and the poor may have been excluded from the prevailing consensus.[53] Thinkers of the New Left in the 1960s expressed serious doubts that liberal democracy was the good society itself in operation. During the 1960s and 1970s many Western governments experienced problems arising from industrial relations, race relations, conditions of urban life, the Vietnam war, and education. New issues of social and political concern, such as those identified by the second wave of feminism and the ecology movement, refused to allow a complacent political consensus to develop. In the 1970s the New Right emerged to challenge the postwar consensus on the mixed economy and welfare state.

Both Lipset and Bell have recently returned to their original end-of-ideology theses, reconsidering them in the light of the criticisms offered of their work and the political events which are often taken to constitute, in part, the basis for criticism.[54] Neither finds good reason to withdraw or revise fundamentally their respective original ideas and arguments. Both are keen to clarify their positions so as to render irrelevant what they take to be seriously mistaken criticism. Although neither Lipset nor Bell is likely to recruit many new supporters, a new version of the end-of-ideology thesis has attracted much popular and critical interest. In the summer of 1989 Francis Fukuyama, at the time an official in the US State Department, published an article, proclaiming 'the end of history as such: that is, the end point of mankind's ideological evolution'.[55] Fukuyama distances himself somewhat from the earlier thesis by noting that he refers 'not to an "end of ideology" or a convergence between capitalism and socialism . . . but to an unabashed victory of economic and political liberalism'. This final triumph of liberalism is facilitated, says Fukuyama, by the 'total exhaustion of viable systematic alternatives',[56] and here there are echoes of Bell's earlier argument. Fukuyama also echoes Bell in limiting his thesis to the 'more developed states of the world', noting that 'the vast bulk of the Third World remains very much mired in history'.[57] Among the consequences of this end of history, which Fukuyama seems not to welcome with any great relish, is the end of philosophy,[58] and so presumably the end of political philosophy. In this respect the end-of-history thesis is similar to the earlier end-of-ideology thesis. Fukuyama's article received much press coverage and popular support, coming as it did just prior to the collapse of communism in East Europe and chiming as it did with hopes of a new world order. However, it too has been subject to criticism, both theoretical and empirical.[59]

THE REVIVAL OF POLITICAL PHILOSOPHY

The heyday of logical positivism and linguistic analysis is past and few now accept all the arguments once offered for the impossibility of normative political philosophy. The influence of analytic philosophy remains, and conceptual analysis is a prominent aspect of political theory, but now the rigour of the analytic style is even applied to substantive normative theory. No longer do many, if any, political scientists accept the end-of-ideology thesis and the particular argument that normative political theory is redundant and eclipsed by empirical political science. Some enthusiasm remains for the application of scientific method in the study of politics, and many political scientists still self-consciously attempt to remain value-free, but few are now prepared to argue that normative theory has no legitimate place in the study of politics. In short, political philosophy is no longer thought to be dead. In 1962, six years after he announced the death of political philosophy, Peter Laslett, in his introduction to the second series of *Philosophy, Politics and Society*, acknowledged that in addition to a great interest in the philosophy and methodology of the social sciences there was a discernible interest once more in normative political philosophy.[60] By 1967, in the introduction to the third series of *Philosophy, Politics and Society,* Laslett acknowledged there was 'little purpose in labouring the point that political philosophy in the English speaking world is alive again'.[61] The revived discipline is, Laslett believes, not quite its former self. 'There has been little reversion to the sort of *a priori* sociology and disguised prescriptivism for which the traditional theorists have so often been attacked.'[62] Such is the chastening impact of logical positivism, linguistic analysis, and the behavioural revolution in political science. Final confirmation of the revival of political philosophy is commonly taken to be marked by the publication in 1971, and the subsequent massive impact, of John Rawls's *A Theory of Justice.*[63]

I do not wish to deny the revival of interest in political philosophy, and indeed I welcome it, but the supposed revival of the discipline is, I believe, an illusion. Before there can be a revival there must be a death, and I do not believe that political philosophy did die or could ever die. I do not wish to deny the near-fatal influence of positivism and historicism on normative political philosophy. It is not difficult, however, to list a number of substantial works of political philosophy produced in the 1950s and 1960s, when it was assumed that the discipline was dead: Jacques Maritain, *Man and the State* (1951); Leo Strauss, *Natural Right and History* (1953); Eric Voegelin, *Order and History* (from 1956); Bernard Jouvenel, *Sovereignty* (1957); Hannah Arendt, *The Human Condition* (1959); Friedrich Hayek, *The Constitution of Liberty* (1960); Michael Oakeshott, *Rationalism in Politics* (1962); Herbert Marcuse, *One Dimensional Man* (1964); and some of the work of C.B. Macpherson, particularly the essays published as *Democratic Theory: Essays in Retrieval* (1973).[64] Such works tended to be ignored during the ascendancy of the death-of-political-philosophy thesis. John Rawls was publishing, without much recognition, during this period. One article, 'Justice as Fairness', which sets out some core ideas and arguments of *A Theory of Justice* was published in 1958 in *The Philosophical Review,* and republished in 1962 in the second series of *Philosophy, Politics and Society.*[65] This, above all, shows that political philosophy was alive, if not fully well and acknowledged, in the 1950s.

The successful impact of Rawls's *A Theory of Justice* may be due to a number of factors. It is a work of substantive normative political philosophy, which is most welcome after the aridity of much analytic political theory, and which displays high standards of analytical clarity and rigour. He combines in one work the approaches and materials of traditional normative political philosophy and those of more modern empirical social sciences such as economics and psychology. He offers a clear method for political philosophy, in the form of reflective equilibrium. Moreover, Rawls's political philosophy is very relevant to contemporary political concerns. The common belief that political philosophy is stimulated by, and produced in, political crises seems to gain support from the publication of *A Theory of Justice* and a number of substantial works which followed it: Robert Nozick, *Anarchy, State and Utopia* (1974); Ronald Dworkin, *Taking Rights Seriously* (1977); Bruce Ackerman, *Social Justice in the Liberal State* (1980); and Michael Walzer, *Spheres of Justice* (1983).[66] These works have a common theme of social justice, or the distribution of goods in society, which is relevant to the social problems of poverty, the welfare state, discrimination, and industrial relations. These books also deal with issues such as civil disobedience, education, rights of minorities and groups, and duties to future generations, all of which feature as political problems in the postwar world. The problems which stimulate political philosophy also stimulate the post-behavioural revolution in political science and undermine the end-of-ideology thesis.

Alan Ryan argues that in the first decade after its appearance *A Theory of Justice* 'dominated the intellectual lives of political philosophers . . . in the English speaking world' and attributes its success, in part, to the fact that it 'provides an ideology for American liberalism, an ideology of which American liberalism is badly in need'.[67] If Rawls has dominated the discipline of political philosophy, how can Ryan so easily refer to him as an ideologist of American liberalism? Ryan is not clear on this. Other critics of Rawls are more explicit. Bhikhu Parekh acknowledges that Rawls's theory of justice is one of the most impressive achievements of twentieth-century political philosophy, and that for Rawls the discipline is not confined to conceptual analysis and must address itself to substantive questions of moral and political life.[68] Yet Parekh believes that some crucial aspects of Rawls's political thought are ideological and not philosophical. According to Parekh, 'Philosophy is a self-conscious and radically self-critical form of inquiry. Non-philosophical forms of inquiry rest on, and are constituted by, several basic assumptions which they do not and cannot question.'[69] Ideology is such a non-philosophical form of inquiry, which is 'structurally biased' and 'understands man and society within the framework of a set of assumptions characteristic of a specific class, society or epoch'.[70] Parekh argues that 'Rawls's theory of justice rests . . . on liberal assumptions about the nature of man' and that Rawls's formulation of the problem of how individuals will choose principles of justice which are acceptable to all 'only makes sense within a secular, rationalist, pluralist and sceptical *Weltanschauung* characteristic of contemporary Western culture'.[71] The widespread recognition of the revival of normative political philosophy does not dispel fears and suspicions that the discipline may be, at times, little or no more than political ideology. Thus the problem of ideology continues to haunt political thought.

THE PROBLEM OF IDEOLOGY: TOWARDS A SOLUTION

The problem of ideology may be better understood after the completion of the review of various conceptions of ideology in Chapters 2 and 3. At this point, however, a fairly clear indication of the problem is available. The problem of ideology in contemporary political thought is at heart a problem of values. Even after the heyday of positivism there remains the concern that the values of human conduct are not susceptible of rational or scientific proof. Normative thought may be held to have no objective foundation; to lack rational justification; to rest on unquestioned and unprovable assumptions; to be subjective or relative to the interests and positions of particular social groups; to distort the appearances of reality; and to lack universal applicability.

Thus, normative thought may be dismissed as ideology or as being, at least, ideologically distorted. The main problem of ideology is the problem of relativism, according to which there are no absolute and objective standards, and all standards are relative to specific and incommensurable contexts.

If there is a problem of political ideology, as a mode of political thought, then it is to political philosophy and political science, as the other modes of political thought, that one must look for a solution. One attempted solution to the problem of ideology, as noted in this chapter, has been the separation of empirical science and analytic philosophy from normative ideology. This solution, I will argue in subsequent chapters, is invalid. I will argue, among other things, that the study of politics cannot be value-free and that political thought cannot avoid being normative. The proper distinction between political science and political philosophy on the one hand, and political ideology on the other, is not that between facts and values, but between proper and improper political analysis. Thus, the solution to the problem of ideology is not to avoid values, but to find a way of thinking about values that can avoid relativism. What is required is normative analysis which is objective, and not ideological. It is necessary to discover the objective foundations of values so as to determine their validity and so distinguish proper from improper values. This, I will argue, requires practical reason, capable of knowing the objective needs and goods of human nature, and of ordering this knowledge in the provision of appropriate political arrangements. It will also require political judgement, capable of applying general principles of political conduct to particular problems and situations.

2 Conceptions of Ideology: The Marxist Tradition

INTRODUCTION

Ideology is one of the key concepts of modern social and political theory, and also one of the 'most equivocal and elusive'.[1] It is a key concept not only because it is so widely used but also because it is hard to imagine how one could dispense with a concept of the nature and function of ideas in the analysis of social and political life. It is an elusive concept not only because it is defined in so many different ways but also because its many meanings and uses are themselves so often ideological. In the following two chapters I do not seek to offer anything like a comprehensive account of the variety of conceptions of ideology; this would be impossible in the space available.[2] Rather, I seek only to outline the origins of the concept and the development of the main traditions of theorising about ideology; to identify the problem of ideology; to consider possible solutions to the problem; and to provide a basis for the further examination of the relationship of ideology, science and philosophy as modes of political thought. This chapter considers the origins of the concept of ideology and its treatment by some of the main thinkers in the Marxist tradition. The next chapter considers some of the important conceptions of ideology in the non-Marxist tradition. This distinction between the Marxist and the non-Marxist traditions is convenient and not wholly arbitrary. As will be argued, the first substantial theory of ideology is provided by Karl Marx. The concept becomes increasingly important for later Marxists who, despite the many and significant differences in their approaches and formulations, work within a single tradition of dialectical materialism. The non-Marxist tradition of theorising about ideology undoubtedly shows even greater diversity than the Marxist tradition, but even in the former some common ground is apparent. Many members of the non-Marxist tradition formulate their conceptions of ideology in more or less direct opposition to the materialist, and specifically economic, analysis of Marx.

THE ORIGIN OF IDEOLOGY

Although ideology is one of the most elusive concepts in social and political thought, it has, unlike so many other concepts, an origin which can be dated and located quite precisely. It is widely recognised that the term *idéologie* was coined in late-eighteenth-century France in the context of debate about educational and wider social reform. In 1795 the Convention of the French Republic established the National Institute of Science and Arts, which was to provide a national system of higher education, in the tradition of the Enlightenment. Education, in turn, was to provide the intellectual foundation for social reform, in the revolutionary tradition. The National Institute was to teach three classes of subjects: mathematical and physical sciences; moral and political sciences; and literature and fine arts. The second class was divided into six subclasses: analysis of sensations and ideas; morals; social sciences and legislation; political economy; history; and geography.[3] Closely associated with the second class was a group of thinkers who came to be known as the *idéologues*. One of their number was Antoine Louis Claude Destutt de Tracy, who in 1796 or 1797 seems to have coined the term *idéologie* as his preferred name for the analysis or science of ideas, which was to provide the intellectual foundation for the second class. In a proposal to the National Institute Tracy says:

> I would prefer that the name 'ideology', or science of ideas, should be adopted. It is an appropriate name because it does not hint of anything doubtful or unknown; it does not bring to mind any idea of cause. Its meaning is very clear to all, if only that of the French 'idea' is considered, for everyone knows what he means by an 'idea', though few people know what it really is. This is appropriate, for 'ideology' is the literal translation of science of ideas.[4]

Tracy suggests in this quote, and makes explicit in his multi-volume *Eléments d'Idéologie* (1801–15), that the true science of ideas must not start from any presuppositions or innate ideas and must proceed only from that which can be known with certainty. Ideology is to be thoroughly empiricist, sensationalist and reductionist: all human knowledge is to be reduced to experience of the world by means of sense perception. The appropriate method is that of analysis: knowledge is to be broken down to its irreducible component parts in sensation. Thus, ideology is opposed to prejudice and metaphysics, to religion and belief based on unquestioned authority, in short to non-scientific thought. The *idéologues* assumed and argued that the correct reconstruction of society must necessarily proceed from correct ideas and thinking about society. George Lichtheim says of the *idéologues* that their 'attitude was "ideological" in the twofold sense of being concerned with ideas, and of placing the satisfaction of "ideal" aims (their own) ahead of the "material" interests on which the post-revolutionary society rested'.[5] The political significance of the science of ideas is made clear in the words of one of Tracy's fellow *idéologues*, Pierre Jean Georges Cabinis:

> Ignorance perpetuates the misery and the dependence of the poor. It establishes between them and other men relations of abasement and domination, respectively, which even the wisest of laws are impotent to make disappear. Here, then, is that which has been well understood only by the modern philosophers, who have made a true science of liberty. For they have taught us that liberty... can never be conserved or perfected except by the enlightenment of men.[6]

It is possible to be fairly precise about the origin of the term ideology. It would be a mistake, though, to assume that that which is termed ideology dates only from the late eighteenth century. Concern about the nature and function of ideas, and particularly the possible political distortion of ideas and the use of ideas for political purposes, is evident in thinkers much earlier than the *idéologues*. It is fairly common in accounts of the history of the concept of ideology to note that the *idéologues*, in seeking to found a true science of ideas, follow in the path of Francis Bacon. Bacon, writing in the early seventeenth century, attempts to prepare a new approach to human knowledge and a new scientific methodology. In his *Novum Organum* (1620), Bacon seeks to supersede Aristotle's *Organon*, replacing the latter's deductive method with an inductive one. Bacon argues that human knowledge grows not by deduction from propositions which encapsulate what is already known (or presupposed) but by induction from empirical evidence. To establish an empirical, inductive approach to knowledge, it is necessary to identify, and eradicate if possible, those factors which tend to distort human perception and thought. Bacon identifies four kinds of 'idols' which tend to militate against objective knowledge. The idols of the tribe are inherent in human nature and serve to shape and so distort perceptions and thoughts. The idols of the cave are peculiar to individuals, dependent upon individual circumstances and conditions, and productive of eccentric individual views. The idols of the marketplace arise from the social intercourse of humans and particularly from language, which is the means of social intercourse. Language sets constraints on thought, and has particularly adverse effects when imprecise. Finally, the idols of the theatre are the dogmas and principles of older traditions of thought which remain and play upon the mind, interfering with its operation.[7]

Like the *idéologues* after him, Bacon seeks to distinguish a true science of ideas from false, distorted accounts of reality. Where the *idéologues* would claim to differ from Bacon and other earlier empiricists is in their provision of what they take to be the correct analysis of ideas as the antidote to distortion and prejudice. Bacon does not present a conception of ideology, and it would only confuse the study of the concept to identify Bacon's inductive science and the *idéologues*' science of ideas. However, Bacon does raise a number of points which are relevant to the study of ideology: he distinguishes an objective science of reality from distorted consciousness; he identifies certain factors which tend to distort human consciousness; and he locates some of these factors in the social life of human beings.

If Bacon provides evidence of an early concern about the possible distortion of ideas, then Plato provides the earliest possible written evidence of a concern about the possible use of ideas for a political purpose, where use-value overrides truth-value. In Book 3 of *The Republic* Plato's Socrates considers the appropriate hierarchical structure and harmony of the good society, and how to justify this arrangement to the various ranks. He proposes an 'opportune falsehood' or 'noble lie': while all citizens are brothers, yet in their generation the members of the different ranks had metals of different value implanted in their souls. Thus the relative status of each individual is fixed by nature and ought to be recognised and maintained.[8] The noble lie serves a political function in that it provides both an explanation and justification of a particular political arrangement. When Socrates says that the noble lie should be used 'to persuade if possible the rulers themselves, but failing that the rest of the city',[9] he seems to advocate the use or imposition of a ruling ideology. Earlier in *The Republic* Plato prepares a defence of the principle of the noble lie, which is more philosophical than political. In Book 2 Socrates distinguishes a lie in the soul and a lie in words. A lie in the soul is wholly unacceptable because it involves total falsehood in the thinker and all who accept his or her word. A lie in words may be acceptable. It does not involve total falsehood, for the utterer of the lie in words, at least, knows the truth of the matter, and those to whom the lie is uttered may benefit in some way by believing it and acting upon it.[10] The noble lie about the metals in the soul is such a lie in words and is acceptable.

The *idéologues* may have invented the term ideology, but they did not discover the substance of ideology. Moreover, the term they invented very quickly came to be used in a way almost exactly opposite to their intended use. The *idéologues* see ideology as true ideas which promote beneficial social change. The first great theorist of ideology, Karl Marx, sees ideology as ideas which are, in some way, false or distorted, and which support repressive social arrangements. To understand this significant and sharp turnabout in the use of the term ideology it is necessary to pay some attention to the criticism of the *idéologues* launched by Napoleon Bonaparte in the early nineteenth century.

At first the *idéologues*, whose ideas stood in opposition to the traditional ideas of the pre-revolutionary order and to some of the material interests of their own post-revolutionary society, had the support of political leaders, and offered their support in turn. In particular, Napoleon was impressed by the *idéologues* of the National Institute, of which he became a member in 1797; and after he staged his coup in 1799 he received the support of the *idéologues* and the educated middle classes in general. However, by 1803 he had suppressed the vital second class of the National Institute. The practical statesman in power soon found the *idéologues* to be of no help and some hindrance. His critique of ideology includes the following points: ideology undermines Christianity, the traditional religion, which is one of the strongest forces for public order and peace; ideology is, paradoxically, metaphysical, rejecting the traditional laws and lessons of history which are the proper basis for social order, and substituting abstract principles which lead to disorder; and ideology is dangerously democratic, encouraging the belief that the people are the true source of authority.[11] Napoleon's denunciations of the *idéologues* read like the various conservative critiques of the ideas and thinkers that inspired the revolution. The effect of his criticisms is to give the term ideology a negative and pejorative sense. It is precisely this sense that is picked up by Marx and fashioned into the first substantial theory of ideology.

THE GENESIS OF KARL MARX'S THEORY OF IDEOLOGY

I noted in Chapter 1 that the supposed death of political philosophy in the mid-twentieth century has been attributed to the influences of positivism and historicism. When, under the influence of positivism, human reason is denied the ability to deal with both facts and values, and when, under the influence of historicism, human reason is denied the ability to transcend the intellectual categories of its specific time and place, then authentic normative political philosophy becomes difficult if not impossible. Such a debilitation of human reason can also be seen to underlie the modern concept of ideology, according to which at least some social and political thought is non-rational, non-objective and distorted. Marx's theory of ideology can be seen as the outcome of the union of influential strands of thought, of the preceding two centuries, which tend to undermine the traditional notion of human reason. Such an argument is offered, in somewhat different ways, by Bhikhu Parekh and Karl Mannheim.

Parekh argues that what he calls the 'psychological and the historicist attacks on the traditional theory of rationality created a serious intellectual crisis and generated "the problem of ideology"'.[12] The traditional theory of rationality, according to Parekh, holds that

> thinking was essentially a contemplative activity in which the human mind soared above the contingencies of human existence and comprehended its subject matter without being influenced by any extra-theoretical factors issuing from the thinker's background. Thinking, in other words, was regarded as a direct and unmediated encounter between the thinking mind and its objects of thought.[13]

Clearly such a characterisation of something termed 'the traditional view of rationality' is vulnerable to criticism. For example, I should wish to take issue with Parekh's suggestion that reason, traditionally conceived, is theoretical only. Certainly Aristotle, to whom Parekh refers, argues for both theoretical (or speculative) and practical reason, that is, for reason capable both of knowing truth and of ordering knowledge to a good end. However, the strength of Parekh's characterisation is his stress on the link of objectivity and reason.

The attack on this traditional view of reason comes from 'two related but essentially different directions'.[14] First, there is the attack based on a psychological theory of human nature, according to which reason 'was set in motion by human desires; indeed it was created by desires'. Thus, the essential task of reason 'was considered to be to serve passions, to find the best means of gratifying them'.[15] Parekh believes that such a psychological theory of human nature and challenge to traditional human reason was 'initiated by Hobbes, refined by Locke and perfected by the thinkers of the French Enlightenment'.[16] To see more clearly how such a psychological theory contributes to the modern conception of ideology it is useful to add the name of David Hume to the catalogue of attackers of traditional rationality, and to note the comments on Hume of William Oliver Martin.

> Was David Hume essentially a philosopher or an ideologist? He was a philosopher. Given the premises of Locke and Berkeley, that what we know are our ideas and that to be is to be perceived, Hume showed that the consequences land one in scepticism. And other things follow, too, such as reason being the slave of the passions. And who will disagree? This is philosophical reasoning of a rather keen sort. It does not make Hume an ideologist. Even from the standpoint of Hume's intention the most that can be said is that Hume, among others, established the philosophical foundations of ideology. But if, instead of rejecting the premises, a person accepts the conclusions of Hume, thus denying all metaphysical truth, and then uses his reason as a slave of his feelings in order to construct a world in idea to satisfy some practical purpose, then that person becomes an ideologist and not a philosopher.[17]

The second attack on traditional rationality, Parekh argues, comes from 'the historicist school of which Hegel was the great philosopher'.[18] Kant had already reduced the order of the world to the order organised by the human mind. Hegel then reduces human nature to a social creation and society to a historical product. As Parekh says, 'Hegel's philosophy implied that human thought was culturally and historically conditioned and could not transcend the categories and assumptions of the time.'[19] Thus, human reason is mediated not by individual desires and interests but by social ones, and is, moreover, historically relative.

According to Parekh, these two attacks on traditional rationality come together in Marx, 'which is why he is such a central figure in the discussion of ideology'. Parekh explains:

> Marx married liberal psychology to Hegel's historicism. Like Hegel he too divided history into several epochs, but unlike him his principle of division was not cultural but economic. Human thought for him was determined by interests as the liberals had argued; but he defined interest not in individual but in socio-historical terms. Each

> individual thought . . . in terms of the categories characteristic of his class. . . . He remained unable, Marx thought, to transcend the categories and assumptions of his class. . . . Such limited and distorted thought Marx called ideology.[20]

A similar argument is offered by Mannheim, who, although he presents perhaps the most substantial theory of ideology outside the Marxist tradition, acknowledges that the modern theory of ideology was first 'methodically developed by Marxism'.[21] Mannheim identifies three significant steps in the development of a theory of ideology, which is also the 'dissolution of an ontological dogmatism which regarded the "world" as existing independently of us, in a fixed and definitive form'.[22] First, there is the development of a 'philosophy of consciousness', which replaces the 'medieval–Christian objective and ontological unity of the world' with a unity which lies not in the world itself but derives from the organisation of experience imposed by the perceiving subject. Such a philosophy of consciousness is evident in the work of Kant. Second, there is the development of a historical account of consciousness. In the work of Hegel, in particular, the unity of the world which is attributable to the knowing subject is seen as a process of historical transformation. For Hegel, *volkgeist*, or folk spirit, represents the particular, historically differentiated elements of consciousness, which are finally integrated in World Spirit, or the Absolute Idea. Third, there is the crucial development of a social account of consciousness. When the Marxist notion of class comes to replace the Hegelian notion of folk or nation as the bearer of historically evolving consciousness it can be appreciated that 'the structure of society and its corresponding intellectual forms vary with the relations between social classes'.[23]

The arguments of Parekh and Mannheim are not the same, but there are important similarities. They agree that the problem of ideology emerges from the breakdown of traditional notions of an objective world which can be known objectively by human reason able to transcend particular interests and historically limited categories. They agree also that various strands of thought fuse in Marx to produce the first substantial theory of ideology.

MARX'S THEORY OF IDEOLOGY

As is the case with other important concepts, such as the state, class and revolution, there is no single, clear, comprehensive account of ideology on offer from Marx. It is not too difficult, however, to piece together from various sources a substantial theory of ideology. Marx first employs the term ideology in *The German Ideology* (1846; co-written with Friedrich Engels), where he provides his fullest discussion of the concept. To locate the component parts of his theory of ideology it is necessary to refer to earlier works, written at a time before he seems to have been familiar with the term, and later works, in which the term is used very little. The component parts are as follows.

1. Basic to all of Marx's thought is the materialist thesis: 'It is not the consciousness of men that determines their existence, but, on the contrary, their social existence that determines their consciousness.'[24] The material conditions of life, the activities and relationships in which humans necessarily engage in order to maintain the production of life sustaining goods, determines how and what humans think. As the material conditions of life, or economic structure of society, change, so too will the forms of human consciousness and the various superstructural formations to which they correspond.[25] Marx accepts that human thought is unable to transcend the material and historical contexts in which it is formed or determined.

The materialist thesis throws up a number of questions, some of which are dealt with by Marx and some of which are taken up by twentieth-century Marxists as they rework the thoughts of the master. To take what is perhaps the most obvious and troublesome: what exactly is the relationship between the material conditions of life and human consciousness, between the structure and superstructure? It can be assumed, I think, that Marx is not a crude or mechanical materialist. In his *Theses on Feuerbach* Marx seems to argue for a dialectical relationship between material conditions and human consciousness, and for a dialectical unity of theory and practice in revolutionary, practical–critical activity.[26] Moreover, Engels confirms that neither he nor Marx ever asserted more than that the economic factor was the ultimate determining factor in human history. It is not, says Engels, the only determining factor, for human consciousness and superstructural forms can exercise their influence on history.[27] Marx may ultimately be a reductionist, in that ultimately ideas and consciousness can be reduced to the economic factor, but there is room within Marxism for the development of a theory of the relative autonomy of ideas and ideology, as will be seen later in the consideration of the work of more recent Marxists. A further question that arises from the simple statement of the materialist thesis concerns the mechanism by means of which material conditions form or determine ideas. Marx does offer some clues here, and these will be considered as a further component part of his theory of ideology.

2. For Marx, all ideas are in some way and to some extent formed or determined by the material conditions of life, but there is an important distinction between ideas that offer a correct account of social reality, and ideas that do not and so are ideological. This is not simply a distinction between true and false ideas. Nor is it a distinction between ideas that correspond and ideas that fail to correspond to reality. All ideas correspond in some way to social reality, which is their ultimate source. The distinction Marx makes is between correct consciousness and distorted or inverted consciousness. In his early critique of the subject, Marx refers to religion as 'an inverted consciousness' of the world.[28] Religion is not simply false, for despite all its illusions it offers some indication of the truth of social reality. Marx explains that religion is the product of an 'inverted world'. A social reality that produces real human suffering produces also the expression of this suffering and religious illusions about the relief of suffering. In his later work *The German Ideology*, Marx refers to ideology in terms of inverted or 'upside down' consciousness: 'If in all ideology men and their relationships appear upside down as in a camera obscura, then this phenomenon stems just as much from their historical life process as the inversion of objects on the retina stems from the process of direct physical life.'[29]

This notion of inverted consciousness is somewhat puzzling.

At first it might seem that Marx identifies ideology with idealism (with religion being one type of idealism and so ideology). For Marx, the materialist, idealism errs in giving primacy to ideas and seeing reality only as a manifestation of these. This error literally puts things upside down. Engels often seems to identify ideology with idealism. When he refers to ideology as 'false consciousness' he means not, as so many would have it, that ideology comprises beliefs contrary to one's true interests, but that ideology blinds one to the 'real motive forces' of thought (the material conditions of life), such that one imagines 'false or illusory' ones (thought processes themselves).[30] But Marx refers also to inverted social reality. Moreover, in his later works, particularly *Capital*, wherein he is less concerned to attack only Hegelian idealism, he refers to the inversion or reversal of appearances, and so consciousness, of social reality. There is a disjunction between appearance and reality, or between the essence of things and human conceptions of them.[31] Importantly, Marx argues that reversed images or inverted consciousness are not simply errors of a faulty perceptual or conceptual mechanism, but are produced by social reality itself. He says that 'imaginary expressions arise . . . from the relations of production themselves. They are categories for the phenomenal forms of essential relations.'[32] For Marx, then, ideology is distorted consciousness, being an inverted representation of the inverted social reality which produces it. To understand this better, and to gain some appreciation of the mechanism by means of which ideology is produced, it is necessary to move on to the third part of Marx's theory of ideology.

3. Marx's explanation of the production of ideology is offered in the context of his analysis of capitalist economic relations. Capitalism involves the production of commodities for exchange. At the level of exchange, in the marketplace, the value of the commodity tends to be seen as an inherent quality of the commodity. For Marx, the value of a commodity is not inherent, but is, rather, the product of human labour. Thus, in capitalist production and exchange, qualities which are properly human and social are attributed to physical objects. This is what Marx refers to as 'the fetishism

of commodities'.[33] Capitalism contains a feature, commodity fetishism, which inverts human consciousness, and so distorts the appearances of production and exchange. Interestingly, Marx writes of commodity fetishism in terms of a 'mist through which the social character of labour appears to us to be an objective character of the products themselves', and suggests that to find a useful analogy 'we must have recourse to the mist enveloped regions of the religious world'.[34] This would seem to link his early contributions to a theory of ideology and his later economic analysis.

Ideology is inverted consciousness produced by an inverted reality. Capitalism produces ideology. But in what sense is capitalism inverted? Marx cannot mean, surely, that capitalism is literally upside down. Jorge Larrain argues that Marx must be understood as arguing that inversion is related to contradiction; that the material contradictions in capitalism give rise to ideology; and that ideology serves to conceal contradictions.[35] The basic contradiction of capitalism, for Marx, is that between the two main social classes, the bourgeoisie which owns the means of production, and the proletariat which owns nothing but its labour power, which it necessarily sells to the bourgeoisie for a wage. Marx argues that the value created by labour is always greater than the value of the wage paid. Because commodity fetishism attributes value to commodities and not labour, the essentially exploitative relationship between the bourgeoisie and the proletariat is concealed. The operation of competitive markets also serves to distort the appearance of reality. In the labour market, the bargain struck by employer and labourer appears to be both free and equal, but is in fact coerced and exploitative. As Marx puts it:

> This phenomenal form, which makes the actual relation invisible, and indeed shows the direct opposite of the relation, forms the basis of all the individual notions of both labourer and capitalist, and all mystifications of the capitalist mode of production, of all its illusions as to liberty.[36]

The capitalist mode of production is essentially contradictory and so produces, among other things, inverted or distorted consciousness. Ideology, as inverted consciousness, distorts appearances and conceals reality. This might seem to leave ideology as no more than an epistemological category, concerned only with the representation and knowledge of reality. That this is not the case is the substance of a further component part of Marx's theory of ideology.

4. For Marx ideology is a political category. Ideology is concerned not only with misrepresentation but also with power and rule. Marx argues that for those involved in capitalist production, 'their own social action takes the form of the actions of objects, which rule the producers instead of being ruled by them'.[37] As human relations and products are mistaken as relations and objects subject to physical laws, they are seen as being beyond human control and as exerting power over human life. As ideology conceals the social nature of capitalist relations and represents these as natural and unalterable, it serves a political function. Capitalist relations are exploitative and so the bourgeoisie benefits at the expense of the proletariat. As ideology conceals exploitation, presents capitalism as a fixed, natural formation, and denies that capitalism can be changed by human action, it necessarily operates to the benefit of the bourgeoisie. As ideology serves to justify capitalism it operates as a weapon of the bourgeois as it rules over the proletariat.

In a famous passage from the *The German Ideology* Marx offers a general account of the political role of ideology in class society.

> In every epoch the ideas of the ruling class are the ruling ideas, that is, the class that is the dominant material power of society is at the same time its dominant intellectual power. The class that has at its disposal the means of material production also for that reason disposes simultaneously of the means of intellectual production, so that in general it exercises its power over the ideas of those who lack the means. The dominant thoughts are furthermore nothing but the ideal expression of the dominant material relationships; they are the dominant material relationships conceived as thoughts, in other words, the expression of the social relations which make one class the dominant one, and thus the ideas of its dominance.[38]

Ideology is a political category because it represents the

interests of one class in a divided society and facilitates the dominance of this class over others. Marx argues that ideology conceals contradictions by presenting a partial view of reality as total and objective. He says:

> In effect, each new class which replaces the preceding dominant one, is obliged, even if only to achieve its aim, to represent its interests as the common interests of all members of society; that is to say, in terms of ideas, to give its thoughts the form of universality, to present them as the only rational ones, the only ones universally valid.[39]

In capitalist society members of the bourgeoisie will be involved in propagating ideology to serve class interests. But there is no indication in Marx's thought of any conspiracy theory, nor is there any need for one. Ideology is not, ultimately, the product of conscious deliberation or arbitrary fabrication, but the effect of a specific set of social relations.

5. The fifth and final part of Marx's theory of ideology concerns the means of combating and eliminating it. Given that ideology is inverted or distorted consciousness, offering a misleading account of social reality, it might seem that the solution to the problem of ideology is to be found in sound epistemology. When Marx says that 'science would be superfluous if the form of appearance of things directly coincided with their essence',[40] he could be interpreted as suggesting that objective science is the corrective of distorting ideology. To some extent this would be a correct interpretation, for Marx does seem to see his own science of historical materialism as the corrective of bourgeois ideology. However, Marx insists throughout his work that the correction of ideology is a practical and not just a theoretical matter.[41] If ideology is the product of certain material conditions of life, as Marx argues, then the correction of ideology must involve the practical correction of the circumstances that give rise to it. Theoretical criticism alone will not dissolve the material causes of ideology. According to Marx: 'The question of whether human thinking attains objective truth is not a question of theory but a practical question. It is in practice that man must prove the truth.'[42] Political ideology must be fought by political action.

Marx's theory of ideology can now be characterised as distorted consciousness, which conceals the nature of social reality that ultimately produces it, and thus serves the interests, and facilitates the domination, of the ruling class. Marx's conception of ideology is thus negative and restrictive, to use the terms of Jorge Larrain and Martin Seliger respectively. For Larrain, the negative conception of ideology refers to 'a form of false conscious or necessary deception which somehow distorts men's understanding of social reality', whereas the positive conception refers to 'the world-view' or 'the opinions, theories and attitudes formed within a class in order to defend and promote its interests'.[43] For Seliger, the restrictive conception of ideology 'confine[s] the term to specific political belief systems', whereas the inclusive conception applies the term ideology to all political belief systems.[44] Marx's conception of ideology is negative in the sense that ideology is seen as distorted consciousness or knowledge, and so can be contrasted with, and replaced by objective knowledge or science. Marx's conception is restrictive, in the twofold sense that the term ideology is restricted to distorted consciousness; and that not all false consciousness, but only that which serves a political purpose, is ideological.

All such negative and restrictive theories of ideology face a serious problem. If ideology, as distorted consciousness, is to be distinguished from objective knowledge, how is objective truth to be attained? With regard to Marx, why is his dialectical and materialist analysis of society a science, as he would have it, and not just another ideology? How can Marxism claim to avoid the relativism of ideology, wherein all that is taken to be true is related to partial class interests and social position? Nicholas Abercrombie identifies 'two main conventional solutions to this problem, both of which can be warranted from Marx's writings', and terms these 'the Doctrine of Proletarian Truth' and 'the Doctrine of Autonomous Science'.[45] Briefly, the doctrine of proletarian truth holds that the working class comes to have interests and hold views which are universal, and thus escapes distorted, partial class ideas to attain objective truth. The doctrine of autonomous science holds that although no class can avoid distorted class ideas, there is a form of knowledge, science, which can develop, autonomous of social determination. I wish to explore these two possibilities with reference to the work of two twentieth-century Western Marxists, Georg Lukács and Louis Althusser, and to offer a critical assessment of some aspects of the development of the concept of ideology in the Marxist tradition.

As a preliminary to this undertaking, I wish to note that the Marxist tradition of thinking about ideology does not sustain Marx's negative and restrictive conception. Larrain notes that soon after Marx's death the concept of ideology begins to acquire new meanings and, in particular, that there is a move away from the negative towards a more positive (or at least neutral) conception. The positive conception of ideology, Larrain argues, gains intellectual currency with the work of Lenin.[46] For Lenin, ideology is not to be seen in terms of a distorted consciousness of social reality, but, rather, in terms of the political struggle that is social reality. For Lenin there is a bourgeois ideology and a socialist ideology, and, crucially, 'there is nothing in between'.[47] All political thought is ideological, and the two class ideologies play positive roles for their adherents in the class struggle. To abandon, as Lenin does, the negative conception of ideology and the distinction between distorted consciousness and a more adequate view of things is not to dispense with the problem of making such a distinction. To adopt a positive (or neutral) and inclusive conception of ideology is to present oneself with the problem in an even more difficult form. With regard to Lenin, if all political thought is ideological, what good reason does he have for siding with the socialist ideology in preference to the bourgeois ideology? How does one avoid the relativist view that one ideology is as good as another, and the nihilist conclusion of 'a plague on both your houses'? When Lenin argues that history has given the Russian proletariat an immediate, revolutionary task, the fulfilment of which would make it the vanguard of the international working class,[48] he could be interpreted as arguing for the specially privileged role of the proletariat and for the doctrine of proletarian truth. When he argues that scientific socialism, as a revolutionary consciousness, must be brought to the proletariat 'from the outside' by the intelligentsia who develop it 'independently of the spontaneous growth of the labour movement',[49] he could be interpreted as arguing for something like the doctrine of autonomous science. Lenin is ambiguous in response to the problem of ideology.

GEORG LUKÁCS: THE DOCTRINE OF PROLETARIAN TRUTH

The doctrine of proletarian truth is most clearly illustrated by Georg Lukács in the essays that comprise his early work of Western Marxism, *History and Class Consciousness.* He seeks to show why proletarian class consciousness is epistemologically superior to bourgeois ideology. Central to Lukács's theory of ideology is his concept of reification: literally, making thing-like. Starting from Marx's concept of commodity fetishism, Lukács develops a more extensive concept of reification and attempts to show how capitalist society in general, and not just commodity production, operates so as to make human and social relations and products seem like natural, physical things. For example, Lukács argues that in the drive for more efficient production, human activity is rationalised, that is, made more uniform, regulated and measured. This has the effect of making human production seem more mechanical.[50] An aspect of this rationalisation is the increasing division of labour, whereby the work process is broken down into isolated, regulated parts, each seen as autonomous and necessary. In this way the social nature of work and production becomes more machine-like.[51] Beyond the realm of production, life in general becomes bureaucratised, as it is ordered in an increasingly standardised and regulated fashion. This has the effect of dehumanising life.[52] For Lukács, reification involves the concealment of social reality: social relations and products are seen as natural, physical things. Reification involves also alienation: human agency is lost in an objectified world. Finally, reification involves power and domination: social arrangements are taken as given and unalterable and the *status quo* is accepted uncritically, to the benefit of the ruling class.

Perhaps the crucial result of reification is the loss of the view of totality. With a reified consciousness humans cannot see the social totality for what it really is. Lukács's concept of totality illustrates the Hegelian influence on his thinking, or, at least, his interest in the Hegelian background of Marxism. In a later comment on his early work, Lukács claims that it was 'undoubtedly one of the great achievements of *History and Class Consciousness* to have reinstated the category of totality in the central position which it had occupied throughout Marx's works', from which it had been ousted by the 'scientism' of those who stressed the economic determinism of Marx. However, Lukács regrets the Hegelian distortion which influenced him 'to put the totality at the centre of the system, overriding the priority of economics'.[53] The concept of totality can be characterised as follows: the social totality is somehow greater than the sum of its parts, and the component parts can be understood only in terms of the whole; the social totality is created by human actions and relations, and these can be understood only in terms of totality; the social totality is not fixed but dynamic, and can be understood only historically and dialectically; and the totality unites all traditional dichotomies, for example fact and value, subject and object, and theory and practice. Reification entails the loss of the view of totality because it breaks down the whole to isolated parts; it presents human and social relations and products as natural things; and it takes reality as given and fixed and fails to view it historically and dialectically.

In his search for an escape from reification, and for a view of totality, Lukács dismisses modern science. Like other Western Marxists, Lukács criticises twentieth-century positivist science, and makes no claim that Marxism offers objective truth precisely because it is a science. For Lukács, modern science is empiricist and positivist, deals only with appearances and isolated facts, and thus cannot grasp the dynamic nature of totality. Because it is unhistorical and non-dialectical, science cannot grasp the dynamic nature of totality. Also, science accepts the given facts and order of things in an uncritical way, calculates from this basis, and so serves bourgeois interests. Far from being the antidote or corrective of ideology, science is, for Lukács, no more than an ideology. Science serves bourgeois interests and 'capitalist society is predisposed to harmonise with scientific method'.[54]

Lukács also dismisses bourgeois ideology or the bourgeois point of view as a possible escape from reification. Bourgeois interests are set and limited by the constraints of capitalist production, and stand in contradiction to proletarian interests. Thus, the bourgeois point of view is essentially partial and affords no grasp of reality. Moreover, the bourgeoisie has an ahistorical and non-dialectical view of reality. It assumes capitalism is the natural form of society, and fails to appreciate its own history and the possibility of post-capitalist society. The bourgeoisie passes off its own limited interests as universal. Thus, bourgeois consciousness is reified. The bourgeois ideology is false not because it is ideological, but because it is bourgeois. The structural position of the bourgeoisie limits its consciousness and determines that its ideology is false.[55]

The only escape from reification, and the only vision of totality, is afforded by the proletarian point of view. This is so, argues Lukács, because the proletariat is the only universal class whose point of view is not partial but whole and unlimited. Lukács claims the authority of Marx for this account of the specially privileged position of the proletariat. In his early *A Contribution to the Critique of Hegel's Philosophy of Right: Introduction*, Marx argues that the proletariat has 'a universal character because of its universal suffering' and that in emancipating itself from suffering it will necessarily emancipate the whole of humanity.[56] Lukács takes this to mean that the 'self-understanding of the proletariat' is 'simultaneously the objective understanding of the nature of society'.[57] The consciousness of the proletariat, as it destroys capitalism and creates a classless society, is a consciousness of the objective aims of the whole of society. The proletariat unites theory and practice in its vision and creation of totality.[58] The theory which is at once the corrective of reification and the revolutionary consciousness of the proletariat is historical materialism, or Marxism.

Lukács follows Lenin in holding that 'the Party is assigned the sublime role of the bearer of the class consciousness of the proletariat and the conscience of its historical vocation'.[59] Like Lenin, Lukács believes that the proletariat cannot by its own spontaneous devices develop a revolutionary consciousness. Such a consciousness must be brought to the proletariat from outside.[60] This, Lukács came to say, clarifies his original distinction between the actual consciousness which the proletariat may have at any time, and the consciousness which can be 'imputed' to it given its objective relationship to the whole of society.[61] The actual consciousness may be 'false consciousness' in that it may fail to offer an objective account of social reality and a true account of the objective interests of the proletariat. The imputed or ascribed consciousness is that which the proletariat would accept if they were able to understand objectively their position in the totality. Here is a concept of false consciousness, as belief in that which is opposed to one's true and objective interests, which is now fairly common but was never fully articulated by Marx.[62]

According to Lukács, the revolutionary proletarian ideology, which is Marxism and which can be imputed to the proletariat and brought to it by the revolutionary party, is uniquely correct because of the specially privileged, universal point of view of the proletariat. This doctrine of proletarian truth is vulnerable to criticism. There is some now standard criticism of Lukács which holds that his theory of reification and ideology is excessively abstract, and that he fails to offer any clear account of the institutional mechanisms by means of which bourgeois ideology dominates society and the means by which this domination can be challenged.[63] Also, it can be argued that Lukács's position is, for a Marxist, strangely idealist. When Lukács writes of the proletariat that 'the rise and evolution of its knowledge and its actual rise and evolution in the course of history are just the two different sides of the same real process',[64] he seems almost Hegelian. As I have already noted, Lukács came to regret the undue influence of Hegel in his early work, but given what he wrote it is not clear how Lukács can hope to square a Hegelian notion of objective truth, which is actual in the Idea, and a Marxist notion of objective truth, which is supposedly proved in human practice. The most devastating criticism of the doctrine of proletarian truth, though, is that it may rest on no more than a circular argument. Marxism is objectively true because it is the revolutionary consciousness of the proletariat, which has a specially privileged social position as the unique universal class, whose point of view grasps totality and so objective truth. But how do we know that the proletariat has this special privilege? Well, because Marxism tells us so. Roisín McDonough notes that 'it seems that the epistemological validity of Marxism and its claim to be a science are dependent upon the existence of a politically active working class. Once this is no longer identifiable the adequacy of Marxism as a science . . . becomes inexplicable.'[65] Leszek Kolakowski goes so far as to argue that the doctrine of the epistemologically privileged position of the proletariat amounts to little more than the ideological foundation of the desired conclusion that the party, as the embodiment of proletarian consciousness, is always right.[66]

LOUIS ALTHUSSER: THE DOCTRINE OF AUTONOMOUS SCIENCE

The doctrine of proletarian truth is supposed to show that although all other points of view are partial and distorted, that of the proletariat is universal and can grasp the objective truth of social reality. The doctrine of autonomous science is supposed to show that although all other thought is socially determined and so incapable of attaining objective truth, science is free of social constraints and so can reveal the truth of social reality. Something like the doctrine of autonomous science is to be found in the work of Louis Althusser. Althusser establishes a sharp distinction between science and ideology, although in doing so he does not follow Marx in adopting a negative conception of ideology. Rather, he develops a positive conception of ideology in the context of a complex reconstruction of Marxism, which is designed to combat what he takes to be mistaken interpretations of Marx and indeed erroneous formulations by Marx himself.

A useful starting point for a consideration of Althusser's treatment of ideology and science is his reworking of the traditional structure/superstructure model of society. As I have already noted, this model is problematic, particularly with regard to the relationship of the material conditions of life and human consciousness, and of practice and theory.

Althusser seeks to stress and develop the holistic quality of the model he finds in Marx, and offers a theory of the 'social formation', which is a 'complex structured whole' comprising a number of interrelated practices: economic; political; ideological; and theoretical.[67] Althusser defines practice as 'any transformation of a determinate given raw material into a determinate product, a transformation effected by a determinate human labour, using determinate means (of "production")'.[68] In using the term practice Althusser has no wish to deny the significance of appropriate theory; he would deny the validity of the traditional theory/practice dichotomy. Economic practice is the transformation of the raw materials of nature into useful products by human labour organised within 'the framework of determinate relations of production'.[69] Political practice transforms social relations into new ones. Presumably revolution is the highest form of political practice. Ideological practice 'has the function (which defines it) of "constituting" concrete individuals as subjects' and so can be said to transform human consciousness.[70] Finally, theoretical practice works on the raw theoretical material of other practices and transforms this into scientific knowledge.[71] A fuller discussion of the nature and relationship of ideology and science, and the relationship of science to the social formation, is offered later. For the present I wish to consider the interrelationship of the various practices and the nature of the social formation and its causal structure.

Althusser remains faithful to one of the fundamental principles of Marxism: that ultimately economic production determines other aspects of society. The social formation is said to be a 'structure in dominance', wherein economic practice is 'determinant in the last instant'.[72] Yet this ultimate determination or dominance is, for Althusser, rather indefinite. He remarks that 'from the first to the last, the lonely hour of the "last instant" never comes'.[73] Althusser rejects economic determinism and refuses to locate economic practice at the base of the social formation as the sole determinant of the epiphenomenal practices of politics and ideology. Rather, the practices are interrelated in a much more complex way within the structured whole. Each practice is said to be 'relatively autonomous' of the others and the whole, being able to affect or determine the other practices and the whole, in some way.[74] Just as any one practice can affect others and the whole, so in turn it can be affected by others and the whole. The practice, when so affected, can then have further affect on other practices and the whole, and so on. The dominance of the economic practice, such as it is, consists in being able to determine, in the last instant, which particular practice is to be dominant in the social formation.[75] This complexity of the contradictory relationships between practices, each being able to determine others and the whole, and in turn being determined by them, is what Althusser refers to as 'overdetermination'. As a consequence of overdetermination, the development of the social formation and its various parts cannot be simple. Different overdeterminations at different times and in different places produce what Althusser refers to as 'uneven development'.[76]

With such a general theory Althusser feels able to combat some mistaken interpretations of Marx and some mistaken formulations by Marx himself. Clearly economic determinism is mistaken, for although economic practice is dominant in the last instant, other practices in the social formation are relatively autonomous. Equally mistaken is the very different doctrine of humanism, which holds human beings to be autonomous agents of history, capable of realising themselves by their own free actions. Individuals are not free agents and have no essential nature to realise for they are constituted by ideological practice. Empiricism is false because it involves a false distinction between knowing subject and known object, and between subjective theory and objective fact. These distinctions are impossible given the totality of the social formation and the social constitution of subjects. Historicism, the doctrine that history progresses in some fairly clear, predetermined linear fashion, is wrong for historical development is necessarily complex and uneven. Moreover, the historical relativism which is implicit in historicism, according to which truth is merely the self-consciousness of the present, is challenged by Althusser's notion of objective scientific truth. Finally, the Hegelian idealism which had an unfortunate influence on the early Marx is overcome by what Althusser refers to as the 'epistemological break' between ideology and science, achieved by theoretical practice. For a clearer account of some of these points a closer consideration of ideology and science is now required.

Within the social formation ideological practice constitutes concrete individuals as social subjects: ideology produces subjects suitably formed for their roles in society. As a starting point for his analysis of ideology Althusser notes that any social formation must reproduce the conditions of production, for without a mode of production there can be no social formation.[77] The reproduction of the conditions of production requires the reproduction of both the forces and the relations of production. The reproduction of labour power, one aspect of the productive forces, requires the reproduction of both skills and submission to the rules of established order. The reproduction of the relations of production is secured by the state exercising power through ideological practice. Ideological practice helps reproduce the conditions of production by constituting individuals as subjects with appropriate skills, in appropriate numbers, and with the appropriate attitudes to social order and its rules. Ideology 'interpellates' individuals as subjects.[78] Ideology operates through what Althusser calls 'ideological state apparatuses' (thus stressing the political function performed), the most important of which in a capitalist society is the educational system.

In his account of ideology Althusser is keen to distance himself from some traditional notions. First, for Althusser there is no end of ideology. Every society requires ideology to constitute its subjects, and this is true of communist society as it is of capitalist society.[79] Clearly, Althusser holds a positive conception of ideology and not the negative conception attributed to Marx.[80] Secondly, Althusser denies that ideology is merely false consciousness. He states: 'What is represented in ideology is . . . not the system of relations which govern the existence of individuals, but the imaginary relation of those individuals to the real relations in which they live.'[81] Ideology does not provide an objective, scientific account of social reality and the relations of individuals to it. But neither is ideology just a false consciousness of reality. Rather, ideology is what Althusser refers to as the 'lived relation' between subjects and their world.[82] Thus, the crucial significance of ideology is that it has a 'practico-social function' rather than a 'theoretical function (function as knowledge)'.[83] Precisely in this way is ideology distinguished from science. Moreover, this lived relation is 'profoundly unconscious'.[84] Thirdly, for Althusser, ideology is not just a matter of ideas and consciousness. Ideology is a practice, existing in and through material practices and institutions. Ideology has a 'material existence'.[85]

It is clear that for Althusser the relationship of science and ideology is not the simple one of opposition implicit in the negative conception of ideology. Ideology is eternal and so not to be exposed and defeated finally by science. Ideology is not just a theoretical error to be corrected by science. Yet, as I have noted, theoretical practice supposedly transforms the theoretical raw material of other practices into scientific knowledge. This must, for Althusser, be a possibility, for otherwise he, as a social subject, would not be able to free himself from his ideological subjectivity to write a scientific discourse, which is 'subjectless discourse'.[86] Without making his 'epistemological break' Marx would not have been able to free himself from the ideological influence of Hegelianism and Feuerbach to produce the science of historical materialism, which exposes the truth of social reality.[87] Without the science of historical materialism, produced by a practice outside of the proletariat, and brought to, or 'imported' into, the proletariat by the vanguard party, there could be no revolutionary overthrow of capitalism.[88] If science is to make a break from ideology, it would seem to be necessary that science is free of all social determination and outside of the social formation. Althusser would seem to confirm this when he says that science cannot be 'ranged within the category "superstructure"'.[89] This is not to say, of course, that theoretical practice is not part of the social formation. It is to say only that one can distinguish the social conditions of theoretical practice and scientific work, on the one hand, and scientific method and knowledge, on the other. Again, Althusser seems to confirm this when he says that 'theoretical practice is indeed its own criterion, and contains in itself definite protocols with which to validate the quality of its product, i.e., the criteria of the scientificity of the products of scientific practice'.[90] Here, it would seem, is the basis of a doctrine of autonomous science: a science not just relatively but perhaps fully autonomous of the social formation.

Althusser's attempt to construct something like a doctrine of autonomous science is not without severe problems and criticisms. Norman Geras argues that Althusser offers only 'the gesture of an intention but hardly a substantive theory' of theoretical practice and its relationship to other practices. Thus, when Althusser attempts to sustain his thesis on the validity and objectivity of science, he leads one 'straight into the realms of mystery'.[91] Geras's criticisms are well founded, and perhaps not at all surprising. It would indeed be a great surprise if, from a general theory of the social formation and the holistic interrelationship of all social practices, Althusser could conjure up a valid doctrine of autonomous science. His attempt to do so, according to Geras, is nothing more than a lapse into idealism, which is contradictory of his general theory. Moreover, it results in political elitism: having conjured the science of Marxism out of thin air, the party intellectuals impose it upon the working class.[92]

Althusser may have come to doubt and regret his attempt at a doctrine of autonomous science, but his 'self-criticism' serves only to create even more serious problems and invite further criticism. Althusser confesses to what he takes to be his 'theoreticist error' in representing the epistemological break as the opposition between ideology and science. In doing so, he admits, he reduced ideology to mere falsity and theoretical error, and confused its practical function.[93] Althusser now recognises that Marx's epistemological break cannot be reduced to a theoretical break with ideology in general. Marx broke specifically with the reigning bourgeois ideology and this break is not simply theoretical, but political and ideological. Althusser says that Marx 'was able to break with bourgeois ideology in its totality because he took inspiration from the basic ideas of proletarian ideology, and from the first class struggles of the proletariat in which this ideology became flesh and blood'.[94] The problem with this formulation is that it returns to the very problem which initiated this consideration of the doctrine of autonomous science: what good reason is there for anyone to side with the one ideology rather than another, to accept Marxism in preference to the bourgeois ideology? If Althusser abandons hope of autonomous science, which he cannot have, he is left with the problem of relativism, the problem of ideology.

CONCLUSION

Marx's conception of ideology may be seen as the outcome of various strands of attack on traditional notions of an objective world which can be known objectively by human reason able to transcend particular interests and historically limited categories. For Marx, ideology is thought which represents the partial material interests of only one class in society; which facilitates the rule of this class over others; and which distorts social reality. Like others who would seek to maintain a restrictive and negative conception of ideology, Marx is obliged to show how it can be demarcated from, and challenged by a more adequate mode of thought. I have considered two possible arguments from those working in the Marxist tradition, Lukács' universal proletarian truth thesis, and Althusser's autonomous science thesis, and have found both of them wanting. Thus I conclude that the laudable aim of Marx, of distinguishing science and ideology, cannot be sustained by the resources of Marxism. I conclude further that Marxism is unable to substantiate claims to know reality and to distinguish proper from improper standards and plans of human action. Marxism, then, exemplifies, and remains vulnerable to, the classic problem of ideology: relativism. Whether or not there is available an adequate demarcation of ideology and science/philosophy is the subject of further speculation in later chapters.

3 Conceptions of Ideology: The Non-Marxist Tradition

INTRODUCTION

The non-Marxist tradition of theorising about ideology is extensive and very diverse, even if it shares an opposition to the materialist and specifically economic analysis of Marxism. In my selection of some theorists from the tradition I concentrate on their treatment of the relationship of philosophy, science and ideology. Emile Durkheim starts with a standard opposition of ideology and social science, but his restrictive and negative conception is more psychological than sociological. Durkheim may not be able to sustain both a psychological and a negative conception and he moves towards a positive (or neutral) and sociological conception of ideology in his later work, while claiming that his account of the social determination of knowledge is non-Marxist. A more consistently psychological conception of ideology is presented by Vilfredo Pareto. He seems to wish to make a sharp distinction between logical science and non-logical ideology, and yet may be unable to sustain the distinction. Karl Mannheim provides perhaps the most important and influential non-Marxist theory of ideology. Like Marx, Mannheim bases his theory of ideology on the notion of the social determination of knowledge, although he rejects what he sees as the rather narrow economic analysis of Marx. Mannheim sees himself as moving beyond Marx's restrictive conception of ideology to a more radical conception, according to which not just the ideas of one class in society, but all belief, including that of Mannheim himself, is socially determined and so not objective or absolute. Mannheim advances something like an inclusive conception of ideology and yet still wishes to establish a social science that can expose the limitations of ideology. Mannheim highlights the problem of ideology, relativism, more sharply than other theorists and so is obliged to propose a more ambitious solution. This proposed solution is invalidated by his formulation of the problem. Michael Oakeshott distinguishes ideology and the knowledge that properly belongs to politics, and distinguishes also ideology, science and philosophy, but does not seek to maintain anything like a negative conception of ideology. Oakeshott argues that the knowledge belonging to politics derives from the traditional manner of political activity, but does not accept anything like the thesis of the social determination of knowledge. Despite its distinctive character, Oakeshott's political philosophy is troubled by the great problem of ideology: relativism.

EMILE DURKHEIM: SOCIAL SCIENCE AND IDEOLOGY

Emile Durkheim is often and rightly described as one of the founding fathers of modern social science in general, and sociology in particular. In his early and still influential work *The Rules of Sociological Method* Durkheim presents, among other things, an account of ideology which has enjoyed a dominant position in mainstream social science. Very much in the tradition of Bacon, whom he acknowledges, Durkheim establishes a sharp distinction between social science and ideology; between an objective account of social reality and an outlook which leaves a concealing veil between social reality and ourselves. Durkheim looks to social reality in order to map out for sociology a subject matter that is 'peculiarly its own'. This subject matter he terms 'social facts', which have the following characteristics.[1] First, social facts are about society and social behaviour, and so distinct from facts about nature and natural behaviour. For Durkheim, only some aspects of human behaviour are properly the subject matter of social science. Other aspects of human behaviour are the subject matter of psychology and biology. Secondly, social facts are external and objective. That is, social facts exist, or have a reality, not just in the subjective consciousness of the individual but in the society to which individuals belong. Social facts such as laws and customs will conform with subjective consciousness in so far as they have been received from society (or internalised) by individuals. Durkheim goes so far as to claim that 'there are ways of acting, thinking and feeling which possess the remarkable property of existing outside the consciousness of the individual'. Third, social facts are coercive in that they structure and constrain behaviour. When individuals freely conform with social facts the coercive power of the latter is unrecognised. When individuals act against social facts their behaviour is curtailed or penalised. Society provides the necessary means of control. Perhaps the clearest illustration of Durkheim's notion of social facts is to be found in his famous analysis of suicide, wherein he argues that acts of self-destruction are to be seen not simply as individual decisions, but as something affected by social conditions, particularly different forms and degrees of social solidarity. Thus, aggregate suicide rates are indicative of social facts, or external and objective social variables, which impact upon individuals.[2]

Social facts are the proper subject matter of social science, but the objective study of social reality is possible only if one overcomes the problem of ideology and moves beyond ideological analysis.[3] The problem of ideology arises from the fact that before one can have a scientific analysis of any subject matter one necessarily has certain pre-scientific conceptions of it. This is the case because in order to live in the world, and regulate one's behaviour appropriately, one must have some ideas about it even before one knows it properly. These original, pre-scientific ideas and conceptions are closer to one than is the reality to which they refer and so one naturally tends to substitute the former for the latter. Having made this substitution one then tends naturally to analyse ideas instead of the reality which lies behind them. As Durkheim puts it: 'Instead of a science which deals with realities, we carry out no more than an ideological analysis.'[4] Ideological analysis is a problem because it cannot provide objective results. Ideological concepts are 'not legitimate surrogates for things' and so analysis limited to such concepts can never approach an adequate analysis of social facts. Ideological concepts allow us to attune our behaviour to the world in which we live, but they can perform this practical function even if they are theoretically false. Thus, for Durkheim, as for others, the use value of ideology is distinct from its truth value. Because scientific analysis is stimulated by human interests and goals, and is preceded by ideological understanding, there is always the danger that human enquiry will be determined by ideological preconceptions rather than by scientific realities. This is true of the natural sciences and even more so of the social sciences whose subject matter is human behaviour. For Durkheim ideology is distorted consciousness in that it precedes scientific analysis and serves human interests which are not determined by objective enquiry. Ideology is a veil which lies between social facts and human beings, and so conceals social reality.

The solution which Durkheim offers for the problem of ideology is social science. Social science, if it follows certain methodological rules, will be able to cut through ideological preconceptions and distortion and expose social reality as the collection of social facts that it is. In that Durkheim distinguishes social science and ideology, he offers a restrictive conception of ideology. He may also be said to offer a negative conception of ideology, for although ideology permits humans to adjust to their world, thus performing a useful function, ideology also distorts reality and stands in need of correction by social science. In a purely formal sense Durkheim's restrictive and negative conception of ideology is similar to Marx's concept. The most obvious substantive difference between Marx and Durkheim is that the latter rejects the materialism of the former. For Durkheim, social facts are not physical or material facts and cannot be reduced to them.[5] Durkheim, though, may face a problem which Marx may not. Whereas Marx argues that one can eliminate ideology by eliminating the social conditions that give rise to it, Durkheim seems to locate the source of ideology in human nature, such that it cannot be eliminated. Durkheim writes of the human need for orientating, pre-scientific conceptions as if this was a basic need of human nature, and he confirms that having acquired such ideological conceptions 'we *naturally* tend to substitute them for realities'.[6] If Durkheim's ideological conceptions, like Bacon's idols of the tribe, are rooted in human nature, then it seems to be impossible to eliminate them and it is not clear how one could avoid them. Durkheim may be said to have a psychological conception of ideology. Accordingly he may not be able to sustain a negative conception of ideology. Consideration of a later work confirms that he eventually gave up on any attempt to do so.

In *The Elementary Forms of Religious Life* Durkheim does not employ the term ideology, but his subject matter is identified in his earlier *The Rules of Sociological Method* as something consisting of ideological notions.[7] For Durkheim, ideology and religion are similar in that both consist of the original and most basic human ideas and conceptions, which represent the world to human beings and allow them to relate to it. Durkheim says that 'the fundamental categories of thought . . . are of religious origin' and that the 'real function of religion . . . is to make us act, to aid us to live'.[8] One important difference between Durkheim's early concept of ideology and his later concept of religion is that whereas the former could be theoretically false, the latter cannot be. No religion is false; all religions represent reality in some way and give meaning to it.[9] Another important difference is that whereas ideology is identified as having its source in human nature, such that one can say it is a psychological phenomenon, religion has its origin in society and is clearly a sociological phenomenon. Durkheim notes that the original concepts to be seen most clearly in primitive religion are 'what the philosophers since Aristotle have called the categories of understanding'. But whereas such philosophers tend to hold such categories to be innate in the mind, Durkheim holds them to be social. He says: 'religion is something eminently social. Religious representations are collective representations which express collective realities.'[10] If humans did not share such categories and representations, social life would not be possible. Although religion is social and cannot be reduced to arbitrary or false individual choice, Durkheim is keen to distance himself from the historical materialism of thinkers like Marx. The collective consciousness of society is more than a mere epiphenomenon of the material forms of life. It arises from a 'synthesis *sui generis* of particular consciousnesses' and, once realised, its content obeys laws of its own.[11]

A further crucial difference between ideology and religion, for Durkheim, is that the latter is socially necessary and so a feature of all societies. Durkheim says:

> there is something eternal in religion which is destined to survive all particular symbols in which religious thought has successively enveloped itself. There can be no society which does not feel the need of upholding and reaffirming at regular intervals the collective sentiments and the collective ideas which make its unity and its personality.[12]

Durkheim seems to hold that whereas social science could hope to overcome and eliminate ideology, it cannot hope to do the same with religion. Social science can analyse religion but cannot remove the need for it. Science can challenge any religion's specific claims about the nature of things, but cannot deny the existence of religion as a social fact, nor perform, and so substitute for, the active, practical function of religion. In short, science and religion can stand as different forms of consciousness, but not as direct opposites.

Durkheim moves from a restrictive and negative conception of ideology in his early work, *The Rules of Sociological Method*, wherein ideology and social science are contrasted as problem and solution, to a neutral or positive conception in his later work *The Elementary Forms of Religious Life*, wherein religion, a form of ideology, and science are contrasted but recognised as being equally necessary in society. The argument that ideology and science are different forms of consciousness, that science can challenge the theoretical content of ideology but not its need to exist, and that science cannot perform the practical function of ideology, is similar to that advanced later by Althusser, as noted in the previous chapter.[13] But whereas Althusser seems to wish to exempt science from social determination in order to attain objective knowledge, Durkheim argues that science and religion 'come from one and the same source', the social categories of understanding, and that 'the value which we attribute to science depends upon the idea which we collectively form of its nature and role in life; that is as much to say that it expresses a state of public opinion'.[14] Just as Durkheim has an impoverished, purely sociological appreciation of the significance of religion, so he has a similar, inadequate appreciation of science.

VILFREDO PARETO: A PSYCHOLOGICAL CONCEPTION OF IDEOLOGY

Durkheim moves from a negative to a neutral or positive conception of ideology, and from a psychological to a sociological conception. A more consistent psychological conception of ideology, as something originating in a natural disposition rather than social conditions, is to be found in the work of Vilfredo Pareto. Pareto does not employ the term ideology in his large and not always well ordered output, but he does offer an account of how humans theorise about their behaviour and this can be seen to include a conception of ideology. Pareto's account of human behaviour displays two important influences on late-nineteenth- and early-twentieth-century thought: irrationalism, which questions the notion of a rationally ordered world which can be understood by human reason; and psychoanalytic thought, with particular reference to theories of the subconscious dimension of human behaviour.

Pareto argues that human behaviour can be distinguished as logical and non-logical, and stresses that non-logical behaviour plays a large part in social phenomena, including politics. Logical behaviour is that in which the means and the end are considered to be linked logically, both subjectively and objectively, that is, 'not only in respect to the person performing them, but also to those other people who have more extensive knowledge'.[15] In non-logical behaviour, which is not necessarily illogical, this logical link of means and end is lacking. Non-logical behaviour may have an objective end, but this will not coincide with the subjective end entertained by the actor. Pareto explains further: 'logical behaviour, for the most part at least, is the result of a process of reasoning. Non-logical behaviour originates mainly from a definite psychic state: sentiments, subconscious influences and so on.'[16]

Much human behaviour may be non-logical but humans have, Pareto claims, a 'strong tendency to attach logical developments to non-logical actions'.[17] This tendency would seem to be rooted in one of the sentiments which give rise to non-logical behaviour. That is, the tendency to give logical accounts of non-logical behaviour is itself an example of non-logical behaviour. Pareto offers some specific explanations of the tendency of intellectuals to minimalise non-logical behaviour. Theorists seeking to give explanations of human behaviour find it much easier to embody these in a theory if they assume that actions are logical. Also, theorists seeking not just to understand but to evaluate and prescribe behaviour tend to take logic as their sovereign principle, and so advocate logical action. Thus, non-logical behaviour is regarded, implicitly at least, as irrelevant or reprehensible in a well-ordered society.[18]

The means by which non-logical behaviour is passed off as logical behaviour provides the substance for what can be seen as Pareto's conception of ideology. Pareto argues that if one examines the various theories offered as logical accounts of non-logical behaviour there is another important distinction to be found: that between constant and variable elements. The constant elements correspond to, or manifest, the non-logical instincts or sentiments of humanity. These sentiments are not identical with interests, which seem to give rise to logical action.[19] The constant elements are termed residues, for they are what remains when the variable elements are removed. The variable elements of human theorising manifest the human need for logical explanation and serve the purpose of explaining, justifying and demonstrating the constant elements. They are termed derivations because they derive from the constant elements.[20] Pareto produces detailed and seemingly arbitrary classifications of residues and derivations. Included in the first class of residues is an 'urge to seek logical explanations'.[21]

Pareto's editor S.E. Finer argues that the concept of derivation 'corresponds, closely enough, with what we now conceive of as "ideologies"'. John Plamenatz, John Hallowell and Peter Winch claim more specifically that what Pareto calls derivations, Marx and Marxists call ideologies.[22] Pareto's derivations certainly have some of the defining characteristics of ideology. Derivations seek to justify non-logical behaviour by rationalising it or passing it off as rational behaviour. Thus, derivations mask and disguise behaviour and underlying reality. Also, derivations perform a valuable psychological function by giving a supposedly logical account of non-logical behaviour. Thus, they have a use-value, but, as Pareto tirelessly points out, the use-value and truth-value of theories need not coincide.[23] The experimental truth and the psychological or sociological utility of a theory may be not only different from one another, but also contradictory. There is, says Pareto, 'antagonism between conditions of *action* and those of *knowledge*'.[24] If people are to act together in society they must conform to certain rules of conduct. For the purposes of acting it matters not that the rules are true, but that they are useful in facilitating coordinated conduct. To take the time to examine their truth, and particularly to find them erroneous in some way, runs contrary to the demands of action. Thus Pareto considers most political philosophy to be mere derivations: psychologically and sociologically useful, though probably false; and serving to conceal the underlying reality of non-logical behaviour.

In line with his distinction between the use-value and truth-value of derivations, Pareto establishes a sharp distinction between derivations and social science. He identifies the task of his own social study as 'removing "logical" masks to reveal the things that are hidden beneath them'.[25] The appropriate method for the social scientist is the logico-experimental one: theorising must proceed only on the basis of experience and logical reasoning therefrom.[26] This would seem to suggest that Pareto maintains a restrictive, though not necessarily negative, conception of ideology. It is a restrictive conception because Pareto distinguishes ideology (derivations) and social science, restricting the former term to attempted rationalisation of non-logical behaviour. It may not be a negative conception, however, because for Pareto ideology performs a very useful function, regardless of its lack of veracity. The difference here between the early Durkheim and Pareto is that whereas the former is concerned to expose and eradicate the distortions of ideology, the latter accepts that distortions may be more useful than the truth.

However, other remarks by Pareto suggest that he does not hope to offer science as the objective antidote to essentially non-rational ideology. First, Pareto does not claim that his scientific method is 'better' than others, for he considers such comparisons to be meaningless. He says: 'No comparison is possible between theories which are entirely contingent and those which admit of the absolute. They are heterogeneous things, incommensurable with one another.'[27] Pareto disclaims any absoluteness for his science.[28] But, *pace* Pareto, only if one can appeal to absolute standards can one challenge and correct alternative beliefs. If, as Pareto says, science is not absolute, it is no better, nor worse, than any ideology. If science is absolute, then, on Pareto's terms, it is incommensurable with contingent derivations. Second, Pareto claims that his social study will be concerned not with the intrinsic truth of such things as religion and moral belief, but only with their existence as social facts.[29] If this is the case, Pareto is unable or unwilling to distinguish the empirical truth and psychological utility of derivations or ideology, and so his repeated assertion of the distinction is no more than a piece of non-scientific, ideological dogma. Finally, Pareto seems to admit that science may be no more than a derivation or ideology. He concedes that the 'worship of "Reason", "Truth", "Progress" and other similar entities is to be classed as non-logical behaviour'.[30] As these values are usually taken to be essential to science, is one to conclude that Pareto's social science is non-logical and ideological? If Pareto's science is not rational, truthful and progressive, of what value is it?

Although seemingly keen to employ social science to unmask derivations or ideology, so as to reveal underlying reality, Pareto seems to concede that science is not up to the task. It is appropriate that Pareto should seem to make this concession, for, as has been noted before, with reference to Bacon and Durkheim, anyone who entertains a psychological conception of ideology seems bound to concede that ideology is universal and eternal. One cannot hope to eradicate that which is supposedly rooted in human nature. But in all Pareto's psychological talk of human beings possessed of non-rational urges to provide rationalisations of their non-logical behaviour there is a telling contradiction. John Hallowell notes that it is a curious twentieth-century phenomenon that so many intellectuals should be engaged in persuading others *by reason* that humans are essentially not rational. Hallowell continues:

> That rational justification for such a view of man should be thought either necessary or possible is itself refutation of the conclusion these intellectuals seek by rational argument to persuade others to accept. That they should concede, moreover, that men do, in fact, feel some necessity for providing 'good' reasons for 'real' ones, for 'rationalising' their behaviour, says a great deal more about the rationality and ethical sensibilities of men than they intend to concede.[31]

Hallowell correctly argues that it is possible for humans to strive after rationality only if they are essentially rational. If, as Pareto claims, humans are motivated by non-rational forces, then how can anyone, including Pareto himself and all other social scientists, escape the non-rational determination of their thought? On Pareto's terms, how can science be anything other than a derivation or ideology?

KARL MANNHEIM: FROM IDEOLOGY TO THE SOCIOLOGY OF KNOWLEDGE

Karl Mannheim makes a distinction between the concepts 'ideology' and 'utopia'. Both ideological and utopian modes of thought are incongruent with reality,[32] although they are so in different ways, and can be distinguished by their differing political effects or functions. Ideology reflects the thought of a ruling group in society which is 'so intensively interest-bound to a situation' that it is 'simply no longer able to see certain facts which would undermine' its 'sense of domination'.[33] Ideological distortion obscures social reality to the ruling group and others in society and so serves to stabilise it. Whereas ideology can be termed reactionary, utopian thought can be termed reforming or revolutionary. Utopian thought reflects the distorted consciousness of 'certain oppressed groups' who are 'so strongly interested in the destruction and transformation of a given condition of society that they unwittingly see only those elements in the situation which tend to negate it'.[34]

Although Mannheim deals fairly extensively with the concept of utopia, it is his treatment of ideology that most clearly reveals the distinctiveness of his thought. Having distinguished ideology and utopia, Mannheim distinguishes two conceptions of ideology and two formulations of the second conception: that is, the particular and total conceptions of ideology, and, further, the special and general formulations of the total conception of ideology. According to both the particular and total conceptions of ideology, beliefs entertained by individuals or groups are in some way socially determined and are to be understood in terms of the social position of the individual or group. The differences between the two conceptions are threefold. First, the particular conception of ideology designates only a part of the content of the beliefs of an individual as ideological, whereas the total conception designates the entire *Weltanschauung*, including not just the content of belief but also the conceptual apparatus of an individual or group as ideological. Second, the particular conception holds that differences of belief between individuals can be resolved, at least in principle, by resort to 'common criteria of validity' and a 'common theoretical frame of reference'.[35] According to the total conception of ideology such resolution is not possible because different parties, holding different total ideologies, share no common belief system. Rather, the differing parties have 'fundamentally divergent thought systems' and 'widely differing modes of experience and interpretation'.[36] Third, the particular conception of ideology applies at an individual, psychological level, whereas the total conception applies at a historical, social level. According to the particular conception, individuals entertain (partial) ideologies which can be attributed directly to specific interests. That is, conscious lies and unconscious self-deception are distortions of reality which serve one's interests. The total conception of ideology employs a 'more formal functional analysis, without reference to motivation, confining itself to an objective description of the structural differences in minds operating in different social settings'.[37] The total conception of ideology is to be located not in any number of individual members of a social group, but in the group as a whole.

I noted, in the previous chapter, how, according to Mannheim, the concept of ideology develops by three significant steps, the third of which owes much to Marxist social analysis. It should now be clear why Mannheim states: 'It was Marxist theory which first achieved a fusion of the particular and total conceptions of ideology.'[38] Mannheim recognises the significance of the Marxist conception of ideology, but he notes the failure of Marxists to continue the development of the concept. Mannheim notes that Marxists tend to adhere to a 'highly restricted' conception of ideology: they tend to distinguish sharply between the ideological thought of their class opponents and their own non-ideological social analysis. Marxists fail, says Mannheim, to apply their analysis to themselves and so fail to see their own thought as ideological. In Mannheim's terms, when one employs the total conception of ideology, but fails to get beyond a restrictive application of it, one employs only a 'special formulation of the theory'. He continues: 'In contrast to this special formulation, the general form of the total conception of ideology is being used by the analyst when he has the courage to subject not just the adversary's point of view but all points of view, including his own, to the ideological analysis.'[39] Thus, Mannheim advocates an inclusive conception of ideology. He argues that the use of the inclusive, general formulation of the total conception of ideology takes one beyond a theory of ideology to 'the sociology of knowledge'.[40] What was once a political analysis of opponents' ideas becomes a general method of analysis in social and intellectual history.

The sociology of knowledge can function in two ways. First, it can seek to show the 'interrelationship between the intellectual point of view held and the social position occupied'.[41] In this, the analyst is concerned with a sociological examination of the determination of belief, and not with the philosophical evaluation of the validity of belief. Second, the sociology of knowledge can seek to combine such non-evaluative analysis with a concern for epistemology and truth. In this, the sociology of knowledge might be able to contribute social science, as distinct from ideology or utopia.

As I propose to argue later, it is in this second notion of the sociology of knowledge that Mannheim's severe problems rest and are revealed. But first I wish to consider further what is involved in the social determination of knowledge or belief. Any theory of the social determination of knowledge or belief involves two claims: first, that human thought develops not (just) from the nature of its subject matter and in accord with immanent laws and logic, but is influenced by extra-theoretical factors; and second, the extra-theoretical factors are social in nature, such that human thought may be conducted and expressed by individuals, but is mediated or determined by the individual's position in society and role in social processes. Mannheim's theory shows a modification of the first point and a non-Marxist clarification of the second. According to Mannheim, not all knowledge or belief is socially determined. Some propositions in mathematics and economics are so formal and abstract as to be 'completely detached from the thinking social individual', and the quantifiable aspects of natural science are similarly 'largely detachable from the historical-social perspective of the investigator'.[42] Quite why formal and abstract propositions escape social determination is not explained fully, and the granting of this exception by Mannheim may be no more than arbitrary. Mannheim distances himself from the Marxist tradition by arguing not only that all social thought is socially determined, but also that it is determined, in part at least, by non-economic factors. Among the social processes and positions which determine belief, Mannheim mentions competition and generation.[43]

If one takes seriously Mannheim's claim that all knowledge or belief (with the noted exceptions of formal, abstract and quantitative propositions) is socially determined, then one is faced with a severe problem, which may be termed Mannheim's paradox, and which serves to undermine the possibility of any objective knowledge of reality. If all knowledge is socially determined, it is necessarily related to specific socio-historical points of view, and so is merely relative and never objective and absolute. Moreover, the thesis of the social determination of knowledge must itself be only relative and so not objectively true. It would seem that Mannheim's sociology of knowledge collapses into relativism. Mannheim, of course, does not wish to acknowledge such a conclusion. He seeks to avoid what he terms relativism, and to find an escape in what he terms relationism. Relativism, says Mannheim, recognises that all knowledge is relative to specific socio-historical points of view; mistakenly assumes that truth must be fixed and static; and so denies the validity of any standards and the existence of objective order in the world.[44] Relationism also relates knowledge to specific socio-historical points of view, but it does not deny the criteria of rightness or wrongness of belief. Rather, it insists that such criteria are themselves related to socio-historical points of view and that propositions cannot be formulated absolutely but only in terms of the perspective of a given point of view. So far this would seem to be a distinction without a difference. Mannhein has not shown how to determine which one of various related propositions is true, or which one of various socio-historical points of view gives the best perspective on reality.

What the sociology of knowledge can do, says Mannheim, is relate any proposition to the social perspective of the knowing subject, and, from this, 'particularise' its scope and the extent of its validity.[45] The final hope must be that the sociology of knowledge can in some way gather together and synthesise all the various particular points of view. Concerning the possibility of a science of politics, Mannheim says:

> All points of view in politics are but partial points of view because historical totality is always too comprehensive to be grasped by any one of the individual points of view which emerge out of it. Since, however, all these points of view emerge out of the same social and historical current, and since their partiality exists in the matrix of an emerging whole, it is possible to set them in juxtaposition, and their synthesis becomes a problem which must continually be reformulated and resolved.[46]

The stress here on totality is reminiscent of the work of Lukács, considered in the previous chapter. As befits one who early in his career fell under the influence of his fellow Hungarian, Mannheim stresses the historical and emerging total nature of reality, and the dynamic nature of the synthesis required to capture this reality. In an ever-developing world there can be no absolute, permanent synthesis.[47] Whatever its exact nature, and this is never made clear by Mannheim, such a synthesis might in principle be possible if all points of view could be said to be various perspectives on one, real, objective world. One major problem for Mannheim, though, is that according to his total conception of ideology, not just the content of all belief, but also the conceptual apparatus of all individuals must be considered subject to ideological distortion. That is, different social groups will have not only differing beliefs about social reality, but also differing ways of conceiving it. There may be no common concept of reality in society; in effect, then, no common reality; and so no way of achieving a synthesis of views about reality. It is one thing to talk about different perspectives on the one reality, and quite another to talk, as Mannheim may be tempted, about different conceptions of reality and so different realities.

A further problem for Mannheim is that any proposition of any possible synthesis would seem to fall foul of his paradox: it would be articulated by a particular individual or group with a particular socio-historical perspective and so would be particular and partial. Mannheim attempts to sidestep this problem by identifying the executors of the synthesis as the intelligentsia. The intelligentsia is, says Mannheim, a 'relatively classless stratum' which is 'socially unattached'.[48] This is so not just because the intellectuals are drawn from different social classes, but because their participation in a common educational heritage tends to suppress class and other social differences and to promote a unity. Also, intellectuals operate in an environment which encourages a sensitivity to the wide diversity of views, and having no fixed class outlook of their own they are obliged when evaluating views to adopt a 'total orientation'.[49] This notion of a socially detached intelligentsia is attacked by Anthony Arblaster, who notes, among other things, the contemporary educational institutionalisation of intellectuals (in 'bourgeois' institutions at that); the continuing social inequality of educational opportunity; the partisan and even servile performance of intellectuals; and the partial political and economic pressures on education.[50] A further similarity between Mannheim and Lukács becomes apparent when one compares the former's intelligentsia, with its total orientation, and the latter's proletariat, with its universal point of view or standpoint of totality. István Mészáros points to a basic difference, though: 'while in Lukács the standpoint of totality is stressed as a crucial *methodological principle,* Mannheim turns it into a *fictitious sociological entity*'.[51]

It is not clear how, given Mannheim's thesis of the social determination of all social and political thought, there can be any escape from the problem of ideology: the problem of relativism. It is not clear how the quest for reality can escape ideological and utopian distortion.

MICHAEL OAKESHOTT: IDEOLOGY, SCIENCE AND PHILOSOPHY AS MODES OF POLITICAL THOUGHT

Michael Oakeshott advances towards an adequate conception of politics and the knowledge belonging to it by considering and criticising two inadequate conceptions of politics: empirical politics and ideological politics. Empirical politics is politics without a policy, according to which one acts not in accord with, nor in pursuit of, any principle or programme, but merely to satisfy any fleeting, capricious desire. This is an inadequate understanding of politics, says Oakeshott, because 'empiricism by itself is not a concrete manner of activity at all'.[52] Empirical politics is impossible, and any attempt to pursue a style of empirical politics is likely to have unfortunate results: 'to try to do something which is impossible is always a corrupting enterprise'.[53] Moreover, any style of politics which approximates to pure empiricism is to be criticised as approaching lunacy and having a result which 'may be supposed to be chaos modified by whatever consistency is allowed to creep into caprice'.[54] Politics may be the pursuit of desire, says Oakeshott, but the activity of desiring is not entirely capricious. As will be noted later, human activity is structured within traditions and practices.

If empiricism by itself cannot be a concrete manner of activity, then, it might be supposed, it is necessary to add to it some motivating factor. Thus arises the second inadequate understanding of politics: ideological politics. According to this understanding, 'politics appear as a self-moved manner of activity when empiricism is preceded and guided by an ideological activity'.[55] Ideology is here understood as:

> an abstract principle, or set of related abstract principles, which has been independently premeditated. It supplies in advance of the activity of attending to the arrangements

> of society a formulated end to be pursued, and in doing so it provides a means of distinguishing between those desires that ought to be encouraged and those which ought to be suppressed or redirected.[56]

Examples of ideology include single abstract ideas such as freedom, equality and happiness, and systems of ideas such as liberalism, democracy and Marxism.

This concept of ideology as an independently premeditated guide to action is similar to what Oakeshott describes elsewhere as rationalism.[57] Rationalism involves belief in the independence of thought from prejudice, habit, tradition and all authority except reason. Rationalism is both sceptical, in that reason questions all belief, and optimistic, in that reason is held to have power to determine truth and goodness. Although it does not deny nor neglect experience, rationalism tends to reduce it all to fit certain rational principles. When applied to politics, rationalism brings all issues and problems before the tribunal of reason, and advocates rational administration. Rationalist politics is like engineering in that all problems are solved by the application of technique, with no regard paid to such matters as custom and practice. Rationalist politics is both the politics of perfection, in that it involves the calculation of the best solutions for all problems, and the politics of uniformity, in that the best possible solutions are to be applied in the same way in all cases.

Among the faults of rationalism two are relevant to the present consideration of Oakeshott's conception of ideology. First, rationalism elevates reason as the sole and independent authority in human thought and fails to recognise the value and authority of (perhaps localised) traditions and practices. Second, rationalism recognises only one of the two distinct, though inseparable, sorts of human knowledge. Rationalism recognises only technical knowledge, or knowledge of technique, which can be formulated in rules. Rationalism fails to recognise practical knowledge, which exists only in practice and which cannot be formulated in abstract rules.[58] To use one of Oakeshott's famous examples, the technique of cookery may be formulated in a cookery book, but this cannot exhaust the knowledge of a good cook, who has a practical knowledge which exists in the practice of good cookery.

The faults of the conception of ideology outlined above can now be seen. Oakeshott's fundamental argument is that ideology cannot be an abstract, premeditated guide to action. Ideology cannot precede activity, but is, rather, an abstraction or abridgement of practice or a tradition of activity. Political ideology, for example, 'is a system of ideas abstracted from the manner in which people have been accustomed to go about the business of attending to the arrangements of their societies'.[59] As an abridgement of a traditional manner of activity, ideology cannot be an independent standard to which political activity must be made to conform.[60] Oakeshott insists that '*what* we do, and moreover what we want to do, is the creature of *how* we are accustomed to conduct our affairs'.[61] If ideology is taken as a guide to action, it is likely to prove to be both false and misleading. Ideology will be false because no matter how skilfully the abridgement is performed, 'a single intimation is apt to be exaggerated and proposed for unconditional pursuit' and the 'complexities of that tradition' are 'squeezed out in the process of abridgement' and 'taken to be unimportant'.[62] Ideology will be misleading in that of itself it never 'provides the whole of the knowledge used in political activity'.[63] Here Oakeshott seems to employ a criticism similar to that made of rationalism: that ideology advances technical knowledge to the neglect of traditional knowledge.[64] Another danger of ideology is that an abstract or abridgement of one human activity may be offered as a model or guide for another. As an example, Oakeshott suggests that abstracts of war, religion or the conduct of industry may be offered as an abstract of political activity, and such irrelevance is 'one of the defects of the model provided by the Marxist ideology'.[65] A further danger of ideology is that an abridgement of a traditional activity may be transplanted from the society in which it has developed into another society, and this is 'always a questionable enterprise'.[66]

Oakeshott is no friend of political ideology. Yet he does not dismiss ideology entirely. He acknowledges that ideologies have their uses, and his supposedly more adequate account of politics and the knowledge belonging to it suggests that his argument is not so much with ideology as such, but with the improper understanding of it. Oakeshott includes in the uses and benefits of political ideology its ability to give 'sharpness of outline and precision to a political tradition' and its ability to 'reveal important hidden passages in a tradition'.[67] When ideologies are used in this way, as techniques for 'exploring the intimation of a political tradition', and when abridgements of tradition allow for consideration of general principles, they are indeed useful. It is when ideologies are accepted or set up as abstract, premeditated guides to action that they are inappropriate and to be criticised.[68] For Oakeshott, politics is properly defined in terms of tradition or practice. It is the 'common recognition of a manner of attending to its arrangements' that makes a people a single community, and politics, which is 'the activity of attending to the general arrangements' of a community, is 'the pursuit, not of a dream, or of a general principle, but of an intimation' of a tradition.[69] The knowledge that belongs to politics is thus knowledge of the tradition of politics. Ideology is not necessarily opposed to this knowledge; it is just an inadequate abridgement of the tradition which we would wish to know more adequately.

Oakeshott does not dismiss ideology entirely and so it would seem that he does not maintain a strictly negative conception of ideology. To confirm this it will be useful to consider how he distinguishes ideology, philosophy and science, while denying that the latter two, separately or together, can act as correctives of the former. To understand this distinction it is necessary to examine Oakeshott's idealism. This examination will also show how Oakeshott can argue that the knowledge proper to politics is derivative of a tradition, and yet reject the thesis of the social determination of knowledge.

Oakeshott is an idealist in that he holds that 'reality is experience' and 'experience is a world of ideas'.[70] By experience Oakeshott means the 'concrete whole which analysis divides into "experiencing" and "what is experienced"'.[71] Reality is identified with experience 'not because it is made real by being known, but because it cannot without contradiction be separated from knowledge'.[72] Thus, Oakeshott's idealism rejects the traditional empiricist distinction between knowing subject and known object. By world of ideas Oakeshott means 'a coherent world of concrete ideas', which alone is 'independent, absolute and complete', and so not just any arbitrary collection of mere mental fancies.[73] Experience, for Oakeshott, is nothing more or less than 'thought or judgement'.[74] In experience there will always be pursuit of the whole of reality, but experience 'frequently suffers modification or abstraction' or arrest.[75] These modifications or modes of experience attempt to grasp the whole of reality but do so only in terms of limited and unchallenged postulates. The various modes produce only various abstract worlds of ideas.

The modes of experience are, Oakeshott acknowledges, potentially unlimited in number, although in his original work of philosophy, *Experience and its Modes*, he deals only with what he takes to be the three main, highly developed arrests or abstracts of experience: historical, scientific and practical.[76] Historical experience is the whole of experience understood in terms of the past. An understanding of the past is supposedly an understanding of that which is present, in so far as as the whole of experience is seen as a series of connected, changing events. Scientific experience is the whole of experience conceived in terms of quantitative measures and generalisations, which alone permit scientists to explain reality in stable, common and communicable terms. Practical experience is the whole of experience understood in terms of the human will, which determines how the world is to be maintained or changed by practice so as to accord with certain values.

Distinct from the various modes of experience is philosophy (or philosophical experience). Philosophy is 'without presupposition, reservation, arrest or modification' and is 'the attempt to realise the character of experience absolutely'.[77] Philosophy is self-critical and so, unlike the various modes, will tolerate no limiting presuppositions or postulates, and will be satisfied with nothing less than the whole coherent world of ideas. Philosophy is not a particular kind of experience, with its own exclusive source of knowledge, but 'experience become critical of itself, experience sought and followed entirely for its own sake'.[78] The tasks of philosophy seem to be twofold. First, philosophy seeks to extend itself and fulfil its purpose of understanding the whole of experience without modification. Second, philosophy maintains its whole perspective and critically analyses all modified experiences by examining their various postulates.[79]

The various modes of experience are, by their very modified, arrested and abstract nature, inadequate and 'must be avoided or overcome if experience is to realise its purpose'.[80] It is not clear, though, that the whole of experience can be realised. Certainly this cannot be done by means of any relationship of the modes themselves. One cannot simply add all the possible modes together to make the whole of experience, for each mode is not just a slice of reality but the whole of reality organised in a partial way, and 'no collections or combination of such abstractions will ever constitute a concrete whole'.[81] Nor can one substitute one mode for a less adequate mode, or play off one mode against another. According to Oakeshott, each mode is 'wholly and absolutely independent of any other' and each 'insofar as it is coherent, is true for itself'.[82] The criterion of truth for any mode is not correspondence with objective reality, but internal coherence. There are as many standards of coherent truth as there are modes. Thus, the various modes 'cannot collide; they are merely irrelevant to one another'.[83] In modern parlance they are incommensurable, without common standard of measurement, and as such there can be no rational debate between them about their relative adequacy. Even when philosophy is brought to bear on the modes it is not clear that experience can be wholly realised. Certainly philosophy can expose the abstract nature of the modes, but this is all it can do, and this does not amount to eradicating them. Philosophy cannot abolish the modes by replacing them. Again the problem is that the standards of truth of the various modes and of philosophy are incommensurable. The criterion of truth appropriate to philosophy is just another self-contained criterion of coherence. Philosophy has nothing to learn from the modes and it would be improper for philosophy to judge the subject matter of the various modes by philosophical criteria. Any attempt to do so would be an example of *ignoratio elenchi*.[84]

What does this mean for politics and the relationship of

political ideology, political science and political philosophy? Politics would be included in what Oakeshott terms practical experience, in that politics is one aspect of the life consisting of wilful changes in existence directed by considerations of value. The term ideology is not employed by Oakeshott in *Experience and its Modes*, but clearly political ideology is an aspect of practical experience, and it may be likened to what he refers to as the 'world of value'.[85] The world of value is something distinct but inseparable from the world of practical experience and is similar in nature and function to the abridgement of a traditional manner of behaviour which, in *Rationalism and Politics*, is termed ideology. Practical experience cannot be what Oakeshott later refers to as purely empirical activity, and the world of value that moves practical experience cannot be postulated *a priori*, that is, prior to practical experience. The practical experience that is politics and political ideology cannot be corrected or replaced by political science or political philosophy. There may be a political science, in so far as the world of politics can be understood in terms of quantitative measures and generalisations (although Oakeshott would seem to doubt this), but political science and political ideology would be distinct modes of experience, with their own criteria of truth, and so irrelevant to one another and incommensurable. The criterion of truth in the world of value is not correspondence with some objective, external standard, but the coherence of the world of value itself.[86] The criterion of truth in the world of science is not correspondence with objective, external nature, for there is no subject matter apart from our ideas which constitute scientific experience.[87] For Oakeshott, political science cannot be the antidote of political ideology.

Neither can political philosophy correct or replace political ideology. As already noted, philosophy can question the postulates and expose the abstract character of the modes of experience, but cannot replace them. Oakeshott concedes that history and science may disappear (for the world managed without them before they appeared), but not, he argues, because philosophy can take their place. Practice, though, will never disappear for it is 'indispensable to life'.[88] Thus, one can conclude that politics and political ideology are most unlikely to disappear, and it is certain that if political ideology does end it will not have been replaced by political philosophy. So long as politics and political ideology remain as aspects of practical experience, philosophy will remain irrelevant to them, and if philosophy enters political life this 'irrelevance must turn to error and falsehood'.[89] There is, for Oakeshott, a necessary tension between the aims of philosophy and the aims of politics and all practical life.

What, then, is political philosophy, and what can it do? In *Experience and its Modes* Oakeshott dismisses political philosophy as not just an arrest of experience but an indeterminate one, which does not even create a determinate, homogeneous world of experience. Political philosophy is characterised also as pseudo-philosophy. Philosophy is unarrested experience, without reservation or presupposition. When it is limited and qualified as political philosophy it necessarily falls short of its philosophical character.[90] The proper role of political philosophy, then, is not to create a world of value, to tell us what is good and how we ought to behave, but, rather, to analyse the concepts and categories of the political world.[91] In *Rationalism and Politics* Oakeshott confirms that political philosophy is not, and should attempt to become, a normative discipline, determining good and bad conduct, and directing our behaviour. Only the pursuit of the intimation of our political tradition can be relevant in this regard. What political philosophy can do with competence is analyse the concepts and ideas of politics, help straighten political thinking, and generally tidy up political argument.[92] Political philosophy is no more than an explanatory discipline; it can help explain what political life is, but not tell us what it should be.

In *On Human Conduct* Oakeshott refers not to political philosophy, but to theorising about human conduct and in particular civil association, which is what would generally be understood as politics. Theorising entails analysis of the postulates of an ideal character, or essence, of a 'going-on' or experience. Thus, theorising civil association entails analysing the postulates, that is, the underlying and contingent concepts, beliefs, assumptions and so on, of political conduct. Theorising civil association is thus an analytic and explanatory, and not a normative, business. The analysis seems to have moved beyond a rather bloodless conceptual analysis towards a richer contextual analysis. Oakeshott says that theorising a substantive performance is 'concerned to expose the contingently related beliefs, sentiments, understandings, and compunctions of an agent, and to discern the congruity of his action with his diagnosis'.[93]

The starting point for this consideration of Oakeshott was his distinction of political ideology and a more adequate account of politics and the knowledge belonging to it. It should now be clear that Oakeshott does not seek to offer political science or political philosophy as the more adequate form of political thought. He offers only a rather vague and uncertain understanding of a political tradition. Although the knowledge proper to politics is traditional, that is, derivative of a traditional manner of activity, Oakeshott does not accept anything like the thesis of the social determination of knowledge. As an idealist, Oakeshott must reject any such thesis which smacks of materialism and the dualism of practice and thought. He argues only that political knowledge is knowledge of a tradition, and that political values are constituted by, and in part constitute, a tradition. I now wish to conclude by arguing that Oakeshott's supposedly more adequate, non-ideological political thought is troubled by the problem of ideology: relativism.

Oakeshott concedes that his political philosophy, or theorising of civil association, will not reveal objective, external standards of political behaviour. There can be no appeal to natural law, reason, ideal justice, real human and social needs, greatest good, etc.[94] For an idealist, there can be no objective values which exist independently of our consciousness or experience.[95] This does not mean, of course, that political values are simply arbitrary and capricious, being merely irrational preferences or subjective judgements. For Oakeshott, the values of political life can be no more, and no less, than the abridgements of the tradition of political behaviour. Being derivative of a tradition, political values cannot simply be made up by individuals and groups as they choose. The trouble here is, as Oakeshott concedes, that 'a tradition of behaviour is a tricky thing to get to know. Indeed it may even appear to be essentially unintelligible. It is neither fixed nor finished; it has no changeless centre to which understanding can anchor itself.'[96] I concede that traditions may be no more difficult to know than, say, natural law or real human needs, but at least such standards offer, in principle, an anchor for our political understanding and judgement. Oakeshott refuses appeal to objective standards and falls back on tradition, in a conservative fashion, for guidance in the activity of politics.[97] That a political philosophy entails conservative conclusions is not, of itself, sufficient warrant for criticising it. However, a political philosophy which offers no objective standards for the evaluation of politics is vulnerable to the charge of relativism. If political values are derivative of, and relative to, a tradition, and if there are different traditions in politics, then there are no common, objective values outside the various traditions. Oakeshott offers no objective way of dealing either with disputes about the interpretation of tradition within any community, or with disputes in the global sphere of politics between communities with different traditions. Oakeshott's political philosophy seems to break down into irrelevance and incompetence in the face of political conflict between various actors with various political traditions.

CONCLUSION

The four writers considered in this chapter offer various conceptions of ideology and none of them offers a satisfactory account of the relationship of philosophy, science and ideology. In his early work Durkheim offers a negative and restrictive conception of ideology, and a fairly traditional conception of social science as the corrective of ideological distortion. He is unable to sustain this negative and restrictive conception because he tends to see ideology as a psychological category, irremediably rooted in human nature. In his later work, Durkheim offers a more positive and sociological conception of ideology. Primitive religion, which appears to be an example of his earlier conception of ideology, is a social construct and is socially useful. Ideology, in the form of religion, differs from science, but the latter cannot correct or replace the former. Pareto offers a more consistently psychological conception of ideology. Much human behaviour is motivated by non-rational forces, including a desire to make the non-rational seem rational. The variable elements of such attempted rationalisations, derivations, may be seen as ideology. Pareto's conception of ideology is restrictive, in that he seeks to distinguish social science and derivations, but not negative, in that he acknowledges the use-value, if not the truth-value, of derivations. Perhaps because of his psychological conception of ideology, he is unable to sustain an adequate distinction between it and science. He acknowledges that science and ideology are incommensurable; that science cannot distinguish the use-value and truth-value of ideology; and that science may be no more than ideology. Mannheim seeks to move beyond the restrictive and negative conception of ideology and offers an inclusive conception. According to Mannheim's general formulation of the total conception of ideology, human thought, with very few exceptions, is socially determined. This conception of ideology (or sociology of knowledge, as Mannheim terms it) is vulnerable to the problem of relativism. If human thought is socially determined, then it is relative to the social position of various knowing subjects, and so not objective or absolute. Mannheim makes futile attempts to resolve the problem of relativism, by offering the empty distinction between relativism and relationism, and the hopeless synthesis of relative points of view. Oakeshott, like Mannheim, makes no attempt to sustain a negative and restrictive conception of ideology and so is vulnerable to relativism. Oakeshott is critical of political ideology, but not because it is unscientific or unphilosophical. He distinguishes ideology, science and philosophy, while arguing that these are incommensurable forms of thought, none of which can correct the others. Political ideology, or what he terms rationalism, is simply an inappropriate form of political thought. The thought that is appropriate to politics has its foundation not in reason but in specific traditions of politics. Oakeshott's non-ideological political thought is thus relative to differing traditions and so cannot escape the problem of relativism that plagues so many concepts of ideology.

The survey of various Marxist and non-Marxist conceptions of ideology in this and the previous chapter confirms the problems of the phenomenon anticipated at the end of Chapter 1: ideology lacks objective justification; it rests on unquestioned and unprovable assumptions; it represents the partial interests of particular social groups; it distorts the appearances of social reality; and it lacks universal applicability. Above all, though, the survey confirms that the major, central problem of ideology, apparent in almost all conceptions, is relativism.

4 Naturalist Political Science and Political Ideology

INTRODUCTION

It should be clear from the consideration of ideology in the previous two chapters that the possible relations of science and ideology include opposition, difference and identity. The opposition of science and ideology almost invariably involves the distinction of an adequate, objective account of reality, and a distorted, partial account, and the correction of the latter by the former. Such an opposition is prefigured in the work of Bacon, who offers his empirical, inductive science as the corrective of the distorting idols which beset human perception and thought. The opposition of science and ideology is given classic expression in the early work of Durkheim, wherein empirical and comparative social science is championed as the supposed conqueror of ideological analysis as it moves beyond our common, primitive ideas to the social facts which are reality.

In the work of Marx also, it would seem, there is an opposition of science and ideology, in as much as the application of a historical materialist analysis is said to expose the partial distortion of bourgeois ideology, thus revealing the essences which lie behind the appearances. However, Marx insists that the correction and eradication of ideology is not a theoretical but a practical matter, involving the revolutionary change of the material conditions which give rise to ideology. Thus, for Marx, science may properly be said to be different from ideology, and not opposed to it as its adequate corrective. A clear statement of this relationship of difference between science and ideology is found in the work of Althusser. He argues that science may seek to transform the raw materials of ideology into knowledge, but cannot deny the necessity for some form of ideology in all societies, including even communist society. The relationship of difference between science and ideology is maintained also in the non-Marxist tradition. In his later work, Durkheim contrasts science and religion (a form of ideology) but denies that the former can perform the social function of, and so replace, the latter. Oakeshott also contrasts science and ideology, but denies that the former can challenge even the theoretical claims of the latter.

A third possible relationship of science and ideology is that of identity, and again both Marxists and non-Marxists maintain it. Lukács argues that modern, positivist, empiricist science is a form of reified consciousness, which harmonises with capitalism and so is no more than bourgeois ideology. Similarly, Marcuse argues that contemporary science is structured for natural and economic exploitation and is thus merely ideology. Pareto seems to concede that science may be no more than another attempt to provide a logical mask for non-logical behaviour, and that the worship of scientific values may be no more than another non-logical cult.

Chapter 1 noted the argument that empirical political science should be distinguished from normative political ideology, so as to maintain the objectivity of the former and correct the bias of the latter. I noted also the argument that the end of ideology leaves political science as the wholly adequate mode of political thought. Thus, contemporary political science is seen as being different from and opposed to political ideology. A further argument which I noted is that for political science to achieve success it should adopt the methods of the natural sciences. The present chapter is concerned with the nature of what might be termed naturalistic political science and its demarcation from, and correction of, political ideology. A full assessment of the adequacy of a naturalist political science for the study of politics is not available at this stage. This will be available later only when I consider the case for non-naturalist social science in Chapter 5, and present a critique of value-free political science in Chapter 6.

In order to examine naturalist political science it is necessary to consider the philosophy of science which might underpin it. I do not propose to show, nor need I assume, that particular political scientists draw consciously and directly on the work of particular philosophers of science. I assume only that any attempt to build a science of politics will involve some conceptions of the nature of science and scientific method, and that these conceptions are likely to be informed by contemporary philosophy of science. Some of the philosophers of science to be considered have written on the philosophy of the social sciences and on social and political matters. This will be useful, but not essential, for my consideration of the possible application of their thought for political science.

The four philosophers of science chosen for consideration in this chapter, Karl Popper, Imre Lakatos, Thomas Kuhn and Paul Feyerabend, are among the most important and influential of the contemporary period. All four thinkers may be described as post-positivist, in that they seek to move beyond the sort of positivist philosophy that was so destructive of traditional political philosophy and so influential in the demand for a science of politics. But they may share little more than this label, for they are often in serious disagreement with one another. Both Popper and Lakatos characterise science as rational; defend it as the highest form of human knowledge; and offer scientific method as the means of demarcating science from ideology. Popper's method of conjecture and refutation, accepted by many social scientists as the definitive scientific method, requires a crucial human decision in favour of reason and rationality, but he is unable to provide any justification for this choice. Lakatos's constructive criticism of Popper emphasises the need for human decisions and social conventions in science, but he is unable to demonstrate the reasonableness of these. Kuhn develops the conventionalist approach to the extent that he questions the rationality and objectivity of science, and so the demarcation of science and ideology. Feyerabend extends this line of argument, making explicit its relativism, and concludes that science is but one ideology among many.

KARL POPPER: FALSIFICATION AND THE DEMARCATION OF SCIENCE AND IDEOLOGY

Karl Popper believes the demarcation of science and non-science to be politically important. Some influential political theories can be shown to be non-scientific and so bad theories. In particular, Popper believes Marxism to be non-scientific and so unable to offer a correct account of society, and, moreover, dangerous in political application.[1] For Popper, the demarcation of science and non-science, and the choice between competing scientific theories, is a matter of the application of scientific method.

Popper's philosophy of science may be seen as an attempt to overcome, or come to terms with, the problem of induction, while avoiding and correcting the inadequate solutions offered by logical positivism. If the aim of science is to furnish explanations of the events and processes of the world, and if explanation involves covering particular events by general laws or theories, then science must account for these generalisations. One traditional and influential account, exemplified in the work of Francis Bacon, is induction. According to the inductive method one gathers evidence of particular events, and reasons from this to a general theory. There is, though, a problem of induction, identified clearly by David Hume, and now widely recognised. If one is to reason from observation of particulars to general propositions, then one would have to include in the argument additional steps which are not in fact available. That is, if one is to reason from the premise, 'all observed Xs are Y', to the conclusion, 'all Xs are Y', one would have to include one of the two following premises: either 'all Xs have been observed'; or 'all unobserved Xs are like all observed Xs'. The first alternative is not available because one cannot observe future events, and the second is an improper assumption of that which one is trying to prove. The logical positivists offer the principle of verification as a solution of the problem of induction. As noted in Chapter 1, they argue that the mark of a scientific hypothesis is not that in practice it is supported by all the necessary evidence, but that in principle one can state what evidence is relevant to its verification.

Popper rejects the logical positivists' attempt to deal with the problem of induction. He argues that both in practice and in principle it is impossible to verify any generalisation. What one can do, and do easily, is falsify generalisations. No amount of supporting evidence can verify a proposition; one piece of contradictory evidence can falsify it. Noting the marked asymmetry of verification and falsification, Popper rejects the former and offers the latter as the method of science. The task of science is to propose solutions to problems and to test rigorously these conjectures by deducing from them particular propositions which can be tested against the evidence of the world. The conjectures or hypotheses cannot be proven true, but can be proven false. Tested and unfalsified hypotheses are accumulated as fallible theories, and so the stock of scientific knowledge builds upon itself. The mark of a scientific proposition is not that it is, or can be proven, true, but that it is formulated in such a way as to be testable and falsifiable. Non-science, or ideology, consists of propositions which cannot be subjected to scientific testing and falsification.[2]

Popper may be termed a post-positivist philosopher of science. In addition to his rejection of the principle of verification, he rejects certain key positivist beliefs. Popper rejects the extreme empiricism of positivism, by rejecting the identification of all non-science as nonsense, and by retaining metaphysics, to some extent. He wishes to accept certain abstract, theoretical, scientific entities. Popper rejects also the sharp positivist distinction between theory and observation, according to which the latter is held to be the objective test of the former. He recognises the priority of theory in science and the theory-laden nature of observation. That is, he accepts that the evidence one gathers may be determined by one's theoretical preconceptions. However, Popper accepts certain key positivist beliefs. He has no doubt that science is pre-eminently rational and the highest form of human knowledge, and, importantly, he accepts the logical distinction of facts and values.

I do not propose to offer anything like a thorough and comprehensive critical examination of Popper's philosophy of science. In the next section I consider Imre Lakatos's account of the problems of various forms of falsificationism.

For the present, I propose to consider a number of issues, including fallibilism, relativism, rationality and values, which touch on my general concern with the relation of science and ideology.

Popper is committed to fallibilism: 'the view, or the acceptance of the fact, that we may err, or that the quest for certainty (or even the quest for high probability) is a mistaken quest'.[3] Given this, one may ask, as indeed Popper asks himself, whether or not his fallibilism entails relativism:

> the theory that the choice between competing theories is arbitrary; since either, there is no such thing as objective truth; or, if there is, no such thing as a theory which is true or at any rate (though perhaps not true) nearer to the truth than another theory; or, if there are two or more theories, no ways or means of deciding whether one of them is better than another.[4]

Popper seeks to combat relativism by arguing that fallibilism does not threaten, but rather presupposes, truth; that human knowledge develops and grows; and that human knowledge can be considered objective.

That fallibilism presupposes truth rather than entails relativism is easily shown, thinks Popper, because 'the idea of error implies that of truth as the standard of which we may fall short'.[5] Relativism, Popper argues, must retreat as human knowledge advances towards truth.[6] Science commences from a problem, resulting very often from the failure of an earlier explanatory theory, and proposes and tests a new solution. In this way one learns from one's mistakes: moving on from earlier ones and being inspired to move on from present ones. Human knowledge, although never infallible, represents always an advance on previous knowledge. By clearing away error one advances towards truth, and although one may never arrive at certainty, one can and must continue to travel and make progress. Popper advances from the notion of progressive, cumulative knowledge to the notion of objective knowledge, independent, in some way, of human thought. His theory of objective knowledge is presented in terms of three worlds: world 1, consisting of physical objects and processes; world 2, consisting of human experience and consciousness; and world 3, consisting of objective knowledge.[7]

This third world is said to be objective because it is autonomous from subjective human consciousness, and its content, human knowledge, is properly measured by something other than subjective belief.

Popper attacks epistemological relativism by appealing to an objective and rational method for testing theories; a method which requires no, and can tolerate no, subjective element of crucial significance. Whether or not such a non-subjective method is available to Popper is a matter for consideration later. At this point I wish to argue that Popper's fallibilism leaves him in no position to talk about theory choice, far less objective knowledge. One can choose between competing theories only by subjecting their respective contents to the measure of truth. Since Popper is a fallibilist, and so does not expect theories to be absolutely true, he refers to the choice of theories according to their 'approximation to the truth' or 'verisimilitude'.[8] But if one can have no access to the truth, then one cannot know whether or not a proposition approximates to the truth. It may be the case that the notion of fallibilism presupposes the notion of truth, but if this standard is in principle unattainable, then it is an impracticable standard, and so not a means for theory choice nor a measure of objective knowledge.

Popper also attacks moral relativism, which he sees as following, at least in part, from epistemological relativism. Popper notes that human values change; that the relevance of morality may be determined by situations; that there always exist 'irresolvable clashes of values'; and 'that clashes of values and principles may be valuable, and indeed essential for an open society'. But, Popper continues, this is quite distinct from relativism; that is, from 'the doctrine that any set of values can be defended'.[9] This distinction is not clear, though. If Popper believes that morality may be relative to different situations, and that the clash of values is insoluble, then he must believe that there is no objective, absolute standard of morality by which all values may be judged. He must believe that all values are relative and that no set of values is better, nor worse, than any other. Thus, Popper is a moral relativist who has no good reason to object to the view that any set of values may be upheld.

Popper, in classic positivist style, believes in the irreconcilable clash of values, and argues for the separation of facts and values. Popper supports his dualism of facts and values thus:

> standards are of our own making in the sense that our decision in favour of them is our own decision, and that we alone carry the responsibility for adopting them. The standards are not found in nature. Nature consists of facts and of regularities, and is in itself neither moral nor immoral. It is we who impose our standards upon nature, and who in this way introduce morals into the natural world.[10]

Moral knowledge, for Popper, is clearly distinct from knowledge of the natural world, although both are constituents of world 3 of objective knowledge.[11] They are not only different but also unequal constituents, for 'there cannot be a criterion of absolute rightness – even less than a criterion of absolute truth'.[12] There is, then, a distinction and asymmetry between facts and values. Only factual knowledge can have the status of science. For Popper, there can be no science of values.

As noted above, Popper can defend himself against the charge of relativism only if he can show that there can be an objective scientific method. I have argued that Popper is a moral relativist, and now I wish to argue that his supposedly objective scientific method rests upon something like a moral decision, which he cannot show to be objective. Popper's scientific method of conjectures and refutations involves 'unjustified (and unjustifiable) anticipations . . . controlled by criticism'.[13] For Popper, 'there is no better synonym for "rational" than "critical"'.[14] Thus, his scientific method is rational, and the rationality consists in the severe, empirical testing of hypotheses or conjectures in the attempt to refute them. Science depends upon reason for its objectivity; but reason depends upon human choice, which is neither scientific nor objective. Popper says:

> Rationalism esteems argument, theory and empirical examination. But one can't justify one's decision in favour of rationalism by recourse to argument and experience.

> Although even this problem is open to debate, it ultimately demands from us a decision – some decision in favour of faith in reason. . . . This decision in favour of reason is moral and not simply intellectual.[15]

For Popper, then, science, and so objective knowledge, depend upon reason, which is itself dependent upon a moral choice. If, as I have argued, Popper is a moral relativist, unable to demonstrate the validity of any value choice, then so too is he an epistemological relativist, unable to demonstrate the validity of the foundation of his science.

Recognising the need for human decisions, Popper recognises also, if only implicitly, the possibility of wrong decisions being made. This might not be a great problem, he says.

> Admittedly, we must decide. But unless we decide against listening to argument and reason, against learning from our mistakes, and against listening to others who may have objections to our views, our decisions need not be final; not even the decision to consider criticism.[16]

But one can choose against reason, against science and against knowledge; and Popper is unable to demonstrate why such a decision is morally wrong. He is unable, largely because of his dualism of facts and values, to demonstrate why a choice in favour of reason is morally and epistemologically correct for humanity. Science, as outlined by Popper, can hardly claim the status of judge over ideology, for the basis of science is no more objective than the content of ideology.

IMRE LAKATOS: SCIENCE AS HUMAN DECISIONS

Imre Lakatos's philosophy of science may be seen as an attempt both to improve on Popper's falsificationism and to defend the rationality of science against the seemingly relativist work of theorists like Thomas Kuhn. I wish to consider Lakatos before Kuhn because this will allow me to offer a fuller analysis of falsificationism and the supposedly rational model of science before considering the criticisms of these in the work of Kuhn and Paul Feyerabend. Like Popper, Lakatos seeks to offer a method which may demarcate science and non-science, and evaluate competing theories and explanations. Lakatos sees Kuhn as failing to provide a secure basis for either of these two tasks. He does agree with Kuhn, though, that any scientific method must be able to account for the history of science and so he seeks to relate closely the history and the philosophy of science.

For Lakatos, the demarcation of science and non-science is the demarcation of the 'most respectable kind of knowledge' and 'superstition, ideology or pseudoscience'.[17] This demarcation 'is not merely a problem of armchair philosophy: it is of vital social and political relevance', and has 'grave ethical and political implications'.[18] Lakatos's grave concern seems to be based on the fear that incorrect demarcation may lead to science being treated as non-science, and so without due respect and tolerance. Also, Lakatos seems to worry that non-science or ideology, such as Marxism or Freudianism, may not be recognised for the worthless (and presumably dangerous) things they are.[19] It seems likely that the latter concern is more decisive, for Lakatos must recognise that simply attaching the label 'science' to an idea or theory does not protect it from political persecution, and that labels may be challenged by political powers at their convenience. Given the political and moral significance of demarcating science and ideology, it is important to consider how Lakatos thinks this can be done and to consider how successful is his method.

Starting from Popper's falsificationism and seeking to move on, Lakatos notes that falsificationism replaces 'justificationism' and 'fallibilism', both of which describe attempts to prove theories true or even probable. Falsificationism may be distinguished as dogmatic (or naturalistic), methodological, and sophisticated.[20] Dogmatic or naturalistic falsificationism asserts that science proceeds by testing theories against evidence of the world, rejecting theories thus falsified, and replacing them with bolder, testable theories. There are three problems with this approach, according to Lakatos. First, it rests on the false assumption of a natural distinction between theory language and observation language, according to which experience of the world is independent of our theoretical suppositions, and so constitutes an objective test of our theories. Second, even if observation was not theory-laden, it would be false to assume that observation propositions can be proven or disproven by experience. Propositions can be derived only from propositions, not from empirical evidence. The supposed confrontation of theory and empirical reality is non-existent. All propositions are theoretical and so uncertain. Third, even if there was a natural observation/theory distinction, and even if the truth value of an observation proposition could be proven, it would not be possible to extend the method of falsification to all scientific theories. Some (of the most important and respected) scientific theories cannot be falsified by any evidence, because they can be modified by auxiliary hypotheses so as to take account of 'awkward' evidence. Moreover, some types of hypotheses cannot be falsified at all.

These problems of dogmatic falsificationism may seem to leave science undifferentiated from non-science, such that science is unable to justify its claims to knowledge in terms of evidence, rationality and progress. In response to such problems, solutions are offered by methodological falsificationism. This scientific method operates on the basis of certain methodological decisions, which are accepted and justified by convention. Because of the importance of human decisions for this method, it is properly termed 'normative'. Referring to the work of Popper, Lakatos outlines the important decisions or conventions involved. First, some singular statements, 'observational' or 'basic', are held to be unfalsifiable. It is recognised that fallible theories mediate our experience of the world; nevertheless, some basic, observational statements or propositions must be accepted as unproblematic if one is to subject theories to empirical testing. Second, it follows that the accepted basic statements are to be separated from the rest, such that one can distinguish the theory under test from the theories that inform our experience. Given this, the methodological falsificationist differs from the dogmatic falsificationist in that the former is not always prepared to accept one piece of 'falsifying' evidence as decisive. The methodological falsificationist separates rejection and disproof, which the dogmatic falsificationist conflates, and so offers a more liberal criterion for the demarcation of science and non-science. Third, in order to deal with probabilistic theories one accepts certain statistical techniques as capable of furnishing falsifying evidence. Fourth, in order to deal with theories conjoined with auxiliary hypotheses or *ceteris paribus* clauses, one must decide whether or not falsifying evidence applies to the conjunction or to the specific theory. Fifth, one may decide to reject a metaphysical theory, which cannot be falsified, if it clashes with another theory which is falsifiable and corroborated.

As Lakatos notes, 'decisions play a crucial role' in methodological falsificationism, and these decisions are risky 'to the point of recklessness'.[21] The decisions are risky only because they are human decisions made on no secure basis, or at least no basis that can be secured by science itself. Without such risky decisions, however, one cannot go beyond discredited dogmatic falsificationism. Lakatos says: 'one has to choose between some sort of methodological falsificationism and irrationalism'.[22] It seems likely that Lakatos's decision for reason is no more secure or objective than that of Popper.

Leaving aside for the moment the potential problems of risky decisions, I now consider other problems of methodological falsificationism. Lakatos claims that the history of science highlights these. Common to both dogmatic and methodological falsificationism are two characteristics which do not accord with the actual practice of science. First, the test of a theory against evidence is seen as a two-cornered fight, whereas history and practice show that tests are at least three-cornered fights, involving at least two rival theories and evidence. Second, in any test, only conclusive falsification is seen as being significant, whereas in history and practice confirmations are often more interesting.

Assuming one wishes to maintain a rational account of science and its progress, or, as Lakatos puts it, a rational reconstruction of the history of science, it is necessary to modify methodological falsificationism. This modification leads to sophisticated falsificationism, which holds that a theory is scientific and acceptable, as opposed to non-scientific and unacceptable, not if it is falsifiable only, but if it has greater empirical content than a rival theory, and some of this excess content is corroborated. Also, sophisticated falsificationism holds that a theory is falsified not by conflicting evidence only, but by a rival theory, which has greater and corroborated empirical content; which has a greater ability to predict novel facts; and which can explain the success and failure of its rival. Sets of theories, which include related theories together with their auxiliary hypotheses, now replace single theories, and rival sets of theories are termed progressive or degenerating in so far as they succeed or fail in growing in content, scope and productivity.

Among the characteristics of sophisticated falsificationism, compared with naive (dogmatic and methodological) falsificationism, there is one which I wish to note because of its significance for my general concern. According to Lakatos, sophisticated falsificationism has need for fewer decisions. In particular, the fourth and fifth decisions noted above are no longer required. This is so, in the case of the fourth decision, because a theory and its auxiliary hypotheses can be falsified not by evidence but by a more progressive theory set. In the case of the fifth decision, an unfalsifiable theory is now rejected only if it causes a theory set to degenerate and there is a better (metaphysical) theory to replace it. However, the first three decisions must remain, because a scientist or a community of scientists cannot avoid the decisions to hold some observational statements to be true, to hold these to be distinct from theoretical statements, and to accept some means of dealing with, or testing, probabilistic theories. The arbitrariness of the second decision may be mitigated by the introduction of an appeals procedure. Any supposed clash between theory and fact may now be seen as a clash between explanatory and interpretive (or observational) theory. One decides for the theory, explanatory or interpretive, which is more progressive, that is, provides more corroborated empirical content. As Lakatos notes, this appeals procedure does no more than postpone the conventional decision about the acceptance or rejection of basic (observational) statements.

Having prepared the way, in terms of a critique of falsificationism, with reference to Popper, Lakatos now introduces his own 'methodology of scientific research programmes'.[23] A scientific research programme is far more elaborate and substantial than a single theory. It is an organised structure comprising of central theories, auxiliary hypotheses, and methodological rules. The central theory constitutes the characteristic hard core of the research programme. This hard core is '"irrefutable" by the methodological decision of its protagonists'.[24] The hard core is shielded by the protective belt of auxiliary hypotheses, which must change to accommodate anomalies and seemingly falsifying evidence. The methodological rule protecting the hard core is known as the negative heuristic, indicating which paths of research to avoid. The rules indicating which paths to follow, how to modify the protective belt, and how to deal with problems, are known as the positive heuristic. The positive heuristic strives forward almost regardless of 'refutations' and is supported and encouraged by 'verifications'. A scientific research programme is said to be progressive in so far as it produces greater and new empirical content, which is corroborated at some point. A programme is said to be degenerating in so far as it fails to do this and lags behind a more progressive rival.

It is clear that for Lakatos, as for Popper, human decisions play a crucial part in science. These decisions are not the result of scientific deliberation, for they are among the preconditions of science. Naive falsificationism requires five main decisions. Sophisticated falsificationism is able to reduce the number to three, but these remain essential. Lakatos's methodology of scientific research programmes maintains the three decisions and in addition requires the big decision to protect the characteristic hard core of theory from the very principle of falsificationism. Such decisions are risky, but might seem reasonable if they facilitated some sort of scientific success or progress. I say *might* seem reasonable, for there must be some doubt about the reasonableness of decisions whose only confirmation is self-confirmation. The reasonableness of the decisions can be judged only in terms of that which is maintained or supported by them: science.

Leaving aside this doubt, there is a more straightforward problem. If the reasonableness of the prerequisite decisions of science depends upon the progress of science, one requires a clear measure of progress as a measure of reasonableness. Such a clear measure is not available from Lakatos. For him, the progress of a scientific research programme is always a matter of comparison of rival programmes. In order to be judged more progressive than a rival, a programme must have greater 'heuristic power', such that 'not only novel facts but, in an important sense, also novel auxiliary theories are anticipated'.[25] Such a comparison cannot be made on the basis of, and no programme can be falsified by, any instant, crucial experiment: '*there are no such things as crucial experiments*, at least not if these are meant to be experiments which can instantly overthrow a research programme'.[26] The success of a research programme cannot be judged on the basis of any one piece of evidence at any one point in time. Nor can the apparent advantage of one programme over another be taken to be decisive, for any lagging programme may stage a comeback.[27] Rather, the comparison of programmes and the choice of the more or most progressive one can be done only with difficulty over a long period of time and with hindsight.[28] But how long does one have to wait before making a judgement? As Paul Feyerabend asks critically: 'if you are permitted to wait, why not wait a little longer?'[29] Indeed, one could wait for ever and not be able to evaluate competing programmes.

For Lakatos, the appraisal of rival research programmes is difficult, of indefinite duration, and inconclusive. In short, he offers no adequate means of evaluating research programmes in terms of their progressiveness. If, as I argued, the reasonableness of the human decisions underlying science might be judged in terms of the success or progress of science, then without an adequate measure of scientific progress there can be no measure of the reasonableness of the decisions. The crucial decisions are not themselves scientific; they cannot be shown to be reasonable. The decisions are therefore no better than ideology. If science rests on something no better than ideology, then science cannot be demarcated from ideology, nor be the antidote of ideology.

THOMAS KUHN: INCOMMENSURABILITY AND THE PROBLEM OF RELATIVISM

Thomas Kuhn's philosophy, sociology and history of science poses a threat to the rationality which Popper and Lakatos seek to defend. It may be argued that Popper and Lakatos leave themselves vulnerable to such a threat. Certainly Kuhn offers his account of science as a criticism of, and alternative to, that of Popper.[30] Whereas Popper sees science as progressing by means of rational criticism of hypotheses in an open environment, Kuhn sees science as consisting of periods of puzzle-solving, structured by the uncritical and dominant outlook of a closed community of scientists, punctuated by revolutions, which change the structures of thought, and which are not necessarily progressive. Kuhn's arguments are partly theoretical, but his greatest reliance is on historical evidence and argument which, he thinks, indicates that science has not been conducted as Popper suggests. This observation prompts the question, noted by Paul Feyerabend, of whether Kuhn is offering methodological prescriptions for, or historical descriptions of, the conduct of science.[31] Whatever Kuhn intends, and he may be offering both in an ambiguous way, his work is critical of the rationality of science.

According to Kuhn, most science is 'normal science', by which he means research firmly located within a given theoretical and methodological outlook of a community of scientists.[32] Such an outlook is termed a 'paradigm'. Kuhn's failure to define clearly the term paradigm, and his loose, sometimes confusing, use of the term, is notorious.[33] However, I think it is possible to arrive at an instructive notion of the term. A paradigm is based upon a recognised scientific achievement, which serves as the basis for further research; it offers a set of assumptions, suggestions and theories about the nature of the world; it defines a set of problems capable of being solved by the scientific community; it indicates which techniques and methods may be used in the search for solutions to the problems; and as a belief system it operates as the defining characteristic of a community of scientists and the curriculum for the instruction of new scientists. The relationship of the community of scientists to their paradigm is almost that of the classic totalitarian society to its single, dominant and all-pervasive ideology. The dominance of the paradigm is such that normal science is largely confined to the solving of puzzles and is seldom, if ever, innovative. The work of normal scientists is that of determining the significant facts, matching facts to theories, and articulating theories.

Since normal science is not innovative, it will not seek novel facts or theories, and if it is successful it will discover none. However, in the conduct of scientific research novelties of fact do appear and novelties of theory may be required. According to Kuhn, novelties which do not accord with the expectations and theories of the given paradigm constitute 'anomalies'. Whereas for Popper such anomalies would count as falsifying evidence, for Kuhn they are resisted by scientists, keen on preserving their paradigm. Anomalies can be resisted only so far and for so long: until such time as their accumulation causes a crisis in normal science. Faced with such a crisis, the community of scientists can reject the given paradigm only if it can, at the same time, accept a new one. Any new paradigm will be accepted only if it can show itself capable of accommodating and accounting for old anomalies, thus providing a new foundation for the conduct of science. A change of paradigms, or paradigm shift, constitutes a 'scientific revolution'. Scientific revolutions are 'non-cumulative developmental episodes in which an older paradigm is replaced in whole or in part by an incompatible new one'.[34]

Kuhn's attack on the rationality of science relates both to the demarcation of science and non-science, and to the choice of competing theories. For Kuhn, science, as normal science, is that which is agreed on by the community of scientists, and so the demarcation of science and non-science is a matter of social convention rather than rational argument. Since science is defined by social convention, all philosophy of science is merely conventionalism. On this matter, Kuhn may be seen as exposing the vulnerability of both Popper and Lakatos. For Popper, the defining characteristic of science is rationality, which is not determined by science, but is, rather, a matter of non-scientific moral choice. For Lakatos, science rests on a number of human decisions, which cannot be shown to be rational or scientific. For both, science rests upon non-scientific decisions reached by scientists, but remains, supposedly, rational. For Kuhn, science is purely conventional and so not objective and rational.

For Kuhn, theory choice is really paradigm choice, and is, again, not a matter of rationality but of social convention. As noted above, paradigms are incompatible; moreover, 'the normal-science tradition that emerges from a scientific revolution is not only incompatible but actually incommensurable with that which has gone before'.[35] Paradigms are incommensurable, that is, without any objective, common standard of measurement, because all standards of measurement are relative to particular paradigms. There can be no rational debate between competing paradigms because there can be no appeal to rational standards outside the terms of the debate. Kuhn says:

> As in political revolutions, so in paradigm choice – there is no standard higher than the assent of the relevant community. To discover how scientific revolutions are effected, we shall therefore have to examine not only the impact of nature and logic, but also the techniques of persuasive argumentation effective within the quite special groups that constitute the community of scientists.[36]

In reviewing the issue of incommensurability in the Postscript to the second edition of *The Structure of Scientific Revolutions,* Kuhn concludes that social persuasion is the only process for theory choice, given the absence of any objective standards rooted in nature or logic. He says:

> There is no neutral algorithm for theory-choice, no systematic decision procedure which, properly applied, must lead each individual in the group to the same decision. In this sense it is the community of specialists rather than its individual members that makes the effective decision.[37]

Science has reached a sorry state when theory choice is conducted on the basis of a technique of persuasion shared with advertisers and salespeople. If no single individual can make a proper choice then neither can any particular group of them. It is strange that the scientific revolutionary Kuhn should share with Edmund Burke, the conservative opponent of political revolution, a disdain of the individual's 'private stock of reason' and an esteem of prejudice, or 'the general bank and capital of nations, and of ages'.[38]

In a lecture delivered eleven years after the publication of *The Structure of Scientific Revolutions* (and three years after the revised second edition) Kuhn makes an unsuccessful attempt to rescue his account of theory choice from criticism.[39]

What Kuhn does is to add something new to his account. In particular, he seeks to identify the characteristics of a good theory, which may act as the 'standard criteria for evaluating the adequacy of a theory'. The five characteristics he identifies are accuracy, consistency, scope, simplicity and fruitfulness.[40] Elsewhere, Kuhn notes that 'such reasons constitute values to be used in making choices rather than rules of choice'.[41] As values rather than rules, such reasons may prove problematic in two ways. First, scientists may differ as to how much weight to attach to each reason, relative to others, when faced with competing theories displaying varying characteristics. Second, although scientists may share values, they may apply them in different ways. Thus, there is at least some element of subjective, non-scientific choice in the assessment of theories.[42] There can be objective choice of theories only if the characteristics of a good theory can be shown to be determined by something other than arbitrary human decision or social convention. Kuhn cannot show this. Indeed, Kuhn argues that 'the experience of scientists provides no philosophical justification for the values they deploy' and that 'those values are in part learned from that experience, and they evolve with it'.[43] Those values upon which scientists base theory choice evolve and change just as theories do. It is only because values evolve and change less rapidly than do theories that the former can be said to be, in some fashion, the basis for choosing the latter. This basis is a most unsatisfactory one. One cannot judge properly the merit of a theory in terms of a value which is itself relative to changing theory.

Lakatos accuses Kuhn of reducing science to irrationality and of making scientific revolutions, and, by implication, theory choice, 'a matter of mob psychology'.[44] Lakatos may be right, but he may be in no position to criticise others. That theory choice is dependent upon human or social decisions, which are not themselves scientific, nor capable of being shown to be rational, is a position which Kuhn shares with Popper and Lakatos. Both Popper and Lakatos, as I have noted, require non-scientific human decisions to facilitate theory choice, and even the former is prepared to admit that such decisions may be communal: 'the acceptance or rejection of basic statements is a matter for something like a scientific jury – the scientific community (which may or may not come to an agreement)'.[45] For all three theorists, theory choice rests on values which are relative to particular communities of scientists, and so not objective. None of the three can offer a sound justification of non-scientific values, nor show why human beings should act in accord with them.

Kuhn's inability to secure a rational demarcation of science and non-science, and a rational basis for theory choice, and his acknowledgement of the need for unjustifiable decisions and conventions, stem from the primacy he gives to paradigms. Thought is determined by the dominant paradigm; paradigms come and go; and so thought is not rational nor objective. Kuhn says there is 'no theory-independent way to reconstruct phrases like "really there"; the notion of a match between the ontology of a theory and its "real" counterpart in nature now seems to me illusive in principle'.[46] That is, there is no objective reality, and so no objective measure of thought to be found there. There can be no rational criticism of a theory in terms of a test against the evidence of the objective real world. From Popper's and Lakatos's refusal to separate theory and observation, and from their thesis of theory-laden observation, Kuhn makes the move to the thesis of theory-determined observation. For Kuhn, there can be no escape from the paradigm so as to test the paradigm. Thus, science cannot be the opposite or corrective of ideology, for science cannot claim any greater rationality than ideology. For Kuhn, indeed, any scientific paradigm may be no more than 'a value system, an ideology'.[47] Scientific paradigms may be said to be ideological in that they are non-rational, consist of thought mediated by a social group, and exercise a dominance over social groups. I believe Alan Ryan is correct when he says:

> If Kuhn's picture of science were correct, its implications for any attempt to turn the social and political sciences into 'normal' sciences would be extremely alarming. So far from the new science being a way out of ideological conflict, it seems that it emeshes us more deeply than ever. Indeed the situation is worse than ever, with the added anxiety that our ideological preconceptions may become

invisible to us, since we cannot see our conceptual spectacles except on those rare occasions when we try on different ones.[48]

PAUL FEYERABEND: SCIENCE AS IDEOLOGY

Paul Feyerabend makes no attempt to contrast science and ideology, and so does not offer the former as a corrective of the latter. He states clearly: 'science is one ideology among many'.[49] Moreover, science is not necessarily the best of the various ideologies, and 'is inherently superior only for those who have already decided in favour of a certain ideology'.[50] Feyerabend concludes thus, having denied that science can, or should, be 'rationalistic' in practice, and having denied that there can be a single, proper scientific method. His arguments are both theoretical and historical. The various rules and standards which are usually taken to constitute rationality have no justification outside of the tradition which upholds them, and so 'rationality is one tradition amongst many rather than a standard to which other traditions must conform'.[51] The evidence of history shows that scientific methods, constructed from various rules and standards, have not been applied consistently and would have arrested the progress of science if they had been.[52] In opposition to scientific enquiry bound by methodological rules and regulations, Feyerabend advocates an 'anarchist theory of knowledge', the permissive principle of which is 'anything goes'.[53]

I do not propose to offer a comprehensive account of Feyerabend's theoretical and historical arguments. Rather, I propose to consider some of his arguments which have a critical impact upon some of the positions of Popper, Lakatos and Kuhn, as noted above. I wish to argue that some of the rather startling conclusions, or, perhaps, presuppositions, of Feyerabend are more or less easily established developments or criticisms of those vulnerable positions.

Feyerabend recognises Lakatos's methodology of scientific research programmes as 'the most advanced and sophisticated methodology in existence today'.[54] Thus, he would tend to accept the validity of Lakatos's constructive criticism of Popper's falsificationism. Feyerabend considers

Popper's falsificationism to be condemned by history, in that theories have declined without necessarily having been formally falsified, and many important theories have withstood supposed falsification. Against Lakatos, Feyerabend argues that the decisions upon which science rests, and the rules according to which it operates, cannot be shown to be rational. Feyerabend notes that one of the familiar rules or standards of science is that which holds that experience or facts measure theories and that theories which do not accord with the facts should be rejected. This is something like the basic rule of falsificationism. Against this, Feyerabend proposes the counter-rule that one should 'introduce and elaborate hypotheses which are inconsistent with well established theories and/or well established facts'.[55] He goes on to offer a theoretical defence of the counter-rule and then to show that it is supported by scientific practice in history. He argues that theories which contradict existing theories can produce evidence and facts not available in any other way, and that evidence required to refute an existing, well-confirmed theory is sometimes unearthed only by means of an incompatible theory. Failure to propose any new theories merely helps to preserve existing theories and so precludes finding better ones. The proliferation of theories is beneficial for science because it breaks down uniform thought, opens horizons, and encourages criticism. Feyerabend concludes that proposing theories inconsistent with existing theories and facts actually increases 'empirical content' and so, following Lakatos, should be seen as a necessary part of the falsifying process.[56] Yet, far from being accepted and encouraged by falsificationists, such a move is prohibited by their rule which demands consistency with existing theories and facts. This rule, claims Feyerabend, is unreasonable and has, quite rightly, been broken by scientists.

Feyerabend can argue in this way, proposing theories contrary to evidence, because of his less than reverential attitude to facts. Accepting the position of Popper and Lakatos that observation is theory-laden, and the stronger position of Kuhn that the dominant paradigm will determine one's appreciation of the real world, Feyerabend claims that 'facts are constituted by older ideologies'.[57] Facts are not, then, arbiters of theories, but, rather, are dependent on them.

Any inconsistency between the given facts and a new theory is really a clash between an older theory and a new one. Given that no theory ever squares with all the available evidence, one cannot reject a theory on the grounds of inconsistency with the facts and, moreover, one should perhaps welcome such inconsistent theories as an advance on the older theories which constitute the given facts. Feyerabend concludes that there can be no test of a theory which is neutral of the theory itself, and that competing theories are thus incommensurable.[58]

Feyerabend shares with Kuhn certain conclusions which are critical of the positions of Popper and Lakatos: that science is not only based on human decisions, but is wholly socially conventional; that observation is not only theory-laden, but is theory-determined; and that competing theories are not only difficult to evaluate, but are incommensurable. These conclusions are won not by challenging, but by developing, the basic assumptions of Popper and Lakatos, and by making explicit some implicit weaknesses and problems in their work. Feyerabend, in his turn, extends the logic of Kuhn and exposes some of the inherent weaknesses of the latter's work. Kuhn casts doubt on the objectivity and rationality of science, and suggests that science may be ideological. Feyerabend extends the critique of science and method, and claims boldly that science is but one ideology among others. Feyerabend accepts Kuhn's thesis of incommensurability and makes explicit the relativism that is implicit in it. He does not, as Kuhn does, search for some more or less objective measure of theory choice. He sees such a search as futile.

Feyerabend denies that there can be any 'method which turns ideologically contaminated ideas into true and useful theories' and denies also that there can be any 'objective measure of all ideologies'.[59] Since science is no better, nor worse, than ideology, and since no particular theory is better, or worse, than any other, one should, according to Feyerabend, be tolerant of all theories. Feyerabend's general position is accurately defined as tolerant or permissive anarchism. His anarchism is an extension of the liberalism of Popper, which is based on the absence of certainty and absolute truth, and of Lakatos, which is based on the absence of absolute falsity. Liberalism which is tolerant, because it knows no certainty, is always vulnerable to evil and error, and to ideologies which tolerate nothing but themselves. That Feyerabend is able to expose weaknesses and problems in the work of Popper and Lakatos does not, though, place him beyond criticism.

Denying any objective measure of theories, Feyerabend claims that a theory can be refuted only by establishing its internal contradictions.[60] Feyerabend can be caught in this trap of his own making. As noted above, his argument against method involves the claim that the strict application of methodological rules serves only to arrest the progress of science. Progress is something that can be measured only by reference to some methodological rule or standard. Without such a measure, so-called progress is merely change and difference. Thus, Feyerabend contradicts himself by referring to progress and denying the means of measuring it.

Feyerabend may also be caught in something like the 'Mannheim paradox', noted in the previous chapter. If all truth is relative, there being no absolute truth, and if all propositions are equally worthy or worthless, then Feyerabend's account of science is no better, nor worse, than any other. Feyerabend, the epistemological anarchist, may not be troubled by this conclusion. But his readers may properly question the value of his theories and criticism, and doubt the wisdom of a 'flippant Dadaist'.[61] Feyerabend shares with Mannheim an embarrassment about the problem of relativism, and, like Mannheim, seeks to deny it in the name of relationism. Feyerabend seeks to distinguish 'relational judgement' of truth, and 'philosophical relativism', which holds that all ideas are equally true or false, or, more radically, 'that any distribution of truth values over traditions is acceptable'.[62] But for Feyerabend, as for Mannheim, this is a distinction without a difference. If 'truth' is only that of a specific viewpoint or of a specific tradition, and no more, then it is relative, and no more. When Feyerabend's embarrassment about relativism is slightest, he dismisses it as a problem by saying that 'intellectuals are afraid of it because relativism threatens their role in society'.[63] Intellectuals and others are rightly afraid of relativism which encourages an irresponsible attitude towards the crucial intellectual and moral decisions and choices which life demands.

CONCLUSION

None of the four philosophers of science considered above would argue that the methods of natural science can be applied directly and wholly, without qualification, in the social sciences, and one of them, Feyerabend, is, of course, against method in science. Yet all four are prepared to consider the relation of natural science methods and ideology, and all four are keen to minimalise the differences between natural and social science. Popper recognises that there are differences between the methods of the natural and social sciences, just as there are differences between the various natural sciences, but believes that 'fundamentally' the methods are the same and so proposes 'a doctrine of the unity of method'.[64] Popper also stresses the social and political importance of demarcating science (as such) from ideology. Lakatos follows Popper on these two issues, but has been less influential, perhaps, on the work of social scientists. Kuhn writes largely of the natural sciences but has been most influential, perhaps, in the social sciences. Although he is concerned about the application of his thought in areas outside science, and about the subsequent neglect of his argument about the distinctiveness of science, Kuhn recognises that in so far as he 'portrays scientific development as a succession of tradition bound periods punctuated by non-cumulative breaks' his 'theses are undoubtedly of wide applicability'. This is only to be expected because, as Kuhn admits, his theses are borrowed from fields other than the natural sciences, including politics.[65] Feyerabend is against method, but would seem to be against it in both the natural and social sciences, and so would seem to argue for a unity of anti-method.

From this review of the work of four leading contemporary philosophers of science it should be clear that they provide inadequate resources for the construction of a political science which can be clearly demarcated from, and provide an antidote to, political ideology. Popper and Lakatos claim to offer a method which can demarcate science and ideology, but both fail to sustain their claims. Popper fails to offer adequate justification for the important human decisions involved in science. Lakatos confirms and extends the need for human decisions in science, and fails to justify these decisions by failing to demonstrate any clear measure of scientific progress or means of theory choice. Kuhn extends the conventionalism of Popper and Lakatos, and concludes that science is no more than a social convention, and that different social conventions are incommensurable. Kuhn suggests that science may be no more than ideological. Feyerabend confirms that science is no more than ideology, and makes explicit the relativism implicit in the work of Kuhn.

The failure of these four theorists to provide an adequate demarcation of science and ideology is their failure to deal adequately with values. Popper fails to provide any justification for the decision for rationality, which is the essential characteristic of science, for he sees this as an unjustifiable moral choice. Popper is a moral relativist who sees all moral judgements as unjustifiable human decisions. Since his philosophy of science rests on an unjustifiable moral choice, he is no less an epistemological relativist. For Lakatos also, the human decisions underpinning science are not scientific and cannot be shown to be reasonable. Thus, decisions made in science cannot be shown to be better than ideological preferences. Kuhn sees all values, including those of science, to be relative to particular paradigms, which are incommensurable. Extending the logic of this line of argument, Feyerabend concludes that all values are equally worthy or worthless, and that there is no special value in science as distinct from ideology.

The failure to demarcate science and ideology, which is the failure to deal adequately with values, is also the failure to provide an adequate model for the study of politics. Any science of politics constructed on the basis of Popper's philosophy of science is likely to be characterised by value-freedom, or at least the separation or dualism of facts and values.[66] This is likely to be true also in the case of Lakatos. A political science built on the basis of Kuhn's philosophy of science is likely, as Alan Ryan notes, to offer no escape from political ideology. In the case of Feyerabend, there would seem to be no doubt about the identity of political science and political ideology. That the study of politics cannot be value-free is the argument of Chapter 6. That the demarcation of political science and political ideology is the demarcation of proper and improper political values is one of the general arguments of the book.

5 Non-Naturalist and Realist Political Science and Political Ideology

INTRODUCTION

Not all students of politics and society accept that the methods of the natural sciences are applicable in their field, and not all naturalist political and social scientists accept the positivist and post-positivist philosophies of science considered in the previous chapter. These two strands of thought, criticisms of naturalism, and criticisms of positivist and post-positivist philosophies of science, are the concern of the present chapter.

What is referred to as non-naturalism, or anti-naturalism, has a long and varied tradition, but can be summarised briefly as holding that the subject matter of the natural sciences differs from that of the social sciences, and that consequently the methods of the former are not appropriate for the latter. Non-naturalist arguments about subject matter range from those about differences in degree to those about differences in kind between the natural and social sciences. About method, non-naturalist arguments range from those about the difficulty to those about the impossibility of fashioning the social sciences on the model of the natural sciences. There is a wide variety of non-naturalist arguments, but this chapter concentrates on one general, central theme of great importance and influence, which often underlies other arguments. I note some other non-naturalist arguments in passing when considering an example of anti-positivist philosophy of science. The general theme may be formulated thus: whereas the subject matter of the natural sciences acts unconsciously in accord with objective laws of nature and is to be explained in causal terms, the subject matter of the social sciences are conscious human beings who understand what they do and whose action is to be interpreted in terms of the meanings invested therein.

This general notion of the interpretation of meaningful behaviour can be traced back at least as far as late-nineteenth-century theorists such as Heinrich Rickert and Wilhelm Dilthey. Such figures developed the theory of hermeneutics, originally concerned with the interpretation of handwritten texts, especially Bibles, and later concerned with the interpretation of the meaning of human behaviour. From such theorists stems also the method known as *Verstehen*, usually translated as understanding, which is concerned with gaining access to the meanings which humans give to their actions. The concept of *Verstehen* is perhaps most familiar from the work of one of the founding fathers of sociology, Max Weber. He seeks to unite, in some way, *Verstehen* and causal analysis by arguing that any social explanation must be adequate at both the level of meaning and the level of causality. There is doubt and confusion about what exactly Weber meant by this. Naturalists might concede that some form of interpretation may suggest hypotheses about human behaviour, but claim that such hypotheses still have to be tested empirically.[1] Another approach contributing to the general non-naturalist theme of interpretation or understanding is that of phenomenology, developed by early-twentieth-century theorists such as Edmund Husserl and Martin Heidegger. Phenomenology is concerned with the *a priori* examination of the objects of experience (phenomena), seen as essences intuited by the mind. From philosophical phenomenology there derives a sociological phenomenology, exemplified in the work of Alfred Schutz, concerned with the examination of the social world in terms of human consciousness of it. Also influential in the development of the non-naturalist theme of interpretation is mid-twentieth-century linguistic analysis, with its emphasis on the analysis of language as the key to the understanding of meaning. This chapter examines the non-naturalist arguments of Peter Winch, which derive largely from the linguistic philosophy of Ludwig Wittgenstein.[2]

In addition to the challenge of interpretive social science, naturalism would seem to face also the problem of human values. Not only can human beings invest their behaviour with meaning, they can also make choices about acting this way or that and so render their behaviour subject to moral evaluation. Natural science aspires to explanation whereas the study of humanity would seem to involve also evaluation. Most, though not all, naturalist social science aspires to be value-free, and for this reason may be criticised as being inadequate for the study of humanity. Such an argument is noted here and developed more fully in the next chapter.

Interpretive social science poses a challenge to naturalism, but is itself not without problems. In considering some of these problems I note the response of a naturalist and later examine his work in more detail. Roy Bhaskar proposes a naturalist social science critical of interpretive social science, which is based on a realist philosophy of science critical of positivism and post-positivism. Although critical of much interpretive social science, including the work of Peter Winch, Bhaskar is not uncritical of naturalism. I note what he describes as the limits of naturalism. Bhaskar's work is a proper challenge to the errors of positivist naturalism and non-naturalist interpretive social science, but it is not without problems of its own. These problems are most apparent in Bhaskar's interesting claims that his qualified naturalism can expose the falsity of ideology and deal with the problems of human values.

PETER WINCH'S NON-NATURALIST PHILOSOPHY OF SOCIAL SCIENCE

In *The Idea of a Social Science and its Relation to Philosophy*,[3] Peter Winch presents a case against naturalism based on the arguments that the subject matter of the so-called social sciences is different in kind from that of the natural sciences, and that the methods of the natural sciences are wholly inappropriate for the study of society. The proper understanding of social behaviour is, Winch argues further, a matter for philosophy, itself to be understood in a distinctive way. Winch's book has been of great significance in the social sciences in the past few decades, if only because it has been so hotly debated.[4] Winch's arguments are particularly sharp and distinctive challenges to naturalism, albeit arguments which are themselves seriously flawed. Winch is not particularly concerned with the application of his arguments in the study of politics, although he offers a few political examples. He is, he says, concerned with the 'notion of a social study as such' and he doubts that the methodological differences of particular kinds of social study can affect the broad outlines of what he has to say.[5] What Winch says about understanding different forms of life, social institutions and belief systems applies, one must assume, to political systems, institutions, practices and ideologies.

Following the well-established non-naturalist tradition, and making specific reference to Max Weber, Winch argues that the subject matter of the social sciences differs from that of the natural sciences in so far as social behaviour is meaningful. Social behaviour may be said to be meaningful in that it has a meaning not only for those who study it but also, crucially, for those who act or perform it.[6] Whereas the subject matter of the natural sciences behaves according to laws and forces which are external to it and which it cannot understand, human beings act in ways which have some meaning for them, precisely because they understand themselves and their social context.

To understand what Winch means by meaningful behaviour it is necessary to consider the other important influence on his thought: the philosophy of Ludwig Wittgenstein. Wittgenstein's thought underwent at least one significant change, but there is in all his work a common concern with language. In his early *Tractatus Logico-Philosophicus*, published in English in 1922, Wittgenstein presents a picture theory of language: language consists of pictures of facts, collected in propositions, and thus represents reality to us. In his later work, particularly *Philosophical Investigations*, published posthumously in 1953, Wittgenstein corrects himself and offers an account of language in terms of tools to be used and games to be played. Accordingly, language can be used in certain ways in the context of language games played according to certain rules. The use of language is a matter of following certain rules. Language is essentially social in that language games and their rules are established only in a social context or in a form of life. Language serves the purposes of society and the rules of language games operate in a public way. There can be no private language for Wittgenstein.

Winch seeks to develop the linguistic philosophy of the later Wittgenstein by arguing that human behaviour in general, like language in particular, involves the following of public rules. According to Winch, 'all behaviour which is meaningful (therefore all specifically human behaviour) is *ipso facto* rule-governed'.[7] Human behaviour makes sense, or has a meaning, to both actor and observer, only if it is behaviour done in accord, or not, with public rules. Presumably behaviour which is entirely arbitrary and ungoverned by any rule can make no sense and have no meaning to anyone. Winch attempts to clarify the notion of meaningful behaviour as rule-following behaviour in what has become a controversial claim: 'I want to say that the test of whether a man's actions are the application of a rule is not whether he can *formulate* it but whether it makes sense to distinguish between a right or wrong way of doing things in connection with what he does.'[8] The rules need not be fully formulable by those who follow them, nor need they be formally and explicitly formulated by others, but without rules according to which action may be in accord, or not, action cannot be said to be meaningful at all.[9] The rules must be public and social.[10] The rules can exist only in a social context for they are rules about human behaviour and interaction, which is what makes society and is done in society. The rules cannot be private, for if they were there could be no mutual understanding of meaningful human behaviour, and so no social interaction, and so no society. The meaningfulness of behaviour, which may be understood and interpreted, and the actual behaviour, which is observable, are one and the same thing. As Winch puts it: 'the social relations between men and the ideas which men's actions embody are really the same thing considered from different points of view'.[11] The study of society thus involves the interpretation of the meaningfulness embodied in observable behaviour.

It can now be seen why, according to Winch, the study of society cannot be conducted on the model of the natural sciences, or why 'the notion of a human society involves a scheme of concepts which is logically incompatible with the kinds of explanation offered in the natural sciences'.[12] If the study of society is not a matter for science, it must be a matter for philosophy. The difference between science and philosophy, for Winch, is that between the empirical/experimental, causal analysis of particular real things and processes on the one hand, and the *a priori*, conceptual study of the nature of reality as such and in general.[13] The study of society as such is not an empirical matter but a conceptual one, concerned with 'the *force of the concept* of reality'; any empirical study would simply beg the question of what evidence is to count as reality. What makes social study essentially conceptual, and little but conceptual, is that social reality is itself constituted by concepts. Thus the study of society is a study of the concept of society, and as such the study of the concepts of those whose behaviour constitutes society.[14] The study of society, then, involves understanding the meaning of human behaviour. By contrast, the scientific study of particular real things or processes involves establishing the causal or statistical regularities according to which those things and processes act in a non-meaningful way. Winch expresses this contrast rather neatly by suggesting 'that social interaction can more properly be compared to the exchange of ideas in a conversation than to the interaction of forces in a physical system'.[15] Winch does not, of course, wish to deny that there are regularities apparent in social behaviour; he denies only that social regularities can be understood in terms of some physical, causal law or statistical regularity operating on humans, beyond their understanding. The regularities of social behaviour are to be understood in terms of the social rules which are conceived by actors, and to which their behaviour conforms, or not. Winch challenges Weber's argument that all social explanations must be adequate at both the level of meaning and the level of causation. Winch questions Weber's suggestion that *Verstehen* is methodologically incomplete and needs supplementing by causal or statistical analyses. According to Winch, no interpretation of human behaviour can be conclusively validated or invalidated by appeal to empirical evidence.[16]

The difference between the causal laws or generalisations of the natural sciences and the interpretations appropriate to the social sciences is clarified by Winch in terms of the issue of prediction and falsification. In the natural sciences, 'a falsified prediction always implies some sort of mistake on the part of the predictor: false or inadequate data, faulty calculation, or defective theory'.[17] It may be recalled from the discussion in the previous chapter that this is certainly the case for Karl Popper. In the understanding of social behaviour this is not the case. The interpretation of how some human agent will behave in the future will involve a study of the concepts in terms of which the agent understands the situation and the decisions to be made. Any prediction made on the basis of this interpretation may turn out to be wrong, but the conceptual base on which it is made remains compatible with whatever decision the agent makes. The interpretation may be faulty, but also the agent may not follow properly the social rule which is acknowledged in the interpretation. The interpretation of human behaviour is a conceptual matter, and not to be falsified or confirmed by empirical evidence.

A further crucial difference between natural scientists and social scientists, for Winch, is that the former impose their explanations upon their subject matter, whereas the latter let the viewpoints of their subject matter structure their interpretation. Winch establishes this difference by means of a consideration of the social behaviour of scientists.[18] It is central to Winch's general argument that all human behaviour is rule-governed, and this is true of the way that natural scientists establish laws and generalisations about natural phenomena. What are to count as identical pieces of evidence supporting a law-like generalisation are determined by the social rules that operate within the community of scientists. Thus, in understanding the behaviour of scientists one must take account not only of the relation of scientists to their subject matter, but also the relation of scientists one to the other, in their community.[19] Whereas natural scientists operate with only one set of rules, those pertaining to the community of scientists themselves, social scientists, necessarily operate with two sets of rules: those governing the operation of social scientists; and those governing the behaviour of the subject matter of social scientists. Thus arises what has been referred to as the problem of the 'double hermeneutic' in the social sciences.[20] The theories of social science are themselves an aspect of a form of life, governed by certain rules. But these theories are about other forms of life governed by other rules. Understanding concepts which are themselves about concepts necessarily presents some problems.

Winch is in no doubt that social scientists must give priority to the rules which govern their subject matter, rather than the rules which govern their own conduct, when offering interpretations of their subject matter.[21] He does not mean that the interpretation of an agent's behaviour must be no more than the agent's own understanding of his or her behaviour. Agents may be unreflective and presumably could be confused about their behaviour. But any more reflective interpretation offered by a social scientist, which might involve concepts taken from a social scientific form of life, must imply a prior understanding of the concepts which belong to the agent's behaviour.[22] Any interpretation or explanation offered by an investigator must be comprehensible not only to others but also to the agent.[23] The investigator need not subscribe to the beliefs of the agent under investigation, but the investigator must seek to understand them in their social context.[24] Where there is a clash of beliefs or standards it would be 'illegitimate' for an investigator to assume that he or she is right and the agent is wrong.[25] It would be improper for an investigator 'arbitrarily to impose his own standards from without. In so far as he does so, the events he is studying lose altogether their character as *social* events.'[26] The error of attempting to apply the methods of the natural sciences in the study of society is apparent, says Winch, in the work of Durkheim. As noted in Chapter 3, Durkheim offers social science as the corrective of pre-scientific ideology. Social scientific concepts and theories offer an objective account of social reality, which is masked by the ideological understanding of agents. Winch would argue that in detaching his analysis from the viewpoint of the agents under investigation Durkheim renders his analysis irrelevant.

CRITICISMS OF WINCH

Winch's work has been subjected to many criticisms, only some of which are directly relevant to my concerns and so will be considered here.[27] Given my concern with the relationship of ideology, science and philosophy as modes of political thought, and the importance of values in political theory, I will consider three interrelated criticisms of Winch: his contrast of philosophy and science as modes of enquiry; his seeming denial of cross-cultural standards of enquiry and evaluation, and the attendant problem of relativism; and his privileging of the agent's point of view.

Winch's argument that the methods of natural science are inappropriate for the study of society rests not only on his notion of society but also on his notion of science. If his conception of science is questionable, then so too are his arguments against naturalism. Roy Bhaskar argues that Winch's 'anti-naturalist stance is based on an untenable theory of science', which is Humean, empiricist and positivist.[28] Bhaskar notes that one of Winch's main anti-naturalist arguments is that social scientific explanations cannot be reduced to the causal generalisations of natural science, which are based on observed regularities or constant conjunctions of perceived causes and effects. As noted above, Winch does wish to argue that the task of social science, which is really philosophy, is the analysis of the conceptualisations of agents, and not the causal analysis of the relation of social behaviour and some supposed external moving force. In his insistence that social behaviour and the ideas which such behaviour embodies are really the same thing considered from different points of view, Winch seems to deny that behaviour and ideas (such as motives and reasons) can be distinguished as (constantly conjoined) effects and causes.[29] Winch's argument against causal analysis in the social sciences does seem to be an argument against the Humean, empiricist, positivist model of causal explanation. In the preface to the second edition of *The Idea of a Social Science and its Relation to Philosophy*, Winch acknowledges this: 'I found myself at times denying that human behaviour can be understood in causal terms, when I should have been saying that our understanding of human behaviour is not elucidated by anything like the account of "cause" given by Hume.'[30] Bhaskar argues that there may be no need to accept Winch's attack on naturalism if there is available a more adequate theory of science than that originally identified by Winch. As Bhaskar would put it, if there is available a more adequate non-empiricist, non-positivist science, there may be the possibility of naturalism. The adequacy of Bhaskar's alternative realist theory of social science is considered later in this chapter.

If, as Winch argues, social behaviour must be understood in terms of the social rules and concepts peculiar to a form of life, and if different forms of life are evident in our world, then he would seem to suggest that cross-cultural analysis and explanation is not just difficult but impossible. Applying the principles of *The Idea of a Social Science and its Relation to Philosophy* in the field of social anthropology and to the problem of how to understand a primitive, alien society, Winch says: 'the concepts used by primitive peoples can only be interpreted in the context of the way of life of these people'.[31] To engage in any cross-cultural study one would necessarily have to determine similarities and differences, but such determinations could be made only on the basis of some rule, and such a rule would be peculiar to a distinct culture or form of life. Winch would seem to argue that cultures are incommensurable, in the way that paradigms are for Thomas Kuhn. As Alasdair MacIntyre points out, if one accepts Winch's claim that one cannot go beyond a society's own self-description, and if one accepts that there are no culturally independent standards or criteria of judgement, then cross-cultural comparison would be rendered logically impossible. As such comparison does seem to be possible, one can question Winch's claim.[32]

Winch's denial of the availability of culturally independent criteria of judgement ensnares him in the classic problem of relativism. Winch acknowledges that 'we should not lose sight of the fact that the idea that man's ideas and beliefs must be checkable by reference to something independent – some reality – is an important one. To abandon it is to plunge straight into an extreme ... relativism, with all the paradoxes that involves.'[33] It is precisely because Winch denies there can be any reality independent of culture-bound concepts, and claims that all is relative to our culture-bound concepts, that he may be charged with what Ernest Gellner terms 'profound conceptual relativism' and 'symmetrical relativism ("symmetrical" in the sense of being egalitarian as between cultures, refusing to judge any of them in terms of another or in terms of a supposedly external norm)'.[34] Stemming from this basic conceptual and cultural relativism there is ontological relativism: 'The world *is* for us what is presented through . . . [our] concepts.' 'Reality is not what gives language sense. What is real and what is unreal shows itself *in* the sense that language has.'[35] There is epistemological relativism: 'The concepts we have settle for us the form of experience we have of the world.'[36] There is logical relativism: 'criteria of logic are not a direct gift from God, but arise out of, and are only intelligible in the context of, ways of living or modes of social life'.[37] And there is, importantly, moral relativism: 'there is an irreducible historical contingency in the norms that a society adheres to'.[38] It is hardly surprising there should be moral relativism, for Winch argues that the problem of morality involves not so much the evaluation of human behaviour but more the understanding of it.[39] The reduction of moral evaluation to mere understanding is an improper move, which seriously devalues an important aspect of human life. The fact that Winch makes the move indicates that he considers moral evaluation, like social understanding, to be bound up in the particular concepts of particular societies. Winch even claims that between those who share a common culture there may be irresolvable moral disputes.[40]

Winch, like many other theorists, seeks to avoid the charge of relativism. The vain attempts of Mannheim and Feyerabend have been noted in previous chapters. Winch's attempt may be no more successful. His attempt involves an *a priori*, rationalist argument to the effect that no matter how they differ, all societies must entertain certain common standards, and that such standards must be natural rather than conventional. For example: 'the notion of a society in which there is a language but in which truth telling is not regarded as the norm is a self-contradictory one'.[41] Winch, following Wittgenstein, argues that in any use of language in society there necessarily is a distinction between telling the truth and telling lies, and that such a distinction makes no sense without some norm or rule of truthfulness embodied in society. Similarly, for Winch, 'to say of a society that it has a language is also to say that it has a concept of rationality'.[42] Such rationalist arguments are perfectly valid, and are a minimal stance against relativism. However, Winch undermines such arguments with his insistence that human behaviour is to be understood in terms of the concepts peculiar to the culture in which such behaviour is performed. If standards such as truth-telling and rationality are universal, they must transcend all particular cultures and forms of life. A further problem for Winch is that the supposedly universal standards are purely formal and the particular content of the concepts of truth-telling and rationality differs from society to society.[43] If there is no common substantive content to the supposedly universal standards of truth and rationality, they are largely redundant.

I turn now to the problems arising from Winch's argument that understanding human behaviour must start with the agent's point of view and indeed conclude in concepts which are compatible with the agent's own. I consider here the work of Charles Taylor, a political philosopher who shares with Winch an opposition to naturalism and a commitment to the interpretation of human behaviour in its social or community context, but who is nevertheless critical of some aspects of Winch's work. Taylor criticises naturalistic social science for merely elaborating the obvious; for failing to address the interesting questions; and for its reductionism.[44] Naturalism fails to appreciate the significance of human agency, and in particular the fact that human agents are not only capable of self-understanding but are actually constituted by this. Naturalism also fails to appreciate that human agency necessarily involves evaluation of the worth of certain things.[45] An adequate human or social science must, for Taylor, involve something like interpretation or understanding together with evaluation. Taylor criticises also what he refers to as 'atomism', a political (and also scientific) theory which views society as composed of independent individuals. Atomism fails to appreciate the significance of community. For Taylor, not only self-understanding but also the community is 'constituitive of the individual, in the sense that the self-interpretations which define him are drawn from the interchange which the community carries on'.[46]

In outlining what he takes to be an adequate social science, Taylor has reason to criticise Winch. Studying human beings as agents whose self-understanding is constitutive of their behaviour does not mean adopting the agent's point of view, and this for two reasons. First, adopting the agent's point of view might render enquiry unilluminating because often agents are wrong, confused or deluded about their behaviour. Second, adopting the agent's point of view would render impossible a scientific study when dealing with a so-called primitive society which had not yet adopted a scientific point of view.[47] Taylor argues that interpretive social science must grasp the agent's point of view in order to identify its subject matter, but should seek to 'make the agent's doings clearer than they were to him'.[48] Taylor makes reference to Marxist theory which claims to reveal the reality masked by appearances. Certainly, if one were to adopt the agent's point of view it would be impossible to distinguish false consciousness and true consciousness, and impossible to uphold, as I wish to do, a negative and restrictive concept of ideology.[49]

In refusing to adopt and be satisfied by the agent's point of view, Taylor is not, of course, retreating to the naturalist method which claims to disregard all points of view in the name of scientific objectivity. The agent's point of view has some significance, and, says Taylor, 'allegedly neutral scientific languages, by claiming to avoid understanding, always end up being unwittingly ethnocentric'. The terms of such languages 'all reflect the stress on instrumental reason in our civilisation since the seventeenth century', and are dependent on 'self-definition of an individualistic kind'.[50] If one is not to adopt the agent's point of view, must one adopt one's own? Is one then committed to ethnocentricity? No, Taylor responds. It is an error 'to hold that the language of cross-cultural theory has to be either theirs or ours'.[51] Taylor advocates what he calls 'a language of perspicuous contrast'. This language would allow one to formulate both another way of life and one's own as alternative possibilities, in relation to some human constants in both, and to criticise the self-understanding of others while amending one's own.[52] This interpretive method, employing a language of perspicuous contrast, helps one avoid, says Taylor, both 'a supposedly neutral social science' and 'a debilitating relativism'. He concludes: 'understanding is inseparable from criticism, but this in turn is inseparable from self-criticism'.[53]

Taylor's version of interpretive social science is, I think, of some value for a number of reasons: it offers a further critique of naturalism, showing that naturalism not only incorrectly neglects agents' self-understanding but also betrays the objectivity and neutrality it proclaims; it offers a critique of Winch's interpretive method, which accepts the incorrigibility of the agent's point of view and necessarily leads to relativism; and it stresses the critical and evaluative, as well as interpretive and explanatory, nature of social enquiry. However, Taylor is not beyond criticism. His social scientific method would seem to limit enquiry to a comparison of principles and practices evident and available in particular communities. It is hard to see how one could transcend particular cultures in one's search for a more adequate self-understanding. Indeed, Taylor, the communitarian, seems to regard with suspicion all attempts to secure culturally transcendent standards. He is prepared to say, with Winch, that there is a plurality of standards of rationality, but wishes to move beyond Winch to argue, puzzlingly, that precisely because standards are incommensurable, transcultural judgements can be made. But such judgements seem to rely on little more than empirical evidence of how the standards and practices of one culture come to attract the attention of other cultures. Taylor also admits that such transcultural judgements may themselves be incommensurable. He claims that in transcultural judgement 'there is no such thing as a single argument proving *global* superiority'.[54] Taylor may be critical of the culture-bound nature of Winch's social science, but he may himself be no less relativist.[55]

In conclusion, Winch poses a proper challenge to the sort of naturalism that neglects the distinctive, meaningful character of human behaviour. However, Winch may throw out the naturalist baby with the positivist bathwater, and his sort of non-naturalist interpretive social science seems to entail relativism and deny the possibility of criticising agents' points of view. For Winch, all ideas and beliefs are relative to their social context, and there are no transcultural standards of belief. When studying society one must work with the agent's point of view and not subject it to rational criticism. Thus, although Winch does not offer a theory of ideology, he would seem to accept, implicitly, the inclusive conception of ideology and deny, implicitly, the negative and restrictive conception which I wish to uphold. For Winch, there can be no scientific or philosophical critique of ideology, or of ideas of any sort. For Winch, philosophy is '*uncommitted* enquiry'.[56] This means that philosophy, and social science which is philosophy, elucidates various forms of life and belief, and treats them all equally and uncritically. Philosophy and social science, for Winch, cannot aspire to be normative and deal with the problem of human values.

ROY BHASKAR'S REALIST NATURALISM

As noted above, Roy Bhaskar criticises Peter Winch's antinaturalist stance by arguing that it is based on an untenable, positivist notion of science. In a number of recent publications Bhaskar has established an alternative non-positivist, realist theory of science, and has argued that on the basis of such a science there can be a qualified naturalist social science. Moreover, this naturalist social science, according to Bhaskar, can provide a moral critique of society and a theory for human emancipation.[57] Bhaskar's realist theory of science is opposed to positivism, then, and to the post-positivist philosophies of science of theorists such as Popper, Lakatos, Kuhn and Feyerabend, considered in the previous chapter. Bhaskar's qualified naturalist social science is opposed to the errors of the hermeneutic and interpretive approaches, including that of Winch, and also to the value-free stance which such approaches often share with positivism. Bhaskar's normative, realist social science involves a critique of ideology and a notion of real, as opposed to false, human interests, which owes much to some aspects of the Marxist tradition, considered in Chapter 2 above. Bhaskar's realist theories of science and social science have much to commend them, in so far as they seek to sustain an account of objective reality, both natural and social, upon which one might build sound critiques of prevailing erroneous doctrines and, in particular, a critique of ideology. However, Bhaskar's theories have flaws, particularly concerning objective human nature and values.

Bhaskar defines scientific realism as 'the theory that the

objects of scientific enquiry exist and act, for the most part, quite independently of scientists and their activity'.[58] Scientific realism is not the only form of realism and is to be distinguished from, for example, predicative realism, which asserts 'the existence of universals independently (Plato) or as the properties (Aristotle) of particular things', and perceptual realism, which asserts 'the existence of material objects in space and time independently of their perception'.[59] Scientific realism may take a number of forms, and that which Bhaskar offers is termed transcendental realism. Transcendental arguments are concerned with demonstrating what the world must be like in order for certain sorts of experience and knowledge to be possible. Thus, the transcendental argument which supports scientific realism consists of 'an elaboration of what the world must be like *prior* to any empirical investigation of it and *for* any scientific attitudes or activities to be possible'.[60] For Bhaskar, science is possible only if there exists a reality, structured in a certain way, which is independent of scientific enquiry and is accounted for by our scientific theories. Bhaskar's transcendental realism is a philosophy of science, or as he prefers it, a philosophy for science, according to which philosophy and science share the same subject matter and differ only in terms of method. He says: 'that the world is structured and differentiated can be established by philosophical argument; though the particular structures it contains and the ways in which it is differentiated are matters for substantive scientific investigation'.[61] Philosophy, for Bhaskar, is an *a priori* discipline,which serves as underlabourer or midwife to science.[62] Winch objects to such conceptions of philosophy and its subordinate relationship to science. Yet both Winch and Bhaskar sharply distinguish *a priori* philosophy and empirical science, and thus vitiate their respective attempts to establish an adequate study of human behaviour.

According to Bhaskar the transcendental realist argument demonstrates that reality is structured and differentiated in three overlapping domains: the real, the actual and the empirical. The domain of the real consists of causal structures and generative mechanisms; the domain of the actual consists of the events, and patterns of events, generated by the distinct structures and mechanisms; and the domain of the empirical consists of our experiences of the distinct events.[63] Bhaskar argues that science, and in particular experimentation, makes sense only if there are objects of scientific knowledge, causal laws, which are other than human experiences and also other than the particular patterns of events. There must, argues Bhaskar, be intransitive mechanisms which tend to operate in certain ways so as to generate the flux of events of which we can have experience.[64] It is the task of science, and in particular of experimentation, to control and study nature so as to identify the causal properties or ways of acting of things. The three domains of reality, although causally linked, are seldom in phase and indeed it is the activity of science that tends to make them so.[65]

Any realist theory would seem to entail a distinction between independent reality and the human thoughts and investigations of which it is independent. For Bhaskar, there is the crucial distinction between the intransitive and transitive objects of human knowledge: between the real world which would remain as it is even if humans ceased to exist and could not know it, and the human knowledge of the world which, because it is a social product, is subject to change.[66] This distinction is also expressed by Bhaskar as one between the intransitive, ontological, and the transitive, epistemological dimensions of the world: between the independent real world as it exists, and human knowledge of the real world.[67] In addition to these two dimensions there is also what Bhaskar refers to as the metacritical dimension of discourse in which transitive human knowledge is critically and self-reflexively scrutinised.[68]

The distinction in question is further expressed by Bhaskar as one between ontological realism and epistemological relativism (or epistemic relativity).[69] The real world may exist as it does, independent of human thought, but humans can know it only through particular descriptions which, being social products, are subject to change. Thus, human knowledge is relative to criteria which change in time and space. Ontological realism and epistemic relativity would seem to presuppose one another according to Bhaskar. There can be an independent reality only if it is distinguished from, and irreducible to, our knowledge and investigations of it. Human knowledge changes, and such change is intelligible only in terms of an intransitive reality of which we claim to have knowledge.[70] Epistemic relativity entails the rejection of any correspondence theory of truth, according to which a proposition is true if it corresponds with reality. For Bhaskar, a proposition is true if and only if the state of affairs that it describes is real, but the relationship here cannot be one of correspondence. Rather, 'the judgement of the truth of a proposition is necessarily intrinsic to the science concerned'.[71] As science changes, so knowledge and truth are relative. To deny epistemic relativism, Bhaskar says, is to embrace 'some type of epistemological *absolutism* (which, by a short route, invariably results in some kind of idealism)'.[72] For Bhaskar, to claim absolute knowledge is, clearly, to identify knowledge with reality, or reduce ontology to epistemology. I do not see why one need draw this conclusion. If there exists an objective, absolute reality, then there can be, in principle if not always in practice, objective, absolute knowledge which corresponds to this. There is no need to reduce reality to knowledge of it. Indeed, just as there can be an objective reality only if it is distinguished from our knowledge of it, so we can have objective knowledge only if there exists a distinct objective reality which is the measure of our knowledge. Leaving this matter aside, it is interesting to note that Bhaskar denies that epistemic relativity entails judgemental relativism, according to which all beliefs are equally valid and there is no good reason to prefer one to another. There can be rational standards of judgement, Bhaskar says, although such standards are 'intrinsic to the science concerned' and so remain 'historically situationally specific'.[73] It is not clear how epistemic relativity differs from judgemental rationality, and I return to this problem later.

It can now be seen how Bhaskar's scientific realism differs from, and is critical of, other philosophies of science. As Bhaskar notes, the mainstream of modern philosophy of science is empiricist and positivist. Within this tradition the objects of knowledge are atomistic events, and experience of the conjunction of such events presents the only basis for scientific analysis in terms of causal laws.[74] There is a tendency within this tradition towards the 'epistemic fallacy': a tendency to collapse statements about ontology into statements about epistemology.[75] For Bhaskar, causal laws express tendencies of real structures and generative mechanisms, and are not merely empirical regularities.[76] Moreover, it is characteristic of the realism which Bhaskar supports that ontology must not be reduced to epistemology. Bhaskar is critical also of the deductive form of explanation, stemming from the empiricist and positivist tradition, and elaborated by contemporary philosophers of science such as Popper. Explanation, argues Bhaskar, must refer to real generative mechanisms, and cannot remain at the superficial level of covering laws and empirical regularities.[77] The other main tradition in the philosophy of science which Bhaskar identifies and criticises is idealist. According to the idealist tradition, the natural world is no more than a construction of the human mind. In a contemporary version of idealism, in the work of Kuhn, the natural world becomes a construction of the collective mind, or paradigm, of the scientific community.[78] The error here, of course, is the failure to distinguish intransitive reality from transitive knowledge.

On the basis of his realist theory of science Bhaskar argues for the possibility of naturalism. By naturalism Bhaskar means 'the thesis that there is (or can be) an essential unity of method between the natural and social sciences'. Naturalism is not to be confused with reductionism, 'which asserts that there is an actual identity of subject matter', nor with scientism, 'which denies that there are any significant differences in the methods appropriate to studying social and natural objects'.[79] Bhaskar offers, then, a qualified naturalism. The qualifications or limits to be placed on naturalism are ontological, relational and critical.[80]

The ontological limits of naturalism arise, of course, from the nature of the subject matter of the human and social sciences. Social structures, unlike natural structures, are action-dependent, concept-dependent and space–time-dependent. Bhaskar clarifies and summarises these points as follows:

(1) Social structures, unlike natural structures, do not exist independently of the activities they govern;
(2) Social structures, unlike natural structures, do not exist independently of the agent's conception of what they are doing in their activity;
(3) Social structures, unlike natural structures, may be only

> relatively enduring (so that the tendencies they ground may not be universal in the sense of space–time invariant).[81]

To understand these peculiarities of social structures it is useful to note Bhaskar's 'transformational model of social activity'.[82] Such a model, Bhaskar argues, avoids the faults of all other models of the relationship of society and individuals. It avoids the faults of both the 'voluntaristic' model of many hermeneutic and interpretive social scientists, according to which social objects are constituted by intentional or meaningful human behaviour, and the 'reification' model, illustrated by the work of Durkheim, according to which social objects are objective things which coerce individuals. It avoids also the faults of any model which seeks to combine these faults. According to Bhaskar's model, individuals do not create society, for social objects always pre-exist them, and society does not exist independently of individuals, for human activity reproduces and transforms social objects. Society and the individual are distinct, and one cannot be reduced to, or explained only in terms of, the other. Yet they are connected in terms of transformation and presuppose one another: society provides the conditions for intentional human activity, which is a necessary condition for society. By distinguishing society and individuals it is possible to argue that human activity is characterised by its intentionality and purposefulness, whilst the transformation affected in the social structure may not be intended. By relating individuals and society in terms of transformation it is possible to argue that people in their conscious activity reproduce unconsciously the structures governing their productive efforts.

On the basis of Bhaskar's transformational model of social activity it can be seen that the generative mechanisms which are the object of social scientific knowledge are dependent on the human action which reproduces and transforms them (while providing the conditions for human action). Also, because social structures are themselves social products, subject to transformation by human action, they can be only relatively enduring and are subject to change in time and place. Further, because they are the products of human activity, social structures are dependent on the conceptions of the conscious human agents who shape them. Bhaskar accepts Winch's notion that the subject matter of the social sciences is concept-dependent, but differs from Winch in arguing that one should not accept that social science 'is *exhausted* by such conceptualisations or that such conceptualisations are *incorrigible*'.[83] Bhaskar criticises the hermeneutic tradition, which includes Winch, for failing to appreciate the validity of scientific realism, and in particular for failing to appreciate that the social conditions for conceptualisations may be real and may exist intransitively or independently of the conceptualisations.[84] Bhaskar, like Taylor, also criticises the hermeneutic tradition for failing to appreciate that the conceptualisations of agents 'may be false or in an important sense inadequate'.[85] The full significance of this critical point is considered later.

The main epistemological limit on naturalism stems not from the fact that the objects of social scientific knowledge are beyond perception, but that they manifest themselves only in open systems. In the natural sciences, with the exception of astronomy, it is possible, by means of experimentation, to close a system and isolate a generative mechanism, to 'produce' empirical regularities, and to conduct decisive tests of theories. Such experimental closure is inapplicable in the social sciences (or applicable only with disastrous effects). Given the lack of decisive tests in the social sciences, theories and laws based on no more than constant conjunctions of events or empirical regularities are out of place, as is Popper's method of falsification. The criteria for the development and replacement of social science theories must be explanatory only and cannot be predictive.[86]

The chief relational limit on naturalism is the fact that 'the social sciences are part of their own field of enquiry'.[87] In the natural world the intransitive objects of knowledge remain unaware of the scientific theories concerning them, and continue to exist and act independently of such science. In the social world, the objects of knowledge are reproduced and transformed by human agents who themselves may be affected by social scientific knowledge. Thus, although the objects of social scientific knowledge exist intransitively, they are causally interdependent with the knowledge of which they are the object.

For my purposes, the most significant limit on naturalism is the critical nature of social science. Bhaskar argues that this critical limit follows directly from the relational limit: 'the consideration that the subject matter of the social sciences includes not just social objects, including both beliefs and their social causes, but beliefs about those objects permits an explanatory critique of false (and other modes of inadequate) consciousness, and being, entailing judgements of value and action without parallel in the field of the natural sciences'.[88] Social science is not only critical, as is all science, but also offers the possibility of human emancipation. Bhaskar presents his argument in schematic form:

> Let a belief P, which has some object O, have a source (causal explanation) S. I am going to contend that if we possess:
> (i) adequate grounds for supposing P is false; and
> (ii) adequate grounds for supposing that S co-explains P, then we may, and must, pass immediately to
> (iii) a negative evaluation of S...[*ceteris paribus*]; and
> (iv) a positive evaluation of action rationally directed at the removal of S . . . [*ceteris paribus*].[89]

Bhaskar's critical naturalism is an interesting and welcome attempt to deal with the problems of human values and ideology, but unfortunately it is precisely with regard to these issues that some serious problems of his project become most apparent. Perhaps the first problem concerns the notion of false belief or consciousness, which Bhaskar defines as 'disjuncture, mismatch or lack of correspondence (representative adequacy) between belief and object'.[90] This seems to be a most appropriate definition, given the realist distinction between intransitive reality and transitive knowledge thereof. The problem for Bhaskar is that, as noted above, he denies the correspondence theory of truth, which holds that a belief is true if it corresponds with reality. For Bhaskar, truth, or the judgement of truth, is a matter intrinsic to transitive science.[91] As Roger Trigg remarks, 'the nature of reality becomes irrelevant to science if truth is not understood as some form of correspondence with reality'.[92] If Bhaskar is prepared to abandon reality as the ultimate test of the truth of belief, and to leave transitive science as the judge of truth, he will not only have great difficulty in sustaining a theory of false consciousness, but will also be vulnerable to the charge of relativism. I return to this issue of relativism later.

Bhaskar's notion of false consciousness, such as it is, is an aspect of his theory of ideology. He argues that a belief may be termed ideological if, first, the falsity of the belief can be exposed by reference to a better explanation of the subject matter in question, and, second, an explanation can be offered of the causes of the false belief.[93] This concept of ideology clearly underlies the first two stages of Bhaskar's argument for critical naturalism. Again, the theory of ideology would seem to be appropriate. Bhaskar wishes to maintain a negative and restrictive concept of ideology, and to show how ideology can be corrected by means of human action informed by a scientific critique. The similarities between this conception of ideology and that of Marx are acknowledged by Bhaskar.[94] But, if Bhaskar has a problem in sustaining a theory of false consciousness, then he also has a problem in sustaining his theory of ideology. Also, if, as I argued in Chapter 2, there is a problem for the Marxist tradition in demarcating science and ideology, then this is a problem for Bhaskar. If all knowledge is transitive and so fallible, and if the criteria of rational judgement of belief are intrinsic to transitive science, then it is not clear how, for Bhaskar, one can demarcate supposedly false ideology and supposedly true science.

The next step in Bhaskar's argument for critical naturalism involves the bold move from factual explanations to evaluation. Bhaskar offers his critical naturalism in direct opposition to all varieties of value–free social science and theories of the logical fact–value gap. As I noted in Chapter 1, the case for a value-free, neutral social science is promoted by positivism, with its characteristic fact–value distinction. As Bhaskar notes, various hermeneutic criticisms and displacements of positivism, including the work of Winch, also promote value-neutrality in the social sciences.[95] If, for Winch, the agent's conceptualisation or point of view is taken as being incorrigible, then no moral critique would seem to be appropriate in social study. Against value-freedom and the fact–value gap, Bhaskar argues that if one possesses a theoretical exposure and explanation of false consciousness one can, and must, pass immediately, without introducing any extraneous value judgement, to a negative evaluation of the cause of false consciousness and to a positive evaluation of the means of removing the cause. The problem here is that Bhaskar seems prepared to accept the positivist case for a fact–value distinction, only to assert that he can bridge it without any bridging notions. Bhaskar is keen to deny that his negative evaluation of false consciousness and its cause is won by derivation from some prior commitment to the positive evaluation of truth. That truth is good, says Bhaskar, is a condition of all discourse and not a value to be introduced by human choice.[96] That truth is a condition of discourse seems to me to be true, and to be a valid rationalist argument for the universality or absoluteness of at least one value. Yet, as already noted, Bhaskar denies there can be any ahistoric, intransitive standards of truth outside transitive science. Without some objective, absolute standard of truth it is not clear how Bhaskar can substantiate any negative evaluation of falsity.

Bhaskar is concerned to challenge not only value-free social science but also what he terms 'rationalistic intellectualism or *theoreticism* which conceives social science as immediately efficacious in practice'.[97] For Bhaskar, social science, or critical naturalism, operates only as a 'conditioned critique'. It is critical of the conceptualisations of agents, but it is also itself conditioned 'in its genesis, reception and effect, to extra-scientific, extra-cognitive and non-ideational, as well as scientific, cognitive and ideational, determinations'.[98] Bhaskar explains that freedom or emancipation requires something more than knowledge or theoretical insight. To be free is: '(1) to know one's real interests; (2) to possess both (a) the ability and the resources, i.e., generically the power, and (b) the opportunity to act in (or towards) them; and (3) to be disposed to do so'.[99] It does seem reasonable to argue that emancipation requires not just knowledge of good ends but also the willingness and ability to adopt the means thereunto. The problem for Bhaskar is that he cannot sustain a theory of real human interests and moral ends. He defines an interest as 'anything conducive to the achievement of agents' wants, needs and/or purposes' and a need as 'anything (contingently or absolutely) necessary to the survival or well-being of an agent'.[100] So far, so good. But what are *real* human interests and needs, who is to determine them, and how? Given a realist science of society and humanity, supposedly able to conduct a critique of false consciousness, one might reasonably expect an account of real human interests, needs and moral ends. Instead, what Bhaskar says is that what 'constitutes an agent's wellbeing cannot be stipulated *a priori*' and that 'social science cannot determine or uniquely ground values'.[101] Social science is limited or conditioned not only because it has to consider the will, desire and sentiment of agents (who may be 'wrong' about their interests), but also because it seems to have no real, objective human nature as an intransitive object of knowledge. Real human interests, needs and moral ends would seem to be dependent on human nature. As Bhaskar puts it, as 'ontology stands to epistemology, so anthropology stands to ethics'.[102] But anthropology, says Bhaskar, cannot be ahistorical or universal, for whatever common nature humanity may share is 'never expressed in anything but thoroughly socialised, more or less historically specific and very highly differentiated forms'.[103] Thus, any moral values derived from a study of human nature will be historically specific, and not universal.[104] Just as ontological realism entails epistemological relativism, for Bhaskar, so too it entails moral relativism.

CONCLUSION

Bhaskar's scientific realism and critical naturalism offer a telling criticism of the errors of positivist and empiricist naturalism and of its hermeneutic and interpretive displacements. The realist notion of an objective, intransitive reality offers hope for an objective science and philosophy. Building on this, critical naturalism offers hope for an objective social science capable of dealing with human values and the problem of ideology. But, as I have argued, Bhaskar's critical realism seems to be morally inadequate for such a task. At the root of all the problems of critical naturalism considered above is Bhaskar's relativism. The distinction between intransitive reality and transitive knowledge, although acceptable as an account of changing and erroneous belief, seems to entail the unacceptable principle that nothing but transitive knowledge is available. Bhaskar's epistemological relativism is not rescued by his judgemental rationality, for, as he acknowledges, the standards of rational judgement are never anything but historically specific and contained within shifting science. Although Bhaskar would wish to criticise the relativism implicit in the work of Kuhn, it would seem that the former is enmeshed in the same set of problems as the latter. Just as there is epistemological relativism, so too there is moral relativism: Bhaskar cannot provide any vindication of objective, universal human interests, needs and moral values. Yet if objective values are to be secured there is need of a realist theory of human nature. The possibility of such a realism, morally more adequate than Bhaskar's, will be considered in the final chapter.

6 A Critique of Value-Free Political Science

INTRODUCTION

In order to avoid the bias of political ideology, or to avoid what they see as unjustifiable, because unscientific and unphilosophic, value judgements, some students of politics advocate a value-free approach to their subject matter. Chapter 1 noted some of the theoretical support for the modern project of a value-free science of politics. The logical positivists, held responsible for the so-called death of political philosophy, argue that values are non-rational and non-scientific, and so incapable of being proved true or false. In their wake, linguistic analysts characterise normative political theory as ideological, and contrast it with empirical political science. The end-of-ideology theorists declare normative political thought redundant and hold political science adequate for the support of the good society. Behavioural political scientists seek to separate facts and values so as to avoid non-scientific bias and maintain the supposed objectivity of their discipline. Chapter 4 noted that Karl Popper, one of the contemporary philosophers of science who is most influential on political scientists, accepted the dualism of facts and values. Chapter 5 noted that even Peter Winch, who is so critical of attempts to model the social sciences on the methods of the natural sciences, advocated a value-free study of society.

Chapter 4 argued that some leading contemporary philosophies of science were unable to provide a method capable of demarcating science and ideology, or non-science. The inadequacy of contemporary science as a corrective of ideology is at the same time the inadequacy of contemporary science as a model for the study of politics. The correction of ideology requires not a retreat from value-bias to value-freedom, but, on the contrary, a substantive moral science of politics, which allows for a fully rational and objective study of human interests and values. In this chapter I offer a set of arguments which show that the study of politics cannot, and should not, be value-free.

THE CONCEPT OF A VALUE-FREE POLITICAL SCIENCE

The arguments for a value-free study of politics are not original to the twentieth century. Such arguments are at least as old as modern political thought if this can be dated from the Renaissance. The Renaissance neglect or rejection of the medieval approach to political philosophy, according to which the discipline is located somewhere in a theological-philosophical synthesis, is well expressed by Niccolò Machiavelli. In his short handbook of political advice, *The Prince,* Machiavelli says:

> Since my intention is to say something that will prove of practical use to the inquirer, I have thought it proper to represent things as they are in real truth, rather than as they are imagined. Many have dreamed up republics and principalities which have never in truth been known to exist; the gulf between how one should live and how one does live is so wide that a man who neglects what is actually done for what should be done learns the way to self-destruction rather than self-preservation.[1]

If Machiavelli was merely seeking to distance himself from impracticable utopian thinking there would be nothing remarkable about his writing, for many other political theorists have shared this aim. However, in the passage quoted, Machiavelli makes clear that his aim is to distinguish the facts of political life from the values of life in general, so as to establish a value-free political theory. That is, Machiavelli seeks to establish the autonomy of politics from whatever values apply elsewhere in human life. Of course, Machiavelli's political theory cannot be value-free, for politics must have some end which is valued and for which politics is conducted. In the passage quoted, Machiavelli's valued end of politics seems to be self-preservation. Elsewhere in his writings Machiavelli seems to value such ends as political success, the preservation and enlargement of state power, political order, and freedom.[2]

That Machiavelli seeks to separate the facts of politics from the values of human life, and so attempts a value-free political theory, seems to be the interpretation of Francis Bacon, who says 'we are much beholden to Machiavelli and others, that write what men do, and not what they ought to do'.[3] Bacon welcomes such an attempt to base the study of politics on observed facts because he is, as I noted in Chapter 2, an advocate of empirical, inductive science, which alone he holds capable of cutting through the distortions stemming from the idols that beset the human mind. Bacon's advocacy and practice do not always cohere, however, and as one modern commentator says, 'he did not effectively develop his professed principle that the same empirical and inductive method should be applied to man and society as to nature'.[4] In failing to apply fully the empirical method to the study of ethics, for example, and in further failing to distinguish the normative from the factual, Bacon, according to his commentator, 'is doing something objected to in later British empiricists, most notably Locke and Hume'.[5] Hume attempts to work out to consistency the themes of early modern British empiricism, and, as I noted in Chapter 1, provides a basis for the logical positivist attack on normative political philosophy in the twentieth century. Whereas Hume denies that moral distinctions are derived from reason, but maintains that there can be a moral philosophy capable of determining right and wrong conduct, the logical positivist Ayer, who is influenced by Hume, denies both that moral distinctions are derived from reason and that there can be a moral science. A similar position is adopted by Max Weber, one of the greatest proponents of value-freedom in the social sciences. Although Weber's sociology, which attempts to combine both interpretation of meaningful behaviour and causal analysis, is usually seen as being unlike positivist and naturalist social science, his advocacy of value-freedom rests on an attitude to the relation of facts and values which is shared with positivism.

Weber's advocacy of value-freedom in the social sciences stems, in part, from a radical distinction between the realm of facts and the realm of values. This may be illustrated in terms of Weber's distinction between the subject matter of politics and the discipline of political science.

> To take a practical political stand is one thing, and to analyse political structures and party positions is another. When speaking in a political meeting about democracy, one does not hide one's personal standpoint; indeed, to come out clearly and take a stand is one's damned duty. The words one uses in such a meeting are not means of scientific analysis but means of canvassing votes and winning over others. They are not plowshares to loosen the soil of contemplative thought; they are swords against the enemy: such words are weapons. It would be an outrage, however, to use such words in this fashion in a lecture or in the lecture room.[6]

For Weber, it is one thing to conduct a scientific analysis of the facts of any matter, and it is quite another to state one's values or offer a value-judgement about the world around one. The realm of facts and the realm of values, the realm of science and the realm of judgement, 'are quite heterogeneous problems'.[7]

That facts and values are logically separate is not of itself, as Hume might agree, sufficient warrant for denying the possibility of a moral philosophy, or demanding value-freedom in the study of society. Weber's advocacy of value-freedom involves a further radical assumption. Not only are the realms of facts and values heterogeneous, but within the realm of values science has no place, for there is no rational order. '"Scientific" pleading is meaningless in principle because the various value spheres of the world stand in irreconcilable conflict with each other.'[8] Weber assumes that human reason and science cannot operate so as to justify moral distinctions, and that these are merely subjective choices. In the realm of irreconcilable values, 'fate, and certainly not "science" holds sway over these gods and their struggles' and 'the individual has to decide which is God for him and which is the devil'.[9]

Weber's insistence on the incompatibility of different values and his thoughts on the relationship of ethics and politics place him in the tradition of Machiavelli. Like Machiavelli, Weber distinguishes conduct which follows a supposedly

Christian maxim, according to which one should act rightly and leave the consequences of one's actions to God, and conduct which follows the maxim of *Realpolitik*, according to which the responsibility for the predictable consequences of one's actions is to be taken into consideration. According to Weber, 'these maxims are in eternal conflict – a conflict which cannot be resolved by means of ethics alone'.[10]

Because, for Weber, value-judgements are non-rational, non-scientific and ultimately purely subjective, they must not be allowed to intrude upon, and so contaminate, the scientific study of society. The science of society must be empirical and value-free. There is, perhaps, an immediate problem for Weber: his claim that social science should be value-free seems to be a value-judgement.

Weber's account of the place of values in social science is not exhausted by his conception of value-freedom. Weber's sociology is concerned with the meaningful behaviour of social actors, and social behaviour is meaningful in terms of the values of the actors. Although social scientists are prohibited from passing value-judgements on their subject matter, they are required to take note of the values inherent in social life. Thus, Weber seeks to distinguish value-judgement (*wertulteil*) from value-relevance or value-reference (*wertbeziehung*). Weber believes that he can maintain value-freedom and acknowledge that 'the problems of the social sciences are selected by the value-relevance of the phenomena treated'.[11] The selection of the topics for study from the vast range of social reality necessarily involves value-relevance because social reality has meaning to humans only in terms of the values we hold and by means of which we relate to reality. Weber explains this in terms of the 'cultural sciences' in general.

> The *significance* of a configuration of cultural phenomena and the basis of this significance . . . cannot be derived and rendered intelligible by a system of analytic laws . . . however perfect it may be, since the significance of cultural events presupposes a *value-orientation* towards these events. The concept of cultural is a *value-concept.* Empirical reality becomes 'culture' to us because and insofar as we relate it to value ideas. It includes those segments and

> only those segments of reality which have become significant to us because of this value-relevance. Only a small proportion of existing concrete reality is coloured by our value-conditioned interest and it alone is significant to us. . . . We cannot discover . . . what is meaningful to us by means of a 'presuppositionless' investigation of empirical data.[12]

With Kantians, Weber would argue that reality takes on shape and meaning as the result of the operation of human thought. With contemporary critics of positivist philosophy of science, Weber would agree that there can be no exclusive distinction between observation and theory languages.

Against this brief sketch of background ideas I now offer a characterisation of a general conception of value-free political science. The various assumptions, assertions and arguments do not constitute the conception of any one theorist, and in particular not Weber. The general conception may be, though, an example of a Weberian ideal type. Value-free political science may be characterised in terms of the following beliefs:

(a) politics is autonomous, in that moral values are not (all) applicable in political life;
(b) facts and values are logically separate, and the gulf cannot be bridged by reason;
(c) values are non-rational (and probably subjective), and their validity is not susceptible to scientific proof;
(d) various values stand in irreconcilable conflict;
(e) political scientists may refer to political values, but they should keep separate empirical, scientific analysis and non-scientific value-judgement because: (i) it would be improper for any political scientist to claim, or seem to claim, scientific status for any value; and (ii) there is a danger that non-scientific values will distort the conduct of objective scientific enquiry in terms of data collection and analysis.[13]

TEN ARGUMENTS AGAINST VALUE-FREE POLITICAL SCIENCE

I offer a set of arguments, mostly logical or methodological, against the general conception of value-free political science. The package of arguments as a whole concludes that value-freedom is both impossible and undesirable. The arguments are not directed against any one theorist, and in particular not Weber. In those cases where Weber may be seen to anticipate something of the argument the adequacy of his position will be examined. In what follows much use is made of the arguments of Leo Strauss, who has done more than most thinkers this century to challenge the assumptions, assertions and arguments of value-free political science, and to maintain the dignity and status of normative political philosophy. It might properly be said that the Weber–Strauss debate on value-freedom constitutes the intellectual high point of the general dispute. However, Strauss does not exhaust the case against value-freedom, and other important aspects of Strauss's work are not beyond criticism.[14]

1. Politics is Not Autonomous; Political Behaviour is Subject to Moral Evaluation

The claim that the study of politics can and should be value-free may involve, and indeed rest upon, the assumption that the activity of politics is value-free. According to this assumption politics is an autonomous human activity, not subject to, for example, moral principles. Thus moral philosophy is held to be out of place in the study of politics, and politics is thought to be studied properly in terms of distinctly political, amoral principles. That the initial assumption is false is shown by Strauss's reflections on the nature of politics. Politics is an aspect of conscious human activity and so one is led to consider the purposes of such activity. Strauss says:

> All political action aims at either preservation or change. When desiring to preserve, we wish to prevent a change to the worse; when desiring to change, we wish to bring about something better. All political action is then guided by some thought of better or worse. But thought of better or worse implies thought of the good.[15]

Thus, 'political things are by their nature subject to approval and disapproval, to choice and rejection, to praise and blame'.[16] It is precisely because politics is a conscious human activity, and so an activity subject to human choice, that it is subject to evaluation in terms of the moral values of all human life. Politics is neither above nor below the standards of all aspects of conscious human activity.

It might be agreed that politics is subject to some sort of judgement, but argued that the standards of politics are simply incompatible with other human standards, such as those of morality or religion. To achieve political success, it might be argued, one may necessarily have to disregard or infringe some moral principles. This is the attitude of Machiavelli. According to him, 'princes who have achieved great things have been those who have given their word lightly, who have known how to trick men with their cunning, and who, in the end, have overcome those abiding by honest principles'.[17] Machiavelli's cynicism convinces him that one cannot trust others and that consequently one can achieve political success only if one is prepared to practise trickery and deceit. Such political behaviour is not, for Machiavelli, morally bad, for the standards of politics are not the standards of morality. Machiavelli does not deny morality, although he denies moral principles any jurisdiction in politics. Since all citizens will entertain some moral standards, the successful prince will cynically exploit these. 'A prince . . . need not necessarily have all the good qualities . . . but he should certainly appear to have them.'[18]

Jacques Maritain offers a sharp critique of the 'incurable division between politics and morality' articulated by Machiavelli, and the consequent 'illusory but deadly antinomy between what people call *idealism* (wrongly confused with ethics) and what people call realism (wrongly confused with politics)'.[19] Maritain detects a 'paradox' and an 'internal principle of instability' in Machiavellianism. The use of a supramoral art of politics, which abuses the moral values and beliefs of the citizens will lead to the degeneration of their moral culture and practice. With reference to the first quote from Machiavelli in the previous paragraph, Maritain's point can be illustrated by noting that one can deceive and trick only if one is trusted. Continued deceit and trickery will lead eventually to the loss of trust in one by others, such that one can no longer cynically exploit their trust and hope to deceive them. Just as a parasite which destroys its host will itself eventually die, so the autonomous, amoral art of politics 'wears away and destroys its very matter, and by the same token, will degenerate itself'.[20] Maritain concludes that Machiavellianism may seem to be successful, but that such success is merely illusory, since it is only partial and temporary. Ultimately Machiavellianism cannot succeed, for this would mean the ultimate destruction of the good of politics upon which it feeds and so the ultimate destruction of itself.[21] If politics feeds upon some good it follows that lasting political success requires the promotion and maintenance of this good. That is, politics is essentially a moral activity and the true standards of politics are moral standards, applicable in human behaviour generally.

2. Value-Free Political Science is Incommensurate with its Value-Laden Subject Matter

If, as has been argued, politics is a moral activity, then a discipline commensurate with this subject matter must be normative, and not value-free. Clearly, politicians have values and make decisions on the basis of them, and citizens have values which prompt them to demand decisions and which shape their reactions to decisions. Political values are embodied in political institutions and practices, and provide a justification for political change. Equally clearly, a study of politics which refuses, or is unable to include values in its remit is an impoverished discipline, which is likely to miss much of the stuff of politics. As noted in Chapter 1, the desire to get closer to the stuff of politics, by studying not just formal political institutions but also informal political behaviour, is part of the inspiration of behavioural political science. However, as John Hallowell says of positivistic political science, one must question 'whether by ruling out values as objective truths it automatically eliminates much that is pertinent, if not essential, to the understanding of any political process or behaviour'.[22]

A value-free political science need not, however, and possibly would not, seek to exclude values from its field of study.

Weber refers to an 'almost inconceivable misunderstanding' of his work which takes him as implying that 'empirical science cannot treat "subjective" evaluations as the subject matter of its analysis'.[23] I have already noted that central to Weber's philosophy of social science is his claim that science cannot establish the validity of any value. One might wonder, then, how empirical science can treat subjective evaluations. For Weber, values are to be treated as facts: not as objective moral facts, whose objective normative truth can be established, but as mere facts, whose existence only can be established. As Weber says: 'When the normatively valid is the object of empirical investigation, its normative validity is disregarded. Its "existence" and not its "validity" is what concerns the investigator.'[24]

The problem here is not that value-free political science cannot include political values as empirical entities in its analysis, but, rather, that it cannot establish the objective truth of the values as values. Strauss correctly argues that the 'attempt to replace the quest for the best political order by a purely descriptive or analytical political science which refrains from "value judgements" is . . . as absurd . . . as the idea of a medicine which refuses to distinguish between health and sickness'.[25] Specifically, one could argue that it would be absurd, and morally reprehensible, for a political scientist to identify and attempt to analyse a policy of genocide while refusing to comment on the morality of the policy.

3. Impossible to Select for Study Any Important Political Phenomena without the Use of Values

A consistent value-free political science would refrain not only from passing judgement on any political action or event, but also from making any value-judgement as part of its operation. Employing such restraint, value-free political science would be unable to make a most fundamental and necessary value-judgement: that which determines which phenomena, from an infinite range, are sufficiently important to warrant selection for study. Without making such a judgement about what they should study, political scientists would study nothing at all, much as Buridan's ass, faced with two equally succulent bundles of hay, but with no good reason for choosing one rather than the other, chooses neither and so starves to death through indecision.

As I have already noted, Weber anticipates this problem and attempts to overcome it by means of his distinction between value-judgement and value-relevance, such that, without the need to pass judgements upon them, 'the problems of the social sciences are selected by the value-relevance of the phenomena treated'.[26] Weber says, rather cryptically, 'that the expression "relevance to values" refers simply to the philosophical interpretation of that specifically scientific "interest" which determines the selection of a given subject matter and the problems of an empirical analysis'.[27] Weber does not clarify the matter much by his attempt to identify value with interests; it is not clear what specifically scientific interests are or could be. One would wish to know which values guide the choice of subject matter and its study. Elsewhere, Weber provides a clearer answer: 'the choice of the object of investigation and the extent or depth to which this investigation attempts to penetrate into the infinite causal web, are determined by the evaluative ideas which dominate the investigator and his age'.[28] Thus, the choice of subject matter does, admits Weber, require some judgement of the value of the topics and problems. The values which guide investigation are whatever happen to be dominant in the community of social scientists, and, like all values, these are, for Weber, non-rational and subjective, and not susceptible to scientific proof. In this, Weber seems to adopt a position similar to that elaborated later by Thomas Kuhn in his theory of paradigm-directed science, which I noted in Chapter 4. Weber's position is criticised by Georg Lukács as being ultimately destructive of any conception of rationality and objectivity. In a very neat and concise summary of Lukács's critique, Strauss makes this point very clearly:

> Weber more than any other German scholar of his generation tried to save the objectivity of social science; he believed that to do so required that social science be made 'value-free' because he assumed that evaluations are transrational or irrational; but the value-free study of 'facts' and their causes admittedly presupposes the selection of relevant facts; that selection is necessarily guided by reference to values; the values with reference to which the

> facts are to be selected must themselves be selected; and that selection, which determines in the last analysis the specific conceptual framework of the social scientist, is in principle arbitrary; hence social science is fundamentally irrational or subjectivistic.[29]

Ralf Dahrendorf holds that 'value judgements cannot be derived from scientific insights', and that 'it is probably unrealistic to insist that value judgements be eliminated from the choice of subjects; in any case it is quite unnecessary, since the reason why a subject is regarded as worth investigating is irrelevant in principle to its scientific treatment'.[30] Dahrendorf wishes to make a distinction between 'the logic and the psychology of scientific discovery', such that the 'the psychological motives behind the formulation of any scientific theory or hypothesis are irrelevant to its truth or validity', which 'is determined only by empirical test'.[31] In this Dahrendorf is close to Karl Popper, to whom he refers.[32] This distinction between non-scientific theory formulation and scientific theory testing is also apparent in the argument, noted in the previous chapter, of naturalistic social scientists who admit that *Verstehen* may be a useful means of generating hypotheses, but insist that all hypotheses must be susceptible to empirical testing.

There are two obvious problems with such arguments of Dahrendorf and others. First, even if the scientific testing of theories is perfectly objective, and so a safeguard against subjectivity and arbitrariness, it seems absurd to confine objectivity to the testing of theories, and to leave this aspect of science wholly dependent on subjective and arbitrary theory formulation. Could a reputable science consist in the testing of theories about pink unicorns? Second, it cannot be assumed that scientific testing is objective, for the choice of science over non-science, and the choice of rationality over irrationality as the essential characteristic of scientific method, depends on value judgements, which Dahrendorf holds are subjective, being 'neither verifiable nor falsifiable by observable facts'.[33]

The selection of important political phenomena for study by political science, like the basic choice of science over non-science, requires human value-judgement. Political science is constituted by value-judgements and so cannot be value-free. If it is not to be entirely arbitrary its constituent value-judgements cannot be purely subjective.

4. Impossible to Identify and Describe the Subject Matter of Politics without the Use of Values

It is impossible to select any phenomena for study without making a value-judgement about their importance for study. In the case of politics and other human and social sciences, there is a further reason why one cannot avoid values. Politics is a moral activity, and so the identification and description of political phenomena requires some reference to human purposes and values. As Strauss says, 'by defining the state, or . . . civil society, with reference to its purpose, one admits a standard in the light of which one must judge political actions and institutions: the purpose of civil society necessarily functions as a standard for judging civil societies'.[34] Because political activity is not autonomous and is subject to moral evaluation, it is necessary to evaluate it if one wishes to identify and describe it.

Attempts to define politics and the political without use of value terms are likely to be unsuccessful. Harold Lasswell asserts that 'political science, as an empirical discipline, is the study of the shaping and sharing of power'.[35] Lasswell suggests that politics is characteristically about power; that power is an empirical concept; and that the study of politics is empirical and value-free. There are two obvious problems with this position. First, if politics is no more than the shaping and sharing of power, then it seems that for Lasswell, and other supposedly value-free political scientists, there is no distinction to be made between, say, President Calvin Coolidge and Al Capone, both of whom shaped and shared power and maintained some sort of rule in the United States of America in the mid and late 1920s. The distinction between politics and gangsterism is established and maintained only by taking account of the purposes of political rule, which requires reference to unambiguously normative terms such as justice and authority. As St Augustine says: 'Remove justice, and what are kingdoms but gangs of criminals on a large scale?'[36]

Second, power is not a purely empirical concept, as is

demonstrated by Steven Lukes. Lukes distinguishes three dimensions of power and identifies the type of political study capable of comprehending the various dimensions. The 'one-dimensional' view of power is associated with mainstream behavioural political science and 'involves a focus on *behaviour* in the making of *decisions* on *issues* over which there is an observable *conflict* of (subjective) *interests,* seen as express policy preferences, revealed by political participation'.[37] The 'two-dimensional' view of power recognises that power is exercised not just in decision-making but in nondecision-making. That is, those who have political power can determine which potential issues become issues for decision and which issues are excluded from the political agenda. Thus, it is recognised that some subjective interests are excluded from the political arena. This two-dimensional view represents only a qualified critique of behaviouralism, for it is still assumed that nondecision-making is a form of decision-making and that conflicts of subjective interests can be observed.[38]

The 'three-dimensional' view of power, which Lukes advances, denies that the exercise of power is confined to decision-making and agenda setting in cases where conflicts of subjective interests are observable. Power may be exercised where there is no observable conflict of interests, but where there is a potential or latent conflict, 'which consists in a contradiction between the interests of those exercising power and the *real interests* of those they exclude'.[39] The explanation of why some individuals or groups fail to recognise their real interests and so accept the interests of the powerful as their own may involve a number of factors, including both conscious and unconscious manipulation of interests. The distinction between real and apparent interests is essentially normative, for it involves a distinction between what is actually good for a person and what is merely thought to be good. The distinction involves also the consideration of what a person would choose if he or she was fully aware of his or her interests and was not subject to any persuasion or manipulation by others who have different interests. Thus, Lukes acknowledges that his concept of power is 'ineradicably evaluative' but claims that this does not mean that it is not also 'empirically applicable'.[40] It is not only Lukes's three-dimensional, radical view of power which is normative; both the other views are also closely associated with certain moral positions. The one-dimensional, liberal view accepts that what individuals express as their wants are their real wants. The two-dimensional, reformist view accepts that people's interests may not always be treated equally and may not be expressed formally as policy preferences, but may exist as sub-political grievances.

Hallowell also denies that politics can be defined in terms of any supposedly value-free concept such as power, for 'politics so conceived is almost devoid of meaning'.[41] Power is not, he argues, a substantive and tangible thing, which can be accumulated, but a relational concept involving will and action, together with an acknowledgement of its force.

> Now if power is a relational concept rather than a substantive entity, if it exists only in action, it can never be a self-sufficient end. . . . Since no one can be powerful without acting willfully (purposively), there can be no power where there is no purpose. . . . It is the conflict of purposes, of aims and objectives, that characterises politics – not a struggle for a 'power' divorced from all purposeful motivation.[42]

The student of politics, then, is properly concerned with the purposes and ends of human conduct, and the evaluation thereof. Any supposedly value-free study of political things misses the essence of politics. Any refusal to employ value terms makes the study meaningless and impossible.

5. Political Explanation May Require the Use of Values

David Easton, in characterising the assumptions and objectives of behavioural political science, notes that 'ethical evaluation and empirical explanation involve two different kinds of propositions that, for the sake of clarity, should be kept analytically distinct'.[43] Explanation and evaluation of political phenomena may require different kinds of propositions and intellectual operations, but it seems most unlikely that they can be kept analytically distinct, given that they apply to a common subject matter, which, as I have argued, is subject to evaluation and is partly constituted by values. It would seem that just as the choice, identification and description of political things requires the use of values, so too might the explanation of them.

Alasdair MacIntyre argues that 'to insist that political science be value-free is to insist that we never use in our explanations such clauses as "because it was just" or "because it was illegitimate" when we explain the collapse of a regime'.[44] In order to appreciate fully the weight of this argument it is necessary to follow MacIntyre's distinction between 'being just' and 'being thought to be just'. The former requires an objective measure of justice; a matter for normative political philosophy. The latter requires only a measure of public opinion; a matter for empirical political science. Being unwilling or unable to determine whether or not a regime is just, value-free political scientists will not be able or willing to determine whether or not a regime collapsed or changed because of its intrinsic injustice. Rather, they will be prepared to consider only whether or not a regime was thought to be just and whether or not this might be relevant to explaining its collapse or change. But in doing this, value-free political scientists 'are taking sides in an ancient philosophical argument: is it important for the ruler to be just, or is it important for him to be thought to be just?' Their conclusion is 'that justice plays no part and can play no part in political life. The insistence on being value-free thus involves the most extreme of value commitments.'[45] As MacIntyre notes, one need not take sides on this old issue in order to appreciate that value-free political science is committed by its starting point (value-freedom) and not by its empirical findings to the view that it is right.

6. Value-Freedom Involves Relativism, Both Moral and Epistemological

The advocacy of value-freedom rests on the assumption that values are not susceptible to rational or scientific analysis and validation, and are therefore subjective. Being subjective, values are excluded from science so as to maintain the objectivity of enquiry. Value-freedom thus involves the denial that there are any objective and absolute standards of human conduct, and so the assumption that moral values are relative to different, subjective points of view. Value-freedom thus involves moral relativism. It may also involve epistemological relativism. Value-free social scientists are always alert to the dangers of passing moral judgements, and particularly of using the moral perspectives of their own culture to pass judgements on different cultures. To avoid such dangers, value-free social scientists will seek to understand any alien culture only on its own terms. But if one is required to employ only local standards, and to abandon all notions of objective and absolute standards of human behaviour, one may wonder if it is correct to maintain the standard of social scientific enquiry. If the culture one is examining is one in which empirical science is valued less than, say, myth or magic, then perhaps one ought to analyse the culture as it would analyse itself, and so abandon the standard of science. If moral values are seen as being relative to the various moral agents and cultures, so epistemological standards may be seen as being culturally relative. If it is thought there is no objective and absolute moral standard, so it may be thought there is no objective intellectual standard.[46] I offer both a fuller consideration of the nature of relativism and a set of arguments against it in Chapter 8.

7. Value-Freedom Rests on an Unproven and Unprovable Assumption of the Irreconcilability of Value Conflicts

I have noted that Weber's commitment to value-freedom rests not only on the assumption that facts and values are logically separate, but also on the assumption that value conflicts are irreconcilable. For Weber, reason and science cannot derive values from facts, nor can they resolve conflicts between purely subjective value choices. Thus, science should confine itself to the realm of facts and maintain its integrity by avoiding the distortions of subjective values. Strauss argues that 'the assumption that the conflicts between different values or values-systems are essentially insoluble for human reason . . . while generally taken to be sufficiently established, has never been proven'. He goes on to say that the proof of this assumption would require an effort of a very great magnitude and 'a comprehensive critique of evaluating reason', but that all 'we find are sketchy observations'.[47] Empirical evidence indicating widespread and severe value conflicts, no matter how scientific its collection and analysis, does not, and cannot, prove that value conflicts are irreconcilable. Nor does such evidence prove that there is no objective order of values comprehensible to reason. Strauss argues elsewhere:

> As little as man's varying notions of the universe prove that there is no universe or that there cannot be *the* true account of the universe or that man can never arrive at true and final knowledge of the universe, so little seem man's varying notions of justice to prove that there is no natural right or that natural right is unknowable. The variety of notions of justice can be understood as the variety of errors, which variety does not contradict, but presupposes, the existence of the one truth regarding justice.[48]

Humans tend to disagree among themselves not because they all doubt or deny the existence of truth but, rather, because they all value truth and doubt that others have properly identified it.

Weber may be interpreted as being well aware of the force of arguments such as those just offered when he writes 'against the view that the mere existence of historical and individual variations in evaluations proves the necessarily "subjective" character of ethics'.[49] However, Weber's intention seems to be not to press this argument, which might expose the inadequacy of his basic premise of irreconcilability of values, but to make two other points. First, facts and values are logically separate, such that factual evidence establishes not the validity, but only the existence, of values. Second, one should not 'be "scientifically" contented with the conventional self-evidentness of very widely accepted value-judgements', for it is the task of science to question convention.[50] But whatever Weber intends, he certainly does nothing to prove his basic premise that the various value spheres of the world stand in irreconcilable conflict with each other. Nor could Weber furnish any such proof.

To argue that the irreconcilability of value conflicts has not been proven, and indeed cannot be proven by any amount of empirical evidence or by argument, is not, of course, to argue that any objective order of values is easily comprehended by reason. Human beings will disagree about human needs and purposes and fall into error on ethical and political matters, but failure to find agreement on truth does not indicate that there is no truth, nor that the quest for truth is mistaken and should not be attempted. Rather, disagreement about the truth presupposes the truth. Faced with disagreement humans should continue their pursuit of truth and agreement on truth. Strauss says: 'It is prudent to grant that there are value conflicts which cannot in fact be settled by human reason. But if we cannot decide which of two mountains whose peaks are hidden by cloud is higher than the other, cannot we decide that a mountain is higher than a molehill?'[51]

8. Political Science, Like All Sciences, Rests on Certain Methodological Values

I have argued above that the study of politics cannot be value-free, in any consistent and comprehensive fashion, because value-judgements are required to facilitate the choice, identity, description and, perhaps, explanation of its subject matter. To these arguments I now wish to add another, perhaps more fundamental, one: political science, like all sciences, is based on certain methodological values, such as truth, reasonableness, consistency, fruitfulness and simplicity.[52] Such values are employed by every respectable political scientist, if only implicitly. One would be surprised and rightly scandalised to read a piece of research in political science prefaced by its author's remark that the work is wrong, unreasonable and inconsistent. Of the values mentioned, perhaps the most important is truth, for, as Eric Voegelin says, it constitutes science: 'the object of science has a "constitution" . . . the essence toward which we are moving in our search for truth'.[53]

Certain methodological values are embodied in everyday scientific practice, and a basic value-judgement is made, says Hallowell, when a scientist 'chooses the scientific method itself as the most appropriate for his investigations and strives to adhere to its principles'.[54] If, as Weber insists, social scientists are to refrain from making value-judgements in professional practice, then they ought, strictly, to refrain from judging in favour of science itself, or any particular scientific method. As Easton notes:

> Weber's prescription has created an anomalous situation. If he is to continue to argue for the complete exclusion of value dispute from the university, as he does, he cannot remain consistent and still provide any place within the university for social scientists themselves to debate the very conception of science.[55]

If political science is to be value-free, and consistently and comprehensively so, it is unable to defend itself against any threat and is unable to distinguish good and bad professional practice.

Weber is not entirely unaware of the problem of a social science free of the value of truth, and yet he is unable to solve it on his own terms. He says that 'every professional task has its "inherent norms" and should be fulfilled accordingly'.[56] These norms include the separation of facts and values, and the recognition of facts which may be 'personally uncomfortable'. Weber does not say so, but uncomfortable facts ought to be accepted if and because they are true. Later, Weber describes as a misunderstanding of his position, and so dismisses, the supposed objection that science cannot be value-free because 'science strives to attain "valuable" results, meaning thereby logically and factually correct results which are scientifically significant'.[57] Weber explains that he wishes to keep social science free only of 'practical evaluations', which are subjective. It might seem that Weber is seeking to distinguish subjective moral judgements from methodological judgements, which are more objective and therefore acceptable in science. Elsewhere, though, Weber makes it clear that he considers even methodological values to be thoroughly subjective.

> All scientific work presupposes that the rules of logic and method are valid. . . . Science further presupposes that what is yielded by scientific work is important in the sense that it is 'worth being known'. In this, obviously, are contained all our problems. For this supposition cannot be proved by scientific means. It can only be *interpreted* with reference to its ultimate meaning, which we must reject or accept according to our ultimate position toward life.[58]

If it is accepted that it is the truth of scientific work which makes it worth being known, then it must be accepted that Weber is saying that truth, like all our moral values, is no more than a subjective choice. Thus is exposed the contradiction of Weber's value-free social science: it seeks to free itself of potentially distorting, subjective values while being based on one.[59]

Weber is ultimately unable to prove that social science produces results 'worth being known', for he is unable to establish the validity of truth as a basic value. Yet, as I have noted above, Weber is keen to stress the instrumental value or utility of social science. Perhaps Weber, and other value-free social scientists, believe that social science has a value for everyone because it allows them to implement their values, whatever these are. Perhaps it is thought that there can be universal agreement on the value of social science. But, as Strauss observes, 'once we grant this we are seriously tempted to wonder if there are not a few other things which must be values from every point of view'.[60] If empirical truth or factual correctness is a universal and objective value then so too might be moral goodness. If truth is not an objective value, then social science has no solid foundation or constitution.

Weber and other value-free social scientists argue that it would be outrageous for a teacher to disregard or distort evidence in order to advance some personal value. In this they are right, for to disregard the truth is always wrong. But no teacher can be value-free in practice, for no teacher can properly disregard the value of truth: it would be outrageous to do so.

9. Value-Free Political Science Has an Inconsistent Political Bias

A major fear underlies the drive for value-freedom in the study of politics: the fear that the subjective values of the students of politics, if allowed to interfere with their enquiry, will detract from the scientific status and objectivity of their work. The drive for a science of politics is prompted, in part, by the fear of political ideology. In addition to the argument, offered in Chapter 4, that contemporary philosophy of science may not be able to provide an antidote for ideology, it may also be argued that value-free political science, far from avoiding the problem of bias, has an inherent political bias. Such a bias, if it exists, clearly detracts from the professed objectivity of political science. The arguments offered here suggest that the political bias of value-free political science may be conservative or liberal. These two particular conclusions may not be compatible, and the two particular ideologies may not, of themselves, be thought undesirable. The point of the arguments is not that value-free political science has a particular bias, but that it has any bias at all.

Value-free political science is, if it is consistent with its own aims and methods, concerned only with understanding political reality as it is, and not with passing judgement on how it should be. Value-free political science is thus uncritical of its subject matter, the given political reality, and so is, implicitly at least, conservative towards it. Hallowell notes that 'the refusal to pass an ethical judgement is a kind of ethical judgement none the less' and castigates the:

> shallow 'realism' that mistakes the a-moral description of dirty politics for scientific observation and analysis. Such 'realism' overlooks the fact that by emphasising dirty politics and techniques to the exclusion of any consideration of what politics may or ought to be is itself, implicitly at least, condoning such politics by refusing to condemn.[61]

Charles A. McCoy and John Playford, in their reader, *Apolitical Politics: A Critique of Behavioralism,* gather together a number of articles, critical of behavioural political science, some of which 'raise the question of whether an empirical science, which can only study what is and not what will be, much less what ought to be, must be inherently conservative'.[62]

A value-free study of politics, again if it is to be consistent with its aims and methods, is unable to establish any order of political values and so must maintain a scepticism about such matters. But since politics is an aspect of human activity and so necessarily involves some consideration about how human beings should conduct themselves, one may question how such value-judgements will be made. One may conclude that some sort of conventionalism or conservatism will operate, such that the tried and tested will be preferred to the unknown and distrusted. This is the argument of John Stuart Mill in his comment on the link between Hume's epistemology and political philosophy. Mill says of Hume:

> absolute scepticism in speculation very naturally brought him round to Toryism in practice; for if no faith can be had in the operations of human intellect, and one side of every question is about as likely as another to be true, a man will commonly be inclined to prefer that order of things which, being no more wrong than any other, he has hitherto found compatible with his private comforts.[63]

The inability to provide a scientific and rational account of political values need not lead to conservative conclusions, however. The moral relativism involved in value-freedom may coincide with political relativism and pluralism, which are characteristic of liberalism and liberal democracy. Strauss argues that if 'before the tribunal of reason all values are equal, the rational society will be equalitarian or democratic and permissive or liberal: the rational doctrine regarding the difference between facts and values rationally justifies the preference for liberal democracy – contrary to what is intended by that distinction itself'.[64] If all political values and preferences are equally worthy, or worthless, because there can be no rational or scientific means of ordering them, it may be that the bearers of these various values will be treated equally and tolerantly, because there appears to be no good reason to do otherwise.

However, any link between moral relativism and political liberalism is contingent rather than necessary. As Strauss notes elsewhere, according to consistent moral relativism (which might, of course, place no special value on consistency), tolerance is a value equal in dignity to intolerance. In this case, there is no good reason for choosing tolerance over intolerance, and liberalism over tyranny. Of value-free social science, which is unable to help us in our choice of proper political ends, Strauss comments:

> Such a science is instrumental and nothing but instrumental: it is born to be the handmaid of any powers or interests that be. What Machiavelli did apparently, our

> social science would actually do if it did not prefer – only God knows why – generous liberalism to consistency: namely, to give advice with equal competence and alacrity to tyrants as well as to free peoples.[65]

It may be, after all, inconsistency and subjectivity that characterise the choice of liberal democracy by political scientists, whose value-free ideology denies them a rational choice. It may be, after all, that many people are better than their ideology.

The argument that an uncritical, value-free political science may have a conservative bias, and the recognition that moral relativism often coincides with political liberalism, together with the recognition that many supposedly value-free political scientists are liberal democrats, may be reconciled by noting that a conservative bias in a liberal democratic culture will promote a conservation of liberal democratic views. Given that the behavioural revolution in political science, with its commitment to value-freedom, occurred primarily in North America and secondarily in Western Europe, in the post-Second World War period, one might expect the values of the culture of liberal democracy to show through in the discipline.

10. Value-Freedom Rests on the Untenable Assumption that Empirical Science is the Highest Form of Knowledge

The advocacy of value-freedom rests on the assumption of the non-scientific nature of values. This assumption, in turn, rests on a certain conception of science, which is empiricist and positivistic. A science which takes the evidence of the senses to be not only that by which it knows, but also that which it knows, and which accepts only so-called positive facts as proof, may be able to recognise that values exist, but will be unable to establish their validity. The positivism underlying such a conception of science supports also the assumption that empirical science is the highest form of human knowledge, because it is the only form open to objective testing and proof. The demarcation of science and non-science, sought by scientific method, is at the same time the demarcation of knowledge and superstition. Propositions which are not susceptible to testing by scientific method are dismissed as non-scientific and so rejected as claims to knowledge.

The assumption that empirical science is the highest form of human knowledge involves two serious mistakes. First, it involves a neglect of non-scientific or pre-scientific knowledge, which must be the basis of science itself. Voegelin says that 'science starts from the prescientific existence of man, from his participation in the world . . . from his primary grip on all the realms of being that is assured to him because his nature is their epitome'.[66] Science involves speculation on nature, the very existence of which is not susceptible to scientific proof, in the empiricist and positivist conception. In particular, social science involves, says Strauss, the presupposition 'that its devotees can tell human beings from other beings' and 'this most fundamental knowledge' is 'pre-scientific knowledge'.[67] More specifically, 'political science requires clarification of what distinguishes political things from things which are not political; it requires that the question be raised and answered "what is political?" This question cannot be dealt with scientifically.'[68] It is not on the basis of science and the application of scientific method, but on the basis of a pre-scientific knowledge of political things that 'everyone knows that buying a shirt, as distinguished from casting a vote, is not in itself a political action.'[69]

Second, the assumption that empirical science is the highest form of knowledge involves the mistake of neglecting practical knowledge and reason, as distinct from speculative or theoretical knowledge and reason. Empirical science is concerned only with that which is given in, or supported by sense experience. Scientific knowledge is factual, or concerned with how things are. Empirical science neglects practical knowledge, the ordering of human knowledge to the good ends of human action, because it is unable to determine these ends. Practical knowledge is not *a priori*; it must be based, in part, on experience of human beings and their nature. But neither is it entirely empirical; practical reason necessarily moves beyond empirical evidence and makes judgements concerning human ends and goods, which are not explicit in sense data. It is the neglect or rejection of practical reason which lies at the heart of the advocacy of value-free political science. The basic assumptions of value-freedom, the logical gulf between facts and values which cannot be bridged by reason, and the irreconcilability of value conflicts, are specific consequences of this neglect or rejection. Weber's subordination of social science as the handmaid of blind human choices is a specific manifestation of this neglect or rejection.

CONCLUSION

The set of arguments presented above demonstrate that value-free political science is both impossible and undesirable. It follows that the study of politics must be a normative discipline. These conclusions do not, as some might fear, render the study of politics unscientific and unphilosophic, nor do they leave political studies ensnared in the problem of ideology. To deal with the problem of ideology it is necessary not to retreat from value-bias to value-freedom, but, on the contrary, to move to a substantive moral science of politics capable of dealing with human values. The correction of ideology requires a rational and objective study of human needs, which can avoid relativism and so distinguish proper and improper human values. There is no good reason to assume that the study of values is necessarily less objective than the study of facts, just as there is no good reason to assume that facts and values can be easily distinguished in the study of politics. Of course, there is no guarantee that the study of politics will not be subject to some ideological distortion, but this is true for the study of both facts and values. The distinction between empirical political science and normative political philosophy represents a convenient modern division of labour. They are, though, complementary approaches, and ideally are united as moral political science or rational political philosophy, which I take to be one and the same. In order that the study of politics be a normative discipline it must be based on practical reason, capable of knowing the facts and values of politics, and capable of ordering knowledge of politics to the good ends of political activity. Further consideration of this will be offered in Chapter 10.

7 Contemporary Confusion of Political Philosophy and Political Ideology

INTRODUCTION

In the previous chapter I offered criticism of a value-free political science. In the present chapter I examine critically the work of some contemporary political theorists who do not deny that political theory is normative, but who fail to make an adequate distinction between political philosophy and political ideology, or who simply equate the two modes of political thought. Over the past few decades much attention has been given to the methodology of the history of political thought. Important contributors to this project are Quentin Skinner and Richard Ashcraft, who, in their different ways, have stressed the significance of historical and contextual interpretation of texts of political thought. They argue that all political thought is relative to historical or other contexts, and, as a consequence, deny the distinction between political philosophy and political ideology. Perhaps the most significant debate in contemporary political philosophy is that between liberalism and communitarianism. Among a number of key communitarian challenges to liberalism is the argument that there can be no neutral, or universal, or absolute justification for political principles. A clear example of this communitarian challenge is provided by Michael Walzer, who argues that the task of political philosophy is the interpretation of the shared beliefs of particular communities. Again, this argument renders all political thought relative to particular contexts, and so renders vulnerable any attempt to distinguish political philosophy and political ideology. The most fundamental contemporary challenge to any distinction between political philosophy and political ideology is posed by postmodernist and antifoundationalist political theorists. Richard Rorty, in common with other postmodernists, denies the possibility of, and need for, an objective philosophical foundation for politics. This antifoundationalism is profoundly relativist and so leads to the confusion and identity of political philosophy and political ideology.

HISTORY AND POLITICAL PHILOSOPHY: QUENTIN SKINNER

Chapter 1 noted the damage done to normative political philosophy by positivism, linguistic analysis and historicism, in the form of the death of political philosophy thesis and the rise of value-free political science. Chapter 2 noted that the genesis of ideology involves the attack on the traditional conception of human reason by positivism and historicism. Although positivism may no longer be widely accepted, historicism is still prevalent and the influence of linguistic analysis remains in some form. The continuing harmful impact of historicism and linguistic analysis on authentic political philosophy is evident in the work of Quentin Skinner.

In a series of methodological and historical essays published since the 1960s Skinner has argued that there can be no full and proper understanding of political thought that does not involve a very significant historical understanding.[1] According to Skinner the main conclusions on which he would insist are 'that the recovery of the historical meaning of any given text is a necessary condition for understanding it, and that this process can never be achieved simply by studying the text itself'.[2] Attempts to study the text only, in isolation from its historical context, lead, says Skinner, only to historical nonsense and serious errors of interpretation. If one fails to interpret texts and ideas in their proper historical context, one will tend to interpret them in inappropriate contexts and terms. Referring to Thomas Kuhn's notion of the role of paradigms in science, Skinner warns of the danger that the study of texts and ideas will be 'contaminated by the unconscious application of paradigms the familiarity of which, to the historian, disguises an essential inapplicability to the past'.[3] The neglect of the historical contexts of texts tends to produce mythologies rather than good interpretations.[4] What Skinner refers to as the 'myth of doctrines' derives from the assumption, on the part of the historian of ideas, that each classic theorist has a doctrine on the themes taken to constitute the given subject matter. It may lead to the mistake of interpreting some casual remarks by a writer as the doctrine of a theme which the historian anticipated but which the writer could not have intended to convey. Also, it may lead to the mistake of criticising a writer who does not produce a recognisable doctrine for failing to do what he or she had no intention of doing. The 'myth of coherence' involves the assumptions that a theorist's works have an inner coherence and that it is the task of the historian of ideas to reveal or reconstruct this. Thus, coherence may be construed where it does not in fact exist, and apparent contradictions in a theorist's works may be inappropriately removed or resolved by false interpretation. The 'myth of prolepsis' involves disregarding the meaning of the writer in the mistaken attempt to work out the significance of the text, argument or idea for later times. This might lead to the absurd conclusion that thoughts must await the future to achieve their meaning. The 'myth of parochialism' involves the historian of ideas using the terms of his or her own culture for the interpretation of a writer from an earlier, different culture. Misusing his or her historical vantage point the historian may misinterpret the apparent reference and/or sense of some classic text.

Even if all these dangers could be avoided successfully, Skinner says, the textual method would still be inadequate. First, paying attention only to the text might mean neglecting the fact 'that the literal meanings of key terms sometimes change over time', with all the consequent problems of misinterpretation.[5] Secondly, concentrating on the text itself might mean neglecting the 'various oblique strategies which a writer may always decide to adopt in order to set out and at the same time disguise what he means by what he says about some given doctrine'.[6] It is a mistake to concentrate only on the text. It is also a mistake, says Skinner, to concentrate on the supposed 'unit ideas' of intellectual history. This is so not only because unit ideas may not have meanings which remain fixed, but because they have not so much meanings but uses, in that the meanings of ideas are all the uses to which they are put.[7] In this respect, Skinner shares a philosophy of language with the linguistic analysts considered in Chapter 1. A history of all the uses of an idea or term could not be said to constitute a history of a determinate idea.

Having criticised the method of studying only the text, in isolation from its historical context, Skinner does not suggest that one should deny the autonomy of the text and attempt to identify the determination of the text by its context. It does not do to trade one mistake for another. Skinner says: 'The "context" mistakenly gets treated as the determinant of what is said. It needs rather to be treated as an ultimate framework for helping to decide what conventionally recognisable meanings, in a society of *that* kind, it might in principle have been possible for someone to have intended to communicate.'[8] Skinner rejects any deterministic view of context, but argues that an understanding of the context in which any statement is made is crucial to an understanding of the statement. This is the case because any statement, including any statement of political theory, 'is inescapably the embodiment of a particular intention, on a particular occasion, addressed to the solution of a particular problem, and thus specific to its situation'.[9] The intention that the historian must recover, in order to understand the statement, is not just that of its meaning but also that of its 'illocutionary force'. Thus, 'the understanding of texts . . . presupposes the grasp both of what they were intended to mean, and how this meaning was intended to be taken'.[10] The context to be understood is crucially a linguistic one. The reader of a text must first determine the range of meanings which would be possible given the linguistic conventions of the time, and secondly decide which meaning was intended, again given the linguistic context.

My concern here is not the merits of Skinner's detailed arguments about the correct method of interpreting the texts of political theory. Suffice it to say that his general warnings against taking a text out of context and against treating the context as determinant should be heeded.[11] My concern, rather, is the consequences of Skinner's methodology for his characterisation of political theory. Skinner's debt to linguistic analysis and his historicism lead him to confuse political philosophy and political ideology. Skinner declares that his methodological project involves him 'in proposing a more ideological subject-matter for the history of political thought' so as 'more readily to exhibit the dynamic nature of the relationship' which exists 'between the professed principles and the actual practices of political life'.[12] He also says: 'We can hardly claim to be concerned with the history of political theory unless we are prepared to write it as real history – that is, as the record of an actual activity, and in particular as the history of ideologies.'[13] Why does Skinner reduce political theory to political ideology? The answer to this question is suggested by Kenneth Minogue when he says 'presumably... the word "ideology" has been taken to mean thought in response to a situation, by contrast with thinking about timeless essences'.[14] Minogue immediately acknowledges that Skinner does not reduce all theory to ideology, but then very few theorists of ideology would seek to do so. More explicitly, I suggest that Skinner reduces political theory to ideology because his insistence on historical and linguistic interpretation involves, to some extent, the relativism of values which is so detrimental to authentic normative political philosophy.

One of Skinner's starting points in his methodology, as I have noted, is his concern with the priority of paradigms. He warns against attempts to understand another paradigm from the perspective of one's own, and he seems unable to avoid the conclusion that there is no escape from the problem of the incommensurability of paradigms, as noted by Kuhn. That is, for Skinner there seems to be no political thought that is absolute and not relative to some specific context, nor any absolute criterion by means of which one could judge competing political paradigms. For Skinner, correct historical interpretation may be no more than interpretation in terms of the prevailing paradigm of the time and place in which the action or statement in question occurs. Skinner has clarified and corrected his earlier position by denying that he wishes to attribute to any agent 'a privileged access to his own intentions, as a way of "closing the context" in the historical meaning of the text'.[15] This clarification, however, concerns only access to private intentions, and not access to public contexts. Skinner has not changed his position on the significance of context and the need to seek an understanding in terms of contextual conventions.[16]

Skinner identifies the debate in the philosophy of social science between positivists and non-positivists as involving, among other things, contending views on the merits of a correspondence theory and a coherence theory of truth. Thus, positivists test the rationality of the belief of an actor against the available evidence. Critics of positivism, following the work of Kuhn or Winch, deny that there is any available evidence which is not, in some way, culturally determined. Thus, all that can be done to examine the rationality of belief is to consider what counts as evidence within the society in which the belief is held, and to consider how well the belief coheres with others to make a coherent cultural system. According to Skinner: 'The danger with this type of emphasis lies in the tendency to assume that it must follow from this that there cannot be any trans-cultural or trans-historical criteria for applying the concept of rationality at all.'[17] This would seem to suggest that Skinner is keen to avoid the dangers of cultural and historical relativism, yet an examination of his proposed solution of the problem outlined suggests that he fails to do so. Skinner proposes a combination of bits of a correspondence theory of truth with pieces of a coherence theory. The available evidence against which Skinner suggests one might test the correspondence of a belief or action amounts to no more than a 'general awareness of the conventional standards which are generally found to apply to such types of social action within a given social situation'.[18] That is, the available evidence is culturally determined and historically specific. There seems to be no escape from the problem of the relativism of shifting paradigms.

When Skinner deals directly with the question of objective or absolute truth he concludes 'that there may be propositions (perhaps in mathematics) the truth of which is wholly timeless'. In other areas of human enquiry, then, there may be nothing but relative propositions. In particular, the classic texts of social, ethical and political thought reveal 'not the essential sameness, but the essential variety of viable moral assumptions and political commitments'.[19] If Skinner believes that various, and perhaps contradictory political theories are equally viable, and not subject to any absolute evaluation, then he will be tempted to reduce political theory to political ideology.

HISTORY AND POLITICAL PHILOSOPHY: RICHARD ASHCRAFT

Another contemporary writer who argues that political theory must be 'seen in its historical dimensions' and who offers both detailed historical interpretations of seventeenth-century English political thought and methodological considerations, though with nothing of the methodological sophistication of Skinner, is Richard Ashcraft.[20] Ashcraft notes his disagreement with Skinner on the nature of political theory, but, like Skinner, he insists that 'political theory is ideology'.[21] Ashcraft also argues that the identification of 'political theory as ideology' should be the 'recognised starting point for our treatment of political theory'.[22]

Ashcraft insists that political theory is no more than ideology because he seeks to avoid what he takes to be the erroneous view that political theory is philosophy. 'For almost a century', Ashcraft claims, 'the assumptions, methods and arguments of philosophy have dominated the Anglo-American conception of political theory.'[23] In particular, and of late, political theory is dominated by linguistic analysis, such that purely philosophical and logical criteria are used to evaluate political theories, and the task of political theorists comes to be seen as that of sorting out the linguistic and logical muddles of the old masters. According to Ashcraft there are two important and related consequences of this mistaken conception of political theory.

> First, it reflects and reenforces a divorcement of an understanding of political theory in terms of the specific historical-social context within which it arose. Secondly, it severs political theory from precisely those political objectives which, to its author, or to the audience, made the theory a recognisable political force in society.[24]

The close relation of these two consequences is evident from the consideration that the political force of political theory can be recovered and understood only in terms of the historical-social context of the theory.

Ashcraft would be justified in rejecting the influence of an inadequate philosophy, such as linguistic analysis, on political theory. However, what Ashcraft rejects is the influence of philosophy itself. For Ashcraft, the significant aspect of political philosophy is political rather than philosophical, and political theory is practical rather than theoretical. To use his own words, political philosophy is 'an instrument of social change' more than 'a medium of knowledge'.[25] 'A theory is political . . . only in relation to the maintenance or furtherance of the social, political, and economic objectives of a specifically identifiable group within society.'[26] It is to re-enforce this distinctly *political*, rather than philosophical or theoretical conception of political theory that Ashcraft chooses to use the term political ideology. In doing so Ashcraft seems to suggest that political ideology has a use-value rather than a truth-value, or, if ideology does claim to have a truth-value, the concept of truth is subordinated to political use.

In the task of recovering the political force of political theory, by understanding it in its historical-social context, the identification of political theory as ideology is, as has already been noted, a recognised starting point. The student of political theory must seek to understand the political use of ideas by the relevant political groups in the relevant period. At the same time, the student of political theory must also seek to recognise:

> the ways in which one's presuppositions about political theory are structured by the social relationships between political groups in one's own society. Clarity about the origins and nature of one's ideological position will . . . provide the bridge between the 'relevant' past and the 'relevant' present with respect to political theory.[27]

Ashcraft admits that there are difficulties and problems attached to this position, but he fails to appreciate just how difficult and problematic his position is.

By collapsing the distinction between philosophy and

ideology, and by stressing the historical context of all political theory, including one's own, Ashcraft leaves no means by which to establish the validity of competing political theories. Indeed, since validity may be taken to be a philosophical criterion, Ashcraft prefers to write of the 'relevance' of political theory. But relevance must be qualified by quote marks, for it is relative to historical political interests and not a timeless, universal criterion. Given the essentially political character of political theory, whereby the presuppositions of the theory are structured by political relationships (whatever that may mean and however it happens), it seems that the only criterion for the evaluation of political theory is political success in the midst of political struggle. But of course, success is relative to the aspirations of a certain group in time. John Nelson correctly says that 'how Ashcraft could avoid radical relativism can only be guessed, if that'.[28] Ashcraft offers a few unrestrained responses to the criticism of Nelson, but he does not answer the specific accusation of relativism.[29]

If, for Ashcraft, political theory is no more than political ideology, being concerned with distinctly political and not philosophical concerns, then one can question the status of his own writings. Does he produce political ideology and not political philosophy? Does his work have only a political purpose and no epistemological value? It may be that Ashcraft is prepared to accept the labels 'ideologist' for himself and 'political' for his work, yet he could not do so without problems. In particular, since his work involves him in a consideration of the writings of others who would claim to be producing political philosophy and not ideology, Ashcraft must decide how to treat such claims. As another of Ashcraft's critics, Dante Germino, says:

> It would be arbitrary and dogmatic simply to dismiss the claims of the non-Marxists without investigating the epistemological foundations for such a claim. By engaging in such an investigation, however, the Marxists themselves would refute their claim that all thought is ideological. I must reluctantly conclude that in his essay Mr Ashcraft has convicted himself of dogmatism.[30]

I am less clear than Germino that Ashcraft remains dogmatic and never indulges in epistemological considerations. Ashcraft necessarily speculates philosophically on the nature of politics and the good life. Thus, he shows himself to be not simply dogmatic but also inconsistent with his own principle that all political thought is ideological.

Both Skinner and Ashcraft identify political philosophy as political ideology, and neither can offer any means of distinguishing the two modes of political thought. Both writers reduce and limit political philosophy to specific historical contexts, and so both are vulnerable to the charge of relativism. The mistake of both is to treat political philosophy as if it was a historical discipline. As Leo Strauss argues: 'political philosophy is not a historical discipline. The philosophical questions of the nature of political things and the best, or just, political order are fundamentally different from historical questions'.[31] Political philosophy should seek to escape relativism, distance itself from ideology, and seek a universal and objective foundation for politics.

COMMUNITARIANISM: MICHAEL WALZER

An influential contemporary school of thought which denies that political philosophy can provide a neutral, or objective, or universal foundation for politics is communitarianism. Communitarianism is a critique of liberalism and may be as old as liberalism itself, but contemporary communitarianism emerges in response to the liberalism of John Rawls's *A Theory of Justice*, published in 1971. Communitarianism takes many shapes and offers various arguments. Simon Caney conveniently identifies three characteristic component claims of communitarianism: descriptive claims about the nature of persons, who are not independent of, but constituted by, the communities in which they live; normative claims about the value of community, which is denied by liberal individualists; and meta-ethical claims about the status of political principles, which are not universal but confined to the shared values of the community.[32] In considering the impact of communitarianism on consideration about the nature of political philosophy, the most important claim is the meta-ethical one about the status of political principles. The clearest expression of such a claim is offered by Michael Walzer, one of the leading communitarians, and is worth quoting in full.

> One way to begin the philosophical enterprise – perhaps the original way – is to walk out of the cave, leave the city, climb the mountain, fashion for oneself (what can never be fashioned for ordinary men and women) an objective and universal standpoint. Then one describes the terrain of everyday life from far away, so that it loses its particular contours and takes on a different shape. But I mean to stand in the cave, in the city, on the ground. Another way of doing philosophy is to interpret to one's fellow citizens the world of meanings that we share. Justice and equality can conceivably be worked out as philosophical artifacts, but a just or an equalitarian society cannot be. If such a society isn't already here – hidden, as it were, in our concepts and categories – we will never know it concretely or realize it in fact.[33]

For Walzer, philosophy has a tendency to seek universal and eternal truths, and political philosophy has a tendency to judge the principles and practices of particular communities by reference to objective moral reality. But according to Walzer, there is no objective moral reality beyond the everyday concerns of the plurality of particular political communities. He says 'the everyday world is a moral world, and we would do better to study its internal rules, maxims, conventions, and ideals, rather than to detach ourselves from it in search of a universal and transcendent standpoint'.[34] Any attempt to impose supposedly objective and universal philosophical principles on particular communities will involve two dangers. First, it will involve 'overriding' the particular 'traditions, conventions, and expectations' of any community. Second, it will involve the denial of the democratic principle, and the value of the democratic experience, of the community making its moral decisions for itself.[35] For Walzer, then, political philosophers should study particular political communities, rather than some supposedly objective and universal political reality, and they should interpret the political values determined by particular political processes rather than attempt to provide universal philosophical validation for them. Walzer makes a distinction between 'philosophical validation' and 'political authorization' as 'two entirely different things'. He says:

> Authorization is the work of citizens governing themselves among themselves. Validation is the work of the philosopher reasoning alone in a world he inhabits alone or fills with the products of his own speculations. Democracy has no claims in the philosophical realm, and philosophers have no special rights in the political community. In the world of opinion, truth is indeed another opinion, and the philosopher is only another opinion-maker.[36]

Walzer reduces political philosophy to opinion, or, though he does not use the word, ideology.

Walzer acknowledges that his critics have said that his 'argument makes social criticism impossible; it binds us tightly, inescapably, to the status quo. Unless we are in sight of the sun, like Plato's philosopher, we can make no judgement about life in the cave. If we are unable to appeal to the outside, critics inside must turn apologist.'[37] Walzer takes the criticism seriously and seeks to answer it. He claims that there is no advantage to be had from setting out to discover the moral world for we have always lived in it, and there is no need to invent the moral world because it has already been invented.[38] Moreover, the 'problem of disconnected criticism, and thus with criticism that derives from newly discovered or invented moral standards, is that it presses its practitioners toward manipulation and compulsion'.[39] Thus social criticism cannot be wholly detached and objective, and must work from within the particular moral world of the community. Social criticism is a by-product of 'cultural elaboration and affirmation' and 'finds a warrant for critical engagement in the idealism, even if it is a hypocritical idealism, of the actually existing moral world'.[40]

Walzer's model of social criticism might permit the exposure of the hypocrisy of a group which fails to live up to the standards which it has publicly proclaimed, or the identification of the failure of a ruling group to secure the standards generally agreed in society, but little more. His model seems not to allow for radical criticism within any society, nor cross-cultural criticism of any sort. The main problem of Walzer's model of social criticism is its relativism: there is no objective moral reality, and all moral standards are relative to local moral communities. Thus moral standards cannot be applied critically within any society nor at all across societies. The relativism of Walzer's political thought has been rightly criticised by Ronald Dworkin:

> Walzer has not thought through the consequences of his relativism for a society like ours, in which questions of justice are endlessly contested and debated.... For it is part of our common political life, if anything is, that justice is our critic and not our mirror.... In the end... political theory can make no contribution to how we govern ourselves except by struggling, against all the impulses that drag us back into our own culture, toward generality and some reflective basis for deciding which of our traditional distinctions and discriminations are genuine and which spurious.... We cannot leave justice to convention and anecdote.[41]

Walzer's relativism renders him unable both to arbitrate competing political ideas and ideals, and to distinguish political philosophy and political ideology.

POSTMODERNISM AND ANTIFOUNDATIONALISM: RICHARD RORTY

Richard Rorty argues that contemporary political philosophy is a three-cornered debate between: (a) liberals who believe there is a universal, objective philosophical foundation for their political principles and institutions; (b) communitarians who deny the validity of such a foundation and so abandon liberalism; and (c) those, including himself, who seek to preserve liberal institutions while abandoning any universal philosophical foundation for them.[42] Rorty cites Ronald Dworkin as a foundationalist liberal. He identifies the communitarians as including Alasdair MacIntyre, Michael Sandel and Charles Taylor, and notes that although Michael Walzer is taken to be one, the self-image of his preferred society shares much with liberalism. In addition to Rorty himself, nonfoundational liberals include John Dewey, Michael

Oakeshott and, perhaps controversially, John Rawls.[43] Rorty characterises his political thought as 'postmodernist bourgeois liberalism'.[44] To understand the aptness of this chosen label it is necessary to consider the phenomenon of postmodernism and Rorty's antifoundationalism.

Postmodernism is a notoriously vague and fluid term, perhaps because of its adherents' suspicion of authoritative definition, but Stephen White has conveniently identified four interrelated phenomena which constitute what he terms the postmodern problematic: 'the increasing incredulity toward metanarratives, the growing awareness of new problems wrought by societal rationalization, the explosion of new informational technologies, and the emergence of new social movements'.[45] Incredulity towards metanarratives means, according to the originator of the phrase, Jean-François Lyotard, doubt about the ways in which claims to knowledge are legitimated by appeals to some higher discourse. These modern metanarratives include 'the dialectics of the Spirit, the hermeneutics of meaning, the emancipation of the rational or working subject, or the creation of wealth'.[46] Continuing with White's characterisation of the postmodern problematic, incredulity towards metanarratives will cast doubt on the modern project of human improvement and indeed will tend to highlight perceived problems of modernisation and rationalisation. The dominance of a single metanarrative will be challenged by a growing diversity of information sources and claims to knowledge. The notion of general human improvement founded on one theoretical perspective will be met with the suspicion that such a perspective is only partial (probably a white male perspective) and challenged by the rise of a diversity of human groups claiming their own, distinctive ways to a better life.

In political theory, modernism might be said to start in the seventeenth century with Thomas Hobbes's new science of politics, which promises universal peace and prosperity; to continue with the Enlightenment thinkers of the eighteenth century, who stress rational progress; and to culminate in the nineteenth century with Karl Marx's theory of revolutionary emancipation and John Stuart Mill's theory of individual development. Incredulity toward metanarratives is prompted in the late nineteenth and early twentieth centuries, by the irrationalist Friedrich Nietzsche and the existentialist Martin Heidegger, and confirmed by their contemporary heirs such as the poststructuralist Michel Foucault and the deconstructionist Jacques Derrida.

Rorty employs the term 'postmodern' 'in the narrow sense defined by Lyotard as "distrust of metanarratives"'.[47] The postmodernist challenge to political theory, to which Rorty subscribes, is a challenge to the very notion of a foundation for political theory. The notion of an objective, transcultural, rational philosophical foundation for politics, with its appeal to a common human nature, is, Rorty notes, an aspect of the modern or Enlightenment project.[48] For Rorty, politics cannot have, and does not require, any rational philosophical foundation. His argument here is largely epistemological, but since his epistemology is pragmatist he is inclined to argue that his opposition to foundations is concerned with the usefulness and not just the truth of ideas. He argues both that it is philosophically impossible to formulate a foundation for politics, and that this lack of foundation is beneficial for politics. Rorty describes his pragmatist epistemology as antirepresentationalist. Knowledge is not a matter of representing reality, or achieving a correspondence with reality, or 'getting reality right', for there is no reality independent of our thoughts, our language and our culture.[49] There can be no objective philosophical foundation for politics, for both our politics and our philosophy are culturally determined. Rorty says: 'one consequence of antirepresentationalism is the recognition that no description of how things are from a God's-eye point of view, no skyhook provided by some contemporary or yet-to-be-developed science, is going to free us from the contingency of having been acculturated as we were'.[50] The facts that we are denied access to an objective reality, and that we are stuck in our particular culture, are not matters of regret for Rorty.

More recently Rorty has argued that his opposition to foundationalism is not concerned with metaethics and 'questions about realism and antirealism', and that his 'doubts about about the effectiveness of appeals to moral knowledge are doubts about causal efficacy, not about epistemic status'.[51] This apparent change of argument is really more a shift of emphasis. He is not denying his antirepresentationalist epistemology, but stressing his pragmatism, according to which knowledge is 'a matter of acquiring habits of action for coping with reality'.[52] In order to understand Rorty's argument for the utility of antifoundationalism it is necessary to understand his notions of solidarity and ethnocentrism, and his particular solidarity with his own liberal community.

For Rorty there is no objective reality because our reality is dependent on our culture and community. Rather than seek illusive objectivity, we should, Rorty advocates, seek solidarity with our community. We should 'think of our sense of community as having no foundation except shared hope and the trust created by such sharing'.[53] We cannot escape the acculturation of our community, but this is not a problem for our acculturation makes us what we are and provides what is important for us. 'Our acculturation is what makes certain options live, or momentous, or forced, while leaving others dead, or trivial, or optional.'[54] Rorty wishes to stress that members of a community can be regulated and motivated by beliefs which they know to be culturally contingent, and that social life does not require supposedly objective, universal values and principles.[55] Rorty advocates not only solidarity, that is, support for one's culture, but also ethnocentricity, that is, consideration and judgement of all other cultures from the point of view of one's own. Rorty says by way of definition: 'To be ethnocentric is to divide the human race into the people to whom one must justify one's beliefs and the others. The first group – one's *ethnos* – comprises those who share enough of one's beliefs to make fruitful conversation possible.'[56] In his writings Rorty often refers ethnocentrically to 'we', meaning members of the liberal culture of the rich Western democracies, the ethnos with which he identifies.[57] As Richard Bernstein notes, Rorty uses the term 'we' as if he believed there was an essence of liberalism and no serious philosophical disagreement among all those who are termed liberals.[58] Rorty also complicates the matter by describing himself as a social democrat, again as if there were no serious differences between liberalism and social democracy.[59] Rorty suggests why it might be convenient to be ethnocentric and to show solidarity with one's own culture rather than any other, but he fails to provide any moral justification for such behaviour.

Given the lack of access to an objective reality and the effects of acculturation on our thought, Rorty says 'the most philosophy can hope to do is summarize our culturally influenced intuitions about the right thing to do in various situations'.[60] This notion of the interpretive role of philosophy is similar to that held by Walzer. For both Rorty and Walzer philosophy does not discover the truth of objective reality but, rather, makes explicit the shared norms of a community. Rorty recognises that those philosophers who seek a universal foundation for politics tend to be moral realists, who believe that 'true moral judgements are *made* true by something out there in the world', such as human nature.[61] Rorty is an antirealist and antifoundationalist who believes that moral standards are merely the result of the same process of acculturation that produces the rest of social life.

Rorty's 'postmodernist bourgeois liberalism' is well named. He adopts the term 'postmodernist' in order to demonstrate that his liberal society has no, and needs no, universal philosophical foundations. He adopts the term 'bourgeois' in order to emphasise that the institutions and practices of his liberal society are 'possible and justifiable only in certain historical, and especially economic, conditions'.[62] Although Rorty associates himself with postmodernism, he also claims to be 'not fond of the term' and expresses regret at using it.[63] There is at least one good reason for distinguishing Rorty from postmodernism. Although Rorty shares with postmodernism a scepticism about the foundation of the modern, Enlightenment project, he welcomes and seeks to realise the goals and hopes of the project.[64] Thus, Rorty confidently claims something that no self-respecting postmodernist would allow: that 'the culture with which we in this democracy identify ourselves is morally superior to other cultures'.[65] Rorty's antifoundationalism links him with most other postmodernists; his ethnocentrism sets him apart from them.

Rorty seeks to demonstrate the superiority of the liberal culture of the rich Western democracies in terms of its openness, tolerance, freedom, harmony and potential for greater solidarity. Liberalism is best not because it achieves or embodies the supreme foundational value, but, rather, because its lack of foundation is useful for securing moral progress. Although all human communities remain ethnocentric and limited by the bounds of their culture, it is the merit of 'the liberal culture of recent times' that it 'has found a strategy for avoiding the disadvantage of ethnocentrism'. It is in the nature of liberal culture 'to be open to encounters with other actual and possible cultures'. The liberal culture makes 'openness central to its self-image' and 'prides itself on its suspicion of ethnocentrism'.[66] This ethnocentric openness is advantageous in so far as it helps overcome the disadvantages of narrowness and contempt for others which is usually associated with ethnocentricity. However, Rorty recognises that there must be a limit to openness, if only because being open to those cultures which are not themselves open may tempt us to doubt the superiority of our own position. As Rorty puts it, we must avoid becoming '"wet" liberals' and 'so open-minded that our brains have fallen out'.[67] I believe that Rorty is correct in cautioning against unlimited openness, but, as I argue below, his antifoundationalism and consequent relativism leave him unable to substantiate his case. The liberal culture is also tolerant of the diversity of other cultures.[68] Tolerance is supposedly one of the useful consequences of antifoundationalism: in the absence of philosophical foundations people tend to be pragmatic in their search for useful ideas and less inclined to dismiss strange ideas. As with openness, Rorty recognises a necessary limit to tolerance. Liberals must not be so tolerant as to accept the terms of discourse set out by any fanatic they might meet.[69] Again, I argue below that Rorty's relativism causes him problems with this argument.

The liberal culture overcomes the dangers of ethnocentricity and demonstrates its superiority to other cultures by espousing freedom, which it can then extend to others. This is a further supposed advantage of antifoundationalism, which has 'helped us substitute Freedom for Truth as the goal of thinking and of social progress'.[70] Rorty shares with other postmodernist thinkers both the fear that adherence to a metanarrative entails the tyranny of this over all other thought, and the hope that the absence of metanarratives entails equal opportunity for all (non-fanatical) points of view. The unequal distribution of power in liberal societies would seem to deny this hope. Liberal culture is also thought to be superior because it promotes or facilitates harmony among diversity. Rorty argues that both the liberal distinction between the public and private spheres of life, and the liberal ideal of procedural justice permit individuals and cultures to interact in public to their mutual advantage without intruding on each other's privacy and conception of the good.[71] Finally, liberalism is capable of moral progress 'in the direction of greater human solidarity'. This solidarity depends on no foundation such as human nature but, rather, is to be seen as 'the ability to think of people widely different from ourselves as included in the range of "us"'.[72] The ethnocentrism of liberals is supposedly one that permits cosmopolitanism and a solidarity with all peoples. It is the very nature of liberal society which permits it to make moral progress. I have already noted that for Rorty there can be no escape from acculturation. This might seem to deny the possibility of progress, but the acculturation of liberal society is such that it is open to other cultures and so is likely to contain 'splits which supply toeholds for new initiatives'.[73] Moral progress, for Rorty, involves not the discovery of a moral absolute but the imaginative creation of better ideas. I argue below that the notion of moral progress is another problem for Rorty.

The main problem with Rorty's antifoundationalism and his ethnocentric defence of liberalism is relativism. Rorty denies absolute, objective political principles and argues that all political principles are relative to one's culture. This position is relativist, and leaves anyone holding it unable to justify cross-cultural judgements. Yet Rorty seeks to make cross-cultural judgements and demonstrate the superiority of one particular culture, the liberal one, over all others. Rorty, like most relativists, seeks to deny his relativism, and he does this by clarifying what he does and does not believe. He does not hold, he says, the 'self-refuting view' that 'every view is as good as every other'. Nor does he hold the 'eccentric view' that '"true" is an equivocal term, having as many meanings as there are procedures of justification'. The term 'true' means the same thing in all cultures, for 'it is merely a term of commendation', although this univocity of meaning is 'compatible with diversity of reference'. What Rorty does hold is the 'ethnocentric view' that 'there is nothing to be said about . . . truth . . . apart from descriptions of the familiar procedures of justification which a given society – *ours* – uses in one or another form of inquiry'. A pragmatist, Rorty claims, is not making the positive point that something is relative to something else, but, rather, 'the purely *negative* point that we should drop the traditional distinction between knowledge and opinion, construed as the distinction between truth as correspondence to reality and truth as a commendatory term for well-justified beliefs'.[74]

Rorty argues that the distinction between absolutism and relativism is characteristic of the foundationalist attitude he seeks to avoid.[75] Only if one grants the existence of objective reality can one talk of an absolute truth that corresponds to it. If one denies objective reality and absolute truth, then truth is simply that which is true relative to one's culture, and in holding to this one cannot be said to offend against a higher point of view to which one has responsibility. Thus, Rorty says, 'there is no such thing as the "relativist predicament," just as for someone who thinks there is no God there will be no such thing as blasphemy'.[76] But Rorty exposes his relativism in his attempt to deny it. The truth of the existence of God can be established only by reference to objective reality, not the beliefs or doubts relative to any particular individual or community. Similarly, whether or not a statement is true depends on its correspondence to the reality to which it refers and not just the meaning of the term 'true' nor the local cultural convention for justifying truth claims.

Rorty's relativism, and the serious problems it causes him, are evident in the acknowledged circularity of his arguments for the superiority of liberalism. Having denied an objective foundation for all political philosophy, Rorty denies it for his preferred liberalism. He has no objective reason for preferring liberalism over other cultures, and yet he does prefer it. He admits that he asks Western liberal intellectuals to 'privilege our own group, even though there be no noncircular justification for doing so'.[77] This circularity of argument is a problem of relativism. Rorty's belief in the superiority of liberalism is relative to the liberal culture. Rorty fails to demonstrate why members of the liberal culture should show solidarity with it rather than any alternative culture, because he fails to provide it with foundations. His claim that it is a more open, more tolerant, freer and more harmonious culture than others, and so superior to others, can be justified only if it can be demonstrated that openness, freedom, tolerance and harmony are absolutely good qualities. As noted above, Rorty recognises necessary limits to openness and tolerance, and so he does not commit the inconsistency, for a relativist, of elevating openness and tolerance to absolute values. However, he fails to justify these limits by reference to any value higher than culturally approved openness and tolerance. His claim that liberalism is capable of greater moral progress than other cultures has no justification in the absence of an absolute moral measure. Progress properly understood must be movement towards a goal which is known to be worth achieving independently of the process of achieving it. Progress can be made, but the goal of progress must be given.

Richard Bernstein argues that Rorty does not so much answer the charge of relativism as evade it, and that he is right to do so. The charge of relativism or ethnocentrism looses its sting, according to Bernstein, when one realises that there can be no appeal to absolute truth, and that the most one can do is 'play off good and bad forms of ethnocentrism'.[78] But if one's only measure of good and bad ethnocentrism is itself ethnocentric, one is caught in the vicious circularity of relativism. Bernstein does charge Rorty with offering, in his defence of liberalism, 'little more than an *apologia* for the status quo'.[79] It is true that cultural relativists like Rorty have no foundation for supporting objective, cross-cultural judgements and so cannot properly, and often do not, pass critical judgement on their own culture. But Rorty is not content to be an uncritical conservative and welcomes change and moral progress. The criticism that can properly be made of Rorty is that he has no objective standard by which he can distinguish good from bad change, and so no objective criterion for measuring moral progress.

Before the current excitement with postmodernism Leo Strauss had also noted the crisis of modernity as something rooted in a serious doubt about the foundation of political theory. Strauss correctly characterises the crisis of modernism as the problem of ideology. In 1963 he wrote that 'for most political scientists today, political philosophy is not more than ideology or myth'.[80] For Strauss the failure to distinguish political philosophy from political ideology is the 'core' of a modern crisis, which consists in the Western world 'having become uncertain of its purpose', a purpose which was originally universal and concerned with progress towards prosperity.[81] The identification and execution of such a purpose was the task of the 'modern project', which was 'originated by modern political philosophy'.[82] Political philosophy was conceived as one aspect of philosophy and science, themselves conceived as one and the same and concerned with the satisfaction, 'in the most perfect manner', of 'the most powerful and natural needs of men'.[83] 'The modern project', Strauss argues, 'was distinguished from the earlier view by the fact that it implied that the improvement of society depends decisively on institutions, political or economic, as distinguished from the formation of character.'[84] The modern crisis comes about when political philosophy fails to justify the human and social purpose, and is seen to fail. The teaching of modern political philosophy becomes an ideology, 'a teaching not superior in truth and justice to any other among the innumerable ideologies'.[85] The failure of political philosophy to maintain a unity of human and social purpose results from the failure to maintain a unity of science and philosophy, of human nature and nature in general, and of facts and values. Contemporary social science, now uninformed by the wisdom of traditional philosophy, unable to discern the natural good of human beings, and concerned only with the study of the given facts, 'admits and even proclaims its inability to validate any value-judgement proper'.[86]

Unlike the contemporary postmodernists who welcome the loss of the unity of purpose and certainty of modernism, and celebrate the pluralism of values of the postmodern condition, Strauss criticises the relativism and nihilism that follow the deconstruction of authority. Strauss believes that the only solution to the crisis of modernity is to turn away from the Moderns and return to the Ancients, for modernism contains the seeds of its own destruction, in the form of positivism and historicism. The solution to the problem of modernity, which is the problem of ideology, is the recovery of a traditional and substantial conception of human reason, which is not historically relative nor culturally specific. Strauss argues that the only solution to the problem of ideology is the recovery of authentic political philosophy.

Rorty is unwilling and unable to sustain a distinction between philosophy and ideology. His pragmatist antirepresentationalism entails dropping 'the appearance–reality distinction in favour of a distinction between beliefs which serve some purposes and beliefs which serve other purposes – for example, the purposes of one group and those of another group'.[87] Thus, for Rorty ideas are not right or wrong but, rather, useful or not useful. Definitions of ideology, as shown in Chapters 2 and 3, often involve the elevation of the use-value of ideas over their truth-value. In measuring ideas in terms of their social utility rather than their truth Rorty reduces human thought to ideology. He confirms his refusal to distinguish between philosophy and ideology when he refers to the 'uselessness of the notion of "ideology"' and to the 'fuzzy distinction between "ideology" and a form of thought . . . which escapes being "ideology"'.[88]

CONCLUSION

The four thinkers considered in this chapter – Skinner, Ashcraft, Walzer and Rorty – represent various strands of contemporary political thought. What they have in common is an acknowledgement that political thought is normative and cannot be value-free. They also share the problem of relativism, which leads, in all four cases, to the failure to distinguish between political philosophy and political ideology. A critique of relativism is offered in the next chapter. The demarcation of political philosophy and political ideology is considered in Chapter 9.

8 A Critique of Relativism in Political Thought

HOW RELATIVISM ENTERS POLITICAL THOUGHT

In the preceding chapters I have noted that relativism is a problem of ideology and of inadequate conceptions of political philosophy and political science which fail to maintain objectivity. Chapter 1 considered how logical positivists and linguistic analysts tend to dismiss all normative thought as non-scientific and identify it as ideology. Normative thought is held to lack objective verification and to be relative to the non-rational preferences of individuals and groups. Historicism also undermines political philosophy by making all values relative to historical context. One consequence of this attack on normative political philosophy is that even when the revival of the discipline is acknowledged it is suspected of being not much more than ideological. Chapters 2 and 3 noted that the problem of relativism pervades theories of ideology. Marxist theories of ideology seek, but fail, to substantiate their own claims to objectivity and truth, and so fail to demonstrate why Marxism is superior to other bodies of thought. Thus Marxism may be no more than an ideology, whose appeal is relative to a particular social class. Among non-Marxist theories of ideology, Durkheim starts with a negative and restrictive conception of ideology, which he contrasts with social science, but ends with the acknowledgement that both science and ideology are socially functional, relative to particular social formations. Pareto also fails to sustain a negative and restrictive conception of ideology, and seems to accept that reason and science may be no more than derivations, attempted rationalisations of non-logical behaviour. Oakeshott dismisses both empirical and ideological political thought and argues that all authentic political theory is relative to particular traditions of political behaviour. Mannheim argues that nearly all human thought is socially determined and so relative to social conditions.

-He recognises more clearly than the others that ideology poses the problem of relativism, but he fails to resolve it.

Chapter 4 examined possible foundations of a science of politics which, some hoped, would provide an objective antidote to ideology. Both Popper and Lakatos wish to maintain the methodological demarcation of science and non-science, but Popper acknowledges that ultimately science rests on a non-rational value choice, and Lakatos acknowledges the need for non-scientific human decisions in the conduct of science. Extending such conventionalism, Kuhn offers a theory of scientific change which indicates that competing theories are relative to changing and incommensurable paradigms. Feyerabend consolidates this approach and confirms that science is just another ideology and that all truth is relative. Chapter 5 considered the work of Winch, who rejects natural science as a model for the study of society, but whose interpretative social science rests on cultural and conceptual relativism. I considered also the work of Bhaskar, whose critical realist philosophy of science seems to offer the possibility of a naturalist social science which is both objective and normative. Even Bhaskar cannot avoid the problem of epistemological and moral relativism, which are problems also for the concept of a value-free political science, which I criticised in Chapter 6. Chapter 7 examined the work of theorists who do not deny that political philosophy is normative, but who fail to distinguish political philosophy and ideology. The methodological approaches of Skinner and Ashcraft to the history of political thought entail historical relativism. The communitarianism of Walzer and the postmodernist antifoundationalism of Rorty entail cultural relativism.

I have already noted, with reference to Mannheim, Kuhn and Rorty, how many relativists seek to deny their relativism, though without success. I note below that some relativists are not embarrassed by their position and indeed embrace relativism as an appropriate method of study. Other theorists simply deny that relativism is a problem or of any relevance at all to political theory. John Gunnell claims that relativism is a 'philosophical dilemma that has no real practical counterpart' and that 'both philosophically and practically conceived is actually a pseudo-problem that is sustained by the aspirations of rationalism and foundationalism'. His argument is that relativism is 'repressed expression... of the problem of theory and practice', and that only when political theory frees itself from its academic subservience to philosophy, and ceases its vain attempt to provide objective, 'transcontextual' epistemological certainties for politics, can it realise its true relation to the practice of politics.[1] But I have argued that politics (as practice) cannot avoid moral issues, which need to be addressed by (practical) normative political theory, and that the denial of an objective foundation for political philosophy leads to the problem of relativism. Relativism is not a purely philosophical problem, but a problem for politics.

THE NATURE OF RELATIVISM

In order to criticise relativism it is important to avoid, if possible, defining it in such a way that it is necessarily vulnerable to the criticism offered. To avoid winning a facile conclusion on the basis of a contrived definition it is useful to pay attention to the characterisation of relativism offered by thinkers who advocate it, or who see at least some truth in it. However, if relativism is inherently incoherent, it will be impossible to avoid a vulnerable definition. As William Newton-Smith says of relativism, 'it is not easy to formulate the idea so as to make it non-trivial without making it incoherent'.[2] Two writers who advocate relativism, for reasons which will be considered below, are Barry Barnes and David Bloor. They identify three necessary features of relativism.[3] First, relativism starts from the evidence that human belief on any topic varies. It does seem to be an unavoidable and incontrovertible fact that human thought and belief is not uniform but varied, and this fact is very often cited by relativists as part of their case. As will be argued later, this fact of variation of belief, by itself, does not confirm the relativist case, but relativists, including Barnes and Bloor, do not rest their case on this one point.

Second, which of the various beliefs is to be found in a given context depends on, or is relative to, the context of the believers. This is very much the characteristic feature of relativism. It is important to note that this second feature of relativism involves something more than the acknowledgement of the fact that various people entertain various beliefs, relative to their various circumstances. It involves also the denial that there can be anything other than relative belief. Relativists deny that there can be any absolute and universal standards against which any belief can be measured, and argue that all belief is relative to one of a number of different contexts. It is this denial of the possibility of absolute and universal, and unique and objective, standards, independent of context and circumstances, that constitutes the problem of relativism.

Third, relativism necessarily requires a postulate of 'symmetry' or 'equivalence'. That is, if all beliefs are relative to some particular context, then, in the absence of any objective, absolute standards by which to measure them, all beliefs are in some way the same or 'on a par with one another'. Barnes and Bloor insist on the importance of the correct formulation of this equivalence postulate. An incorrect formulation will result in serious difficulties, as they show.

> To say that all beliefs are equally true encounters the problem of how to handle beliefs which contradict one another. If one belief denies what the other asserts, how can they both be true? Similarly, to say that all beliefs are equally false poses the problem of the status of the relativist's own claims. He would seem to be pulling the rug from under his own feet.[4]

Barnes and Bloor think they can avoid the accusation that all relativism is self-refuting by formulating their equivalence postulate to read: 'all beliefs are on a par with one another with respect to the causes of their credibility'.[5] This formulation, though, fares no better than any which refers to equal truth or falsity. If all beliefs are equally credible, because of the variety of otherwise equal contexts to which credibility is relative, then the arguments for and against relativism are equally credible. Thus, we have no means of resolving the conflict of arguments and no warrant for taking relativism more seriously than anti-relativism. Relativism, however one formulates it, undermines itself. Barnes and Bloor cannot solve the problem of defining relativism in such a way that it is both non-trivial and coherent. There is an incoherence in relativism which they cannot avoid.

A writer who sees only some truth in relativism, Bernard Williams, offers a further feature of relativism, which can be usefully added to the definition offered by Barnes and Bloor. Relativism notes the diversity of beliefs; relates them to their particular contexts; and treats all beliefs as equivalent in some way. Relativism seeks to do something else, as Williams notes. 'Its aim is to take views, outlooks, or beliefs that apparently conflict and treat them in such a way that they do not conflict: each of them turns out to be acceptable in its own place.'[6] This involves showing both why beliefs do not in fact conflict and why they may seem to do so. Williams believes that relativism is not wholly successful in this. The attempt, though, involves the following sort of argument. Conflict between two different beliefs can be established only if both can be measured or judged according to one common and objective standard, which is independent of the beliefs. All standards, however, are relative to particular contexts and apply only there; there are no objective standards independent of context. Thus, there can be no conflict between different context-dependent beliefs. Relativists can assert, without contradiction, that two contradictory beliefs can both be true, in their respective contexts, and that a belief can be true in one context and false in another. They can do so only because they reject the notion of objective truth and hold that all standards of truth and falsity are context-dependent. For relativists, apparent conflicts are explained away. The remaining problem for relativists, as Williams notes, is that the more convincing is the argument that beliefs are relative and so not in conflict, the more puzzling it is that people should think that there was a conflict. Again the incoherence of relativism is apparent.

Relativism can now be characterised as involving the following claims:

(a) there is an evident variety of beliefs;
(b) beliefs are in some way dependent upon, or relative to particular contexts or circumstances;
(c) there are no objective, absolute, universal standards of

belief, independent of particular contexts or circumstances;
(d) all beliefs are equivalent in some way;
(e) the apparent conflict between various beliefs from various contexts can be explained away by reference to various context-dependent standards of belief.

Rorty, who was considered in the previous chapter, denies (d) and claims, in his ethnocentric way, that the beliefs of his culture are better than those of other cultures. He argues that one can hold (d) only if one denies (c); that is, one can hold all beliefs to be equivalent in some way only if one has access to some objective measure that can establish such equivalence of truth. I believe Rorty is wrong. It is precisely because of the perceived lack of an objective measure that relativists have no good reason to discriminate between various beliefs. Rorty's ethnocentric preference for some beliefs over others is entirely unfounded and inconsistent with his denial of objective foundations of belief.

To clarify and consolidate the characterisation of relativism it will be useful to distinguish it from that with which it is often confused. First, relativism is not to be confused with subjectivism. Subjectivism holds that belief is relative to the knowing subject, that is, the individual human being, and denies the existence of objective standards of belief which apply to all individuals. By contrast, relativists are often prepared to accept that beliefs and standards are relative not to individuals but to a group of individuals who share a certain context or set of circumstances. All subjectivists are likely to be relativists, but not all relativists are likely to be subjectivists. Subjectivists and relativists are united in denying absolute standards of belief. They may disagree on that to which beliefs are relative. Subjectivists qualify the claim 'proposition *x* is true' so as to read 'proposition *x* is true for individual *A*'. Further, subjectivists will tend to equate the claim 'proposition *x* is true for individual *A*' with that which reads 'individual *A* believes proposition *x* to be true'. In this case, there is no distinction between truth and belief about truth. Consequently, there seems to be no distinction between correct and incorrect belief. Relativists, though, need not equate truth and belief. They can argue that standards of truth are relative to certain contexts shared by groups of individuals. Thus, they can argue that an individual can make a mistake in terms of the local standard of truth of his or her context. Relativists need not assume that all belief is to be taken as true and that truth is simply what any individual happens to believe. However, although relativism and subjectivism are to be distinguished, it is not clear that relativism can prevent slippage into subjectivism and even solipsism (according to which the individual subject is the sole existent). If an individual wishes to establish his or her own unique standards of truth, no relativist would seem to have any good reason to object to this.

Second, relativism is not to be confused with scepticism. Scepticism does not deny the possibility that absolute standards of belief may exist, but denies that human beings can ever know such absolutes with certainty. By contrast, relativism denies the very possibility of such absolutes and holds that all standards are relative to something else. Karl Popper confuses relativism and scepticism when he says that either label may be used to identify the theory which holds that choice between competing theories is arbitrary because: (a) there is no objective truth; or (b) if there is objective truth, there is no theory which is true or nearer to the truth than another theory; or (c) given two or more theories, there is no way of telling which one is better than the others.[7] There is confusion here because anyone who admits that there exists absolute truth cannot at the same time hold that all truth is relative. Certainly scepticism, like relativism, is a menace to the truth, and sceptics may be tempted to accept relativist conclusions, but the two errors are not identical. No good purpose is served by identifying them, for the criticisms of both are not identical.

Thus far I have referred only to the relativism of belief, and to the context or circumstances to which beliefs are relative. It is, of course, possible to distinguish various forms of relativism, inasmuch as different things can be said to be relative to other different things. The two forms referred to most often in the literature of philosophy and social science are epistemological or cognitive relativism and moral relativism. Epistemological or cognitive relativism holds that truth and knowledge are relative to something, and so denies absolute and objective truth and knowledge. Moral relativism denies the existence of good or right as absolute and objective standards of conduct, and holds that all moral judgements are relative to something. In addition, one may find reference to ontological, perceptual and logical relativism and to relativism of reason, according to which, in turn, that which exists, that which is perceived, and the operations of logic and reason are held to be not absolute and objective, but relative to something. Conceptual relativism is ambiguous: concepts may be relative to something else; or other things may be relative to the conceptual schemes by which they are understood. Historical relativism holds that beliefs and behaviour are relative to their historical context. Conceptual schemes and history do not exhaust the list of things to which others may be relative. Martin Hollis and Steven Lukes offer a list of five things to which beliefs might be relative: natural environment; human perceptual and reflective equipment; social context; language; and some all-embracing context, like a form of life.[8] As Hollis and Lukes note, it can be asked whether some of these things, such as language and cognitive context, are themselves relative to other things. Whatever the answer, relativism is not straightforward.

Cultural relativism may have a further significance. If all is relative to a culture, or a form of life, there can be no objective standards for cross-cultural analysis. Accordingly, cultures can be understood only in culturally-dependent terms. Given this, some relativists argue that cultures should be understood only in their own terms, and that it would be methodologically improper to study one culture in terms of another. Thus cultural relativism has come to be seen as a method of social study which advocates the study of a culture only in its own terms.[9] The use of such a method, it is argued, makes for a sensitivity to the peculiarities of the culture under study and avoids the pitfalls of ethnocentricity, the supposedly false assumption that the standards of one's own culture are superior to those of other cultures. The work of Peter Winch, which was examined in Chapter 5, involves something like cultural and conceptual relativism.

Although it is possible to distinguish various forms of relativism, some may necessarily be connected. For example, if one is both a moral cognitivist (holding that moral beliefs are true or false by the standards of knowledge) and a cognitive relativist, one is necessarily also a moral relativist. It might even be the case that all forms of relativism are connected, if only by reduction or extension. Roger Trigg argues that 'conceptual relativism is not just one form of relativism, but is itself the logical outcome of any form of it'.[10] What Trigg refers to as 'ordinary relativism' holds that truth is relative to the conventions arising from human agreement. For relativists, no disagreement between different societies can be settled by reference to a common reality, for that which is taken to be real is also relative to convention. The consistent relativist must recognise that relativism about truth entails relativism about meaning, about the way in which people conceive of their world. The interrelationship of all forms of relativism in modern society is stressed by W.J. Stankiewicz, who cautions against a focus on definitions of various kinds of relativism, for fear of failing to grasp modern relativism in a 'total sense'.[11] He argues that 'pervasive relativism' is established and promoted by factors which form interlocking patterns. Whether or not it is possible to establish that all forms of relativism are interrelated in such a way, all relativism is a problem and is vulnerable to criticism. This does not mean that all the arguments against relativism apply to all forms of it; some of the arguments are necessarily specific. It does mean, though, that it is not possible to accept the positions of Bernard Williams and Steven Lukes, who are prepared to distinguish moral relativism from other forms, and to accept at least some truth in the former while denying it in the latter.[12]

SEVEN ARGUMENTS AGAINST RELATIVISM

I offer a set of arguments against relativism in political thought. Some of the arguments apply to relativism in general; some apply to specific forms of relativism.

1. Relativism Leaves One Unable to Make Real Choices and Renders One Critically Impotent

The initial criticism of relativism is a complaint about its consequences. Faced with conflicting claims about the truth of a matter, or competing explanatory theories, epistemological relativism offers no objective standards of truth and so no way of resolving conflict and competition. Faced with the diversity of moral principles and practices, moral relativism offers no objective standards of human good and so allows for no judgement or criticism. Relativism seems to offer no opportunity for proper choice of belief. The claim is not that relativists, because they hold all beliefs and standards to be equal in some way, have no reason to have a preference for any particular belief or standard. Clearly relativists do hold particular beliefs and accept certain standards, and these are relative to their particular contexts. Rather, the claim is that relativists' beliefs and standards are no more than relative and are limited to their particular contexts. Relativism leaves one able to adopt and apply only localised beliefs and standards. Thus, relativism renders one unable to make any real choice about belief, in terms of objective truth or objective good. What choice one has is arbitrary because unrelated to objective standards. There seems to be no good reason to choose or adopt the localised standards of one context rather than another.

The problem of choice is well illustrated by the inability of value-free social science, which suffers from moral relativism, to provide answers for our moral problems. It is ironic that Max Weber, a chief proponent of modern value-free social science, in an essay entitled 'Science as a Vocation', should quote, with apparent approval, the words of Tolstoy: 'Science is meaningless because it gives us no answer to our question, the only question important for us: "What shall we do and how shall we live?"'[13] Weber does not consider value-free science to be wholly without meaning. Science allows human beings to have some control over life by allowing them to calculate the nature of the world in which they live; science contributes methods for thinking; and, although it cannot determine human ends and goods, science can provide clarity to our calculations about the best means to any end.[14] Value-free social science seems to be at its most useful when offering hypothetical advice of the following sort: '*If* you take such and such a stand, then, according to scientific experience, you have to use such and such a *means* in order to carry out your conviction practically'.[15] For Weber, social science cannot identify the proper ends of human conduct, and can only act slavishly to calculate the best means of attaining the ends chosen subjectively.

Strauss accuses value-free social science of being meaningless and nihilistic, and he makes explicit its 'disastrous consequences'.

> Our social science may make us very wise or clever as regards the means for any objective we might choose. It admits being unable to help us in discriminating between legitimate and illegitimate, between just and unjust, objectives. . . . According to our social science, we can be or become wise in all matters of secondary importance, but we have to be resigned to utter ignorance in the most important respect: we cannot have knowledge regarding the ultimate principle of our choices, i.e., regarding their soundness or unsoundness; our ultimate principles have no other support than our arbitrary and hence blind preferences. We are then in the position of beings who are sane and sober when engaged in trivial business and who gamble like madmen when confronted with serious issues – retail sanity and wholesale madness.[16]

To Strauss's trenchant criticism, one can add the observation that on the basis of value-free political science there can be no policy science. There may be a science of means, but there cannot be a science of ends. The link between value-free political science and policy is ultimately arbitrary because the choice of human goals and so the ordering of the knowledge of political science to these goals is ultimately arbitrary.

Relativism precludes one from passing judgement not only on the beliefs and standards of other contexts but also on those of one's own context. Cultural relativism denies the availability of cross-cultural, objective and universal standards of judgement, by means of which one can judge a supposedly alien culture. As a caution against crude ethnocentrism, cultural relativism may have some value. But it renders one critically impotent in the face of, say, the violation of human rights perpetrated by other cultures. Moreover, relativism renders one unable to make any real criticism of one's own culture. That is, one could attempt to make a criticism of, say, the moral concepts of one's own culture, but this may be dismissed by moral relativists as meaningless, because incommensurable with that which is being criticised. As Steven Lukes says, relativism 'has pernicious practical implications of a conservative and irrational kind, disabling those who succumb to its temptations from criticising what any given society may believe about itself'.[17]

To complain about the consequences of relativism is one thing; to argue against it decisively is another. The complaint can be become an argument if it can be shown that one can do that which relativism seemingly denies, that is, pass judgement on one's own and other cultures. That relativism denies what is done, by denying that which facilitates what is done, is the burden of another argument.

2. The Evident Variety of Belief and Behaviour Does Not Constitute Evidence for Relativism and Indeed Makes Sense Only if Relativism is Denied

The starting point for relativism is often the recognition of the variety of belief and behaviour. It cannot be denied that such variety exists, but this does not constitute evidence for relativism nor warrant acceptance of relativism. That different people do accept different standards of belief and behaviour does not prove that there are no objective and universal standards.[18] Indeed the evident variety can be taken to indicate something else entirely. As I noted in Chapter 6, when considering value conflicts, variety of opinion does not contradict but actually presupposes the truth about which people disagree.

The notion that variety makes sense only in terms of something which is common is the basis for a sharp and conclusive criticism of conceptual relativism offered by Donald Davidson. Conceptual relativism holds, as I noted earlier, that reality is relative to the particular conceptual scheme by means of which it is interpreted. Thus, for the conceptual relativist there are varying points of view, which offer varying accounts of reality, and which seem to pose severe problems of comparison of, and translation between, accounts. Davidson notes clearly the incoherence of this. 'The dominant metaphor of conceptual relativism, that of differing points of view, seems to betray an underlying paradox. Different points of view make sense, but only if there is a common coordinate system on which to plot them; yet the existence of a common system belies the claim of dramatic incomparability.'[19] Davidson proceeds to argue that we cannot make sense of different points of view or different conceptual schemes because we cannot make sense of total or even partial failure of translation between them. This sort of argument will be considered more fully when I come to another criticism of relativism. Davidson's conclusion, and indeed the purpose of his attack on conceptual relativism, is a denial of any distinction between conceptual schemes and reality. To collapse the distinction between reality and conceptual schemes is to go too far just to avoid the problems of conceptual relativism. One can distinguish true and false beliefs only in terms of their correspondence to an objective reality which is independent of one's beliefs. One cannot maintain the notion of objective reality if one does not distinguish it from one's beliefs and opinions about it. As Roger Trigg argues, the notion of different conceptual schemes are dangerous only when reality is no longer thought to be independent of them.[20]

3. Contextual Determination of Belief Does Not Entail Relativism and is Irrelevant to the Determination of the Validity of Belief

If the starting point of relativism is the recognition of the variety of belief, the next step is the claim that the variety is to be explained in terms of the variety of contexts and circumstances to which belief is relative. This step then leads to the claim that there are no standards of belief which are independent of particular contexts and circumstances. Herein lie several unwarranted assumptions. Relativists wrongly assume that because some beliefs are determined by extra-theoretical factors, then all belief is likely to be so. They also wrongly assume that the identification of the contextual determination of belief amounts to a warranted denial of the objective truth of belief. Furthermore, relativists seem to assume that having explained the variety of belief they have removed all responsibility to consider the important question of the objective truth or falsity of belief.

Evidence might indicate that at least some beliefs are relative to context and circumstances. Social scientists might have little difficulty in establishing strong positive correlations, if not causal links, between the social circumstances of believers and their beliefs. But it cannot be shown from any amount of evidence that all possible belief is in some way determined by factors external to the inherent validity of belief. Some belief might follow directly from the inherent logic of previously held belief. That it might also happen to correlate with some social circumstances would be interesting but would not constitute decisive evidence for comprehensive relativism.

Even if one grants that all belief is in some way contextually determined, it does not follow that belief can have no objective validity and that there are no objective standards of belief. The relationship between the social origins of belief and the validity of belief is considered by Karl Mannheim. His rather ambiguous conclusion is that the 'function of the findings of the sociology of knowledge lies somewhere . . . between irrelevance to the establishment of truth on the one hand, and entire adequacy for determining truth on the other'.[21] He seems to mean that by locating all beliefs in their particular social perspectives, the sociology of knowledge both describes belief and exposes the limitations of it. Also, since it might be possible to proceed with some sort of synthesis of all limited perspectives and beliefs, it might be possible to attain some truth independent of particular perspectives. There is no need, though, for such hesitation and confusion. Steven Lukes argues that evidence of the social determination of belief provides no good reasons for seeing standards of truth or validity as variable.[22] First, to establish that the appearance, adoption and maintenance of belief is dependent on some social factor is to offer no proof that the truth or validity of the belief is variable. Even if all belief was causally determined, some people might be lucky enough to be caused to believe what is true. Second, even if it can be established that people have good reasons to adopt certain beliefs because these satisfy their socially and historically determined interests, nothing follows concerning the truth or consistency of what is believed by any particular group of people. Third, the existence of a 'conceptual fit' between beliefs and social factors may show that certain beliefs cohere with other beliefs and other features of society, but in itself has no bearing on the truth or falsity of beliefs. Thus, one can assert that the sociology of knowledge is not relevant to determining the objective truth or validity of belief.

To identify the social origin or causes of beliefs is not to determine the validity or truth of beliefs. Relativism is not established by any evidence of the contextual determination of belief. Nor is relativism warranted in neglecting questions of objective truth. I have already given some attention to Barnes and Bloor's definition of relativism. I now consider their claim that far 'from being a threat to the scientific understanding of forms of knowledge, relativism is required by it'.[23] Starting from the evidence of the diversity of belief, they claim that only a relativist theory of knowledge can offer an account of this diversity, the distribution of beliefs, and the manner of change of beliefs. What they advocate, then, is the sociology of knowledge, and not just a traditional model, but, rather, what is now termed a 'strong thesis' or a 'strong programme'.[24] Traditionally the sociology of knowledge was concerned with what were taken to be probably false or at least controversial beliefs, such as primitive belief systems, religious belief, and political ideology. Some beliefs were taken to be true or uncontroversial, not socially determined, and so excluded from sociological investigation. As noted in Chapter 3, Mannheim excludes abstract disciplines such as mathematics and pure economics, and the natural sciences from his sociology of knowledge. The strong thesis or programme of the sociology of knowledge holds that not just some but all belief, including scientific belief, is socially determined and so relative. Accordingly, and Barnes and Bloor make this clear, there is no objective and context-independent knowledge, and so all distinctions between true and false beliefs, rational and non-rational beliefs, and objective and localised truth are collapsed.[25]

What is the value of this iconoclastic relativist theory of knowledge? Surely very little. It claims to account for the diversity of scientific belief, but it can offer no account of what matters most: the distinction between truth and error. Given that beliefs themselves make claims to truth, and given the diversity of beliefs, the distinction between truth and error cannot be abandoned except in a most careless and irresponsible way. Abandoning the notion of objective truth is unwarranted and runs the risk of encouraging the collapse of science into the sociology of scientific belief. Raymond Aron notes clearly the need to maintain the crucial distinction.

> Sociological study of the origins of concepts should not be confused with the theory of knowledge, i.e. analysis of the transcendental conditions of truth. The conditions for scientific truth are not to be confused with the circumstances of the social advent of truth. It is a dangerous illusion to imagine that there is a sociological theory of knowledge. There is only a sociological theory *of the conditions in which* knowledge develops. The sociology of knowledge *is* knowledge. But knowledge can never be *reduced* to the sociology of knowledge.[26]

There is no adequate defence of relativism as a sound principle of enquiry.

4. Relativism is Self-Refuting and Incoherent

Perhaps the most common and most effective argument against relativism is that it is self-refuting and incoherent. This argument can take many forms, and some are to be preferred to others, but a basic one is as follows. If relativism is true, then all truths are relative. If all truths are relative, then so too is the truth of relativism. Therefore, relativism is no truer than its denial, and so is trivial. If relativism seeks to establish itself as non-trivial and assert the universal and non-relative truth of itself, it must necessarily refute itself. This formulation of the argument recalls an earlier point: it is impossible to formulate relativism in a non-trivial way without making it incoherent.

William Brandon says of the argument from self-refutation that it is 'more a philosophical bludgeon than a rapier.'[27] By considering other formulations of the argument it is, I think, possible to show that criticism can be both sharp and bluntly effective. First, recall Donald Davidson's criticism of conceptual relativism. He argues that the notion of different points of view, relative to different conceptual schemes, makes sense only if there is a common coordinate system on which to plot them. The existence of a common system would refute the claim of conceptual relativism, of separate and incommensurable conceptual schemes. Relativism can make sense only if it can allow for that which would undermine it. Another and very precise formulation of relativism which exposes its inherent incoherence is presented by Germain Grisez. So impressive and clear is it that it is worth quoting in full, without further comment.

> Metaphysical relativism means that all truth – that is, whatever is rationally accepted as true – is a function of a or of b or of c or of . . ., where 'a' and 'b' and 'c' and ' . . .' stand for irreducibly diverse and untranscendably limited principles. But if this position is true, then either the position itself is a function of one (or of a definite, but limited, set) of these principles or the position itself is not a function of such a principle. If the position itself is a function, say, of a, then either the position admits b and c and . . . as equally reasonable or the position excludes b and c and . . . as not true or less reasonable. If the position excludes the alternatives to a, then the position does not really mean that all truth is a function of a or of b or of c or of . . .; what the position really means is that all truth is a function of a. If the position admits the alternatives, then it has comprehended a and b and c and . . . in a single view, and in this unified view the limits of each of these principles (and of any set of them) are transcended.[28]

The arguments of both Davidson and Grisez are concerned with the self-refuting formulation of relativism. Another argument from self-refutation focuses not on the formulation of relativism but on the use of evidence by relativists in their attempt to support their position. Maurice Mandelbaum argues that relativists offer evidence in support of their position not, of course, to convince themselves, but in an attempt to convince non-relativists or others who do not share their particular point of view. But such evidence, if it is to be convincing, has to be interpreted in a non-relativist way. If objective evidence is available, its very existence denies the relativist case that all claims are relative.[29] I noted, in considering the definition of relativism, that one important feature is the claim that apparent contradictions are explained away by reference to separate and incommensurable standards of belief. It can now be seen that such a claim is self-refuting. If one introduces evidence of incommensurable beliefs as support for relativism, one necessarily assumes that such evidence can be understood, and understood in a certain way, by all who heed it. But if this is the case, there exists at least one common standard of understanding and the existence of this undermines the relativist case.

The force of the argument from self-refutation is not felt by all. Mary Hesse detects a fallacy in it. The argument wins its conclusion by demanding of relativism that which is self-destructive. Hesse says that it is fallacious to demand from any statement of relativism a ground or support which is non-relativist. Relativists, it must be recognised, can give only relativist grounds for relativism.[30] I do not deny that relativism cannot give that which is demanded of it. But if relativism cannot supply an objective, non-relativist ground for itself, then relativism is no better than the case against it, and so need not be taken any more seriously than objectivism. If relativism does offer some ground for itself as an account of all knowledge or morality, it offers an objective ground and so refutes itself. Either way relativism denies itself. It denies itself the status of truth or it denies itself coherence.

There are many formulations of the argument from self-refutation. That of Davidson was originally noted in an earlier argument about the variety of beliefs making sense only if one could relate them to some common standard of belief. Further examples will be referred to in later arguments. It might seem that most, if not all of the arguments against relativism are variations of the argument from self-refutation. This may be the case. But for the sake of spelling out clearly the various arguments against relativism they will be kept separate and the argument from self-refutation will be left as the central one.

5. Relativism Denies That which Can and Should be Done, and that by Means of which it is Done

If relativism is true (though it is necessary to be sensitive to the limitations of the truth of relativism and to the impossibility of the objective truth of it), then certain important things seem not to be possible. If epistemological relativism is true, there can be no attempt to resolve conflicts between competing and incommensurable scientific theories. If moral relativism is true, one cannot pass judgement on those who do not share one's values. If conceptual relativism is true, there can be no translation between languages based on different linguistic conventions and concepts. If cultural relativism is true, one cannot interpret alien cultures except in their own terms (granted that which may be problematic, that one can grasp the alien concepts). It might seem as if this argument is about to amount to no more than another complaint about the consequences of relativism. It amounts to more than this, though. The seemingly impossible can be, is, and should be done. There exist the means by which the seemingly impossible can be done and the existence of these refutes relativism.

In a number of papers, Martin Hollis and Steven Lukes argue that there is reason to believe that there exist universal and objective concepts and criteria of truth, logic and rationality, and an objective reality, for these are the prerequisites of such activities as comparing, translating, criticising and understanding.[31] Lukes argues that it is only if one assumes a 'common bridgehead' of beliefs and standards that one can discern that which is uncommon.[32] His argument is not unlike Davidson's about the requirement for a common coordinate system on which to plot different points of view. Moreover, his argument is not unlike that from self-refutation, in that the necessary assumption of a common bridgehead of concepts and beliefs refutes the claim of relativism. Taking the matter of understanding another belief system, Lukes argues that this can be done only if one can translate the other system or language into one's own. This would seem to be a fair point, for only if one can translate a language can one know both that noise and shapes constitute a language at all, and that it differs, if at all, from one's own. Such translation can be done, Lukes argues, only if certain things are the case. First, both belief systems must share at least some criteria of truth, and some concept of the common reality to which it refers, otherwise one simply cannot identify any beliefs of an alien culture. Nothing can be taken to constitute a belief if it does not relate to a common reality and seemingly confirm or deny one's own beliefs. Second, both belief systems must share at least some logical rules, for without the rules of identity and non-contradiction, and the concept of negation, one could not make sense of any alien assertion of belief, or any alien argument. Third, both belief systems must share at least some criteria of rationality, such as what constitutes a good reason for holding a belief, otherwise one could not understand and debate commitment to specific beliefs. According to Lukes, such criteria and concepts of truth, logic, rationality and reality are both universal, because they operate in all languages and belief systems, and fundamental, because they set the constraints to all thought.[33]

Critics of Hollis and Lukes argue that their notion of a common bridgehead of beliefs and concepts is underdescribed and lacks clear boundaries; lacks empirical reality; and refers only to the form and not the content of concepts and beliefs.[34] The criticism of the lack of definition of the supposed common bridgehead is, I think, unfair. Both Hollis and Lukes offer some fairly detailed and clear suggestions about its content and nature. But taking this criticism together with the others, I suggest that they somewhat miss the point of the argument against relativism. Lukes acknowledges that the argument that *some* foundation, bridgehead or common core exists is an *a priori* argument, and that the specific content 'is in a sense an empirical matter, or at least revisable in the light of experience'.[35] Encountering new alien belief systems or problems in our translations might require a revision of our assumptions about the content of the core. It can also be argued that the specific content of true beliefs or specific good reasons for adopting beliefs are a matter for rational discussion based on evidence. And this is a matter for rational discussion between those of differing points of view; it is not to be established by *fiat*, by one culture imposing itself upon another. For the specific content of true belief to be established by rational discussion, certain formal criteria of truth and rationality need to be ever present and available.

As a specific and politically relevant example of the possibility of, and need for, interpretation and judgement of different belief systems or points of view, consider the case of false consciousness. If relativism is true, and all belief is relative to specific, localised contexts, then it makes no sense to talk about identifying and exposing false consciousness. As Lukes says: 'Only by assuming that one has access to a reliable, non-relative means of identifying a disjunction between social consciousness, on the one hand, and social realities, on the other, is it possible even to raise questions about the ways in which misperceptions and misunderstandings of all kinds arise.'[36] Students of politics do refer to false consciousness in offering accounts of political behaviour, and in some cases they are right to do so. That they can do so requires the existence and availability of certain concepts of social reality, truth and rationality. The identification of what is true or false consciousness is a matter for rational discussion. The discussion is likely to cover human interests and the distinction between true and false interests. This involves a discussion of moral values, as Lukes elsewhere acknowledges,[37] and this introduces a serious criticism of his position.

The weakness of Lukes's position is his distinction between cognitive and moral relativism, and his restriction of criticism to the former only. Lukes's reason for conceding some truth at least to moral relativism is that he can see no reason to accept a set of non-relative, objective concepts and criteria of moral truth, moral logic, and moral rationality, analogous to those of cognitive truth, logic, and rationality.[38] He concludes that by contrast to our knowledge of the world, 'moral judgements may be incompatible but equally rational, because the criteria of rationality and justification in morals are themselves relative to conflicting and irreducible perspectives'. Moral concepts are, he says, essentially contestable.[39] Such a concession to moral relativism deserves criticism. First, if cognitive relativism is false, and if morality is cognitive, then moral relativism is false. Thus Lukes's position is tenable only if he can show that morality is non-cognitive, and this he does not do. Second, Lukes acknowledges his own discomfort at resting his case on a fact–value distinction which is largely untenable, and on a denial that contestable moral concepts make sense only if there is some common element to them all.[40] Third, Lukes simply dismisses without argument the notion of a common moral reality. He does not consider the argument that it makes sense to make moral judgements of those who do not share our moral values precisely because we are all human and all share the same human nature, with its moral purposes and standards. This argument is elaborated below.

6. Relativism Does Not Necessarily Support Supposedly Beneficial Political Conclusions, Nor Does its Denial Entail Supposedly Objectionable Ones

Just as relativism is sometimes defended as a sound principle of enquiry, supporting the sociology of knowledge, so too it is sometimes defended as a sound principle of politics, supporting tolerance, liberalism and democracy. A simple expression of such a defence is offered by Hans Kelsen: 'just as autocracy is political absolutism and political absolutism is paralleled by philosophical absolutism, democracy is political relativism which has its counterpart in philosophical relativism'.[41] This claim involves two assumptions. First, it is assumed that those who believe in absolute truth will be encouraged to impose their truth on others and to suppress alternative, and so supposedly wrong, opinions. Second, it is assumed that philosophical relativism encourages the recognition and tolerance of a plurality of equally worthy political ideas. The two assumptions are evident in the contemporary postmodernists and antifoundationalists considered in the previous chapter. First, they fear that adherence to a metanarrative or foundation entails the tyranny of this over all other thought. Second, they hope that the abandonment of metanarratives or foundations allows for the freedom and equality of opportunity of all points of view. The two positions are evident even in those who would not describe themselves as relativists. First, Karl Popper, in an addendum to his criticism of the philosophies of Hegel and Marx and their regrettable political conclusions, says that 'the idea of philosophical absolutism is rightly repugnant to many people since it is, as a rule, combined with a dogmatic and authoritarian claim to possess the truth'.[42] The political manifestation of such dogmatism and authoritarianism is repugnant to Popper, who advocates an open society, along the lines of the open scientific community which takes seriously all theories and puts them all to a rigorous, rational test. Second, Leszek Kolakowski argues that precisely because moral values cannot be proved true by the laws of scientific thought, they cannot be coerced upon the human mind and 'mutual tolerance is therefore necessary'.[43] Both positions are adopted by Bertrand Russell, who argues that the philosophy of empiricism, which is 'halfway between dogma and scepticism', is the counterpart of liberalism, a creed of 'live-and-let-live, of toleration and freedom', and the only 'theoretical justification of democracy'. The only possible theoretical justification of autocracy, Russell argues, is unquestioned dogma.[44]

The defence of relativism as a sound political principle is valid only if it can be shown both that there are necessary links between relativism and certain principles such as tolerance, liberalism and democracy, and that these principles are themselves valuable. Leaving aside the question of how one can demonstrate the value of tolerance, liberalism and democracy, it can be shown that such principles are not entailed by relativism. If all moral values are held to be relative to particular contexts, and if all moral values are thus considered to be equal in some way, it does not follow that one is obliged to tolerate all moral values and not interfere with those who hold different views. As Peter Winch puts it: '*reason* places no premium on tolerance as the appropriate reaction to moral diversity rather than, say, on righteous indignation at the obscene blasphemies of the heathen'.[45] When relativists elevate tolerance to the status of a non-relative principle they engage in self-refutation. If all moral values are relative, there can be no non-relative value of tolerance. If there really is a non-relative, objective value of tolerance, it is not the case that all values are relative. This is the serious confusion of what Bernard Williams terms 'vulgar relativism'.[46] Whether there can be a non-vulgar moral relativism in which there can be some truth is considered below.

Another example of the self-refutation of relativism is what Popper refers to as the 'paradox of tolerance'.[47] If one is to be tolerant of all moral values, then to maintain consistency one must tolerate intolerance. But, of course, tolerance of the intolerant will mean that the tolerant will be destroyed, and their tolerance with them. Popper argues that in the name of tolerance we should claim the right not to tolerate the intolerant. A further example is what Ernest Gellner refers to as the 'dilemma of the liberal intellectual'.[48] If one adopts the method of cultural relativism so as to avoid ethnocentrism and maintain tolerance of diverse cultures, one will find oneself tolerating the intolerant and dealing with cultures which are themselves ethnocentric.

Relativism does not entail the supposedly valuable principle of tolerance. Indeed, relativism may entail undesirable political consequences. I noted in an earlier argument that relativism renders its adherents critically and morally impotent. It can also be argued that relativism renders one politically impotent. The contemporary relativist celebration of difference may mask certain differences which are, objectively, morally improper and intolerable. Relativism may also discourage the proper political activity of attempting to deal with the improper and intolerable behaviour of others. Kate Soper argues that 'cultural relativism . . . by presenting all intervention in the affairs of others as a potentially totalitarian distraint on their autonomy, may all too easily license political inactivity'.[49]

Just as tolerance does not follow necessarily from relativism, so autocracy or authoritarianism does not follow necessarily from the denial of relativism. A commitment to the notion of objective and absolute truth is not the same thing as a commitment to any particular objective or absolute truth. One who denies relativism in the name of absolute truth could, without logical contradiction, claim either that autocracy is absolutely best or that liberal-democracy is absolutely best. The defence of one or the other form of government requires some argument in addition to a commitment to absolute truth. Thus Felix Oppenheim shows that there is no logical link between philosophical and political absolutism.[50] Perhaps it is possible to establish a more positive case, though. An objectivist can argue that truth is in principle attainable by use of reason, and admit that it may be very hard to find or prove with certainty. It would be inconsistent of a rational objectivist to claim, without argument, that he or she is correct and that opponents are wrong. Since rational argument is valued as the means to truth, it becomes the objectivist to welcome argument with opponents. From such an argument Roger Trigg concludes: 'Arrogance is not entailed by any objectivist theory.'[51]

There is no logical link between philosophical relativism and tolerance, liberalism and democracy, nor between the objectivist rejection of relativism and authoritarianism. Nor, it seems, are there any empirical links. History seems to indicate that political theorists and political regimes have not always recognised clear and exclusive links between types of principles and types of practice.

7. Moral Relativism Denies What Exists: a Common Moral Reality and a Common Human Nature

Relative points of view make sense only if they refer or can be referred to something common to them all, and the existence of such a common reality refutes relativism. Specifically, it makes sense to make moral judgements of those who do not share one's moral values only if there exists a common moral reality. This argument may now be elaborated with reference to Bernard Williams's argument against vulgar relativism and for some truth in moral relativism. Vulgar moral relativism fails because it attempts to introduce a non-relative moral value of tolerance of all moral values. Williams argues that moral relativism makes sense only if there can be cases where the moral views of one community can be said to stand in no real confrontation with those of another. Where there can be no real confrontation, there can be no moral appraisal of one community by another, and so moral relativism holds.[52] In real confrontation, the moral viewpoint of one community is a real option for those of another. In this case moral appraisal is possible and so moral relativism is not. In notional confrontation, by contrast, the moral viewpoint of one community is not, and cannot be, a real option for those of another. In this case moral appraisal is not possible and so moral relativism is. A real option is defined as one which can be adopted by a community in its present social and historical conditions, without loss of hold on reality. Can there be, then, cases of merely notional confrontation, where an alternative moral viewpoint is not a real option for a community? Williams considers this question in terms of what he refers to as 'the relativism of distance'.[53] That is, one community and viewpoint may be so distant from another that it offers no real option and so only notional confrontation between them is conceivable. Williams argues that in the modern world spatial distance is irrelevant: 'Today all confrontations between cultures must be real confrontations.'[54] It seems that only temporal distance is relevant, and so only past cultures and future lifestyles could present us with moral viewpoints which stand in merely notional confrontation with our own.

Williams's case for a non-vulgar moral relativism is no more successful than any for the vulgar variety. It does not make sense. I agree with Williams that in the modern world, with its communication features of a global village and its general interdependency, all moral confrontations are real. Thus there is the possibility of objective moral appraisal and there is no truth in moral relativism. This is so not just because of the peculiar features of the modern world, but because its moral agents are all human beings. It makes no sense to conceive of moral points of view which are not real options for us. If there were past communities, or if there can be future communities, whose moral viewpoints are not real options for us, then there must be serious doubts as to whether these were, or can be, communities of human beings. It is, of course, true that over time social, economic and political conditions change, and that moral beliefs change accordingly. It is also true that change can preclude a return to certain conditions. But I have already argued that the evident social determination of beliefs, including moral beliefs, does not establish the relativist claim that there can be no objective moral standards independent of context.

Despite all the change they experience, human beings remain human beings and their behaviour remains subject to evaluation according to the standards of a common human nature and moral reality. As Williams acknowledges, his case for some truth in moral relativism holds only if one necessary condition is granted: 'that ethical realism is false'.[55] He has not refuted ethical or moral realism.

CONCLUSION

The set of arguments against relativism show that it is pernicious, in that it precludes objective epistemological and moral judgement; incoherent, in that any formulation of relativism necessarily undermines itself; unsupported by evidence and argument about the variety of belief and behaviour, about what can and cannot be done, and about its supposed political consequences; and inadequate for the study of politics, in that political and moral problems demand the attention of an adequate normative discipline. In this critique, relativism has been contrasted with objectivism and absolutism. Relativism denies, and is denied by, the existence of absolute, objective and universal standards. Political thought can avoid the problem of relativism if it can entertain the hope of attaining objective knowledge of the nature of politics and the good political order. In the contemporary intellectual climate such a hope is not complete nor widespread. The existence of absolute, objective and universal standards is not, of course, any guarantee that one can know them fully. One's knowledge may fall short of absolute certainty, but it can fall short only because there is a standard to fall short of. In criticising relativism I have not said that the attainment of objective truth is easy or guaranteed. But certainly the denial of objective truth has serious consequences and is incoherent. The possibility of absolute, objective and universal standards of political behaviour, based on a common human nature, and intelligible in moral realism, will be considered in Chapter 10.

9 Demarcating Political Philosophy and Political Ideology

INTRODUCTION

It is necessary to demarcate political philosophy and political science, on the one hand, from political ideology, on the other, not only to save philosophy and science from ideological distortion, but also to provide an antidote for ideology. The problem of ideology is at heart a problem of values and a problem of relativism. Normative thought, precisely because it deals with human interests and values, tends to be most readily dismissed as non-scientific and non-philosophic ideology, or seen as more vulnerable to ideological distortion than other thought. Although the problem of ideology is a problem of values, the solution is not the demarcation of analytic political philosophy, empirical political science and normative political ideology. As I argued in Chapter 6 there can be no value-free study of politics. Normative political thought is essential, but if it is to avoid being dismissed as ideology, it must avoid relativism, which I criticised in the previous chapter. The solution of the problem of ideology must be, ultimately, the solution of the problem of relativism. Thus, the solution of the problem of political ideology is rational normative political thought which can know the objective order of politics; give an objective, absolute foundation to political values; and can distinguish proper from improper political values.

In this chapter I first consider the problems demarcating political philosophy and political ideology, and then offer a set of arguments which indicate how this might be done. In doing this I do not mean to neglect political science, nor to suggest that it cannot play its part in the solution of the problem of ideology. As I noted in Chapter 6, the distinction of political science and political philosophy may be acknowledged as a convenient contemporary division of labour between those who concentrate on empirical analysis and those who concentrate on conceptual and normative analysis. However, there can be no value-free study of politics, and so there can be no absolute demarcation between empirical political science and normative political philosophy. There can be no adequate science of politics which fails to deal with the values of politics, and there can be no adequate political philosophy which does not take account of the facts of political reality. It may sometimes be convenient to distinguish political science and political philosophy, but it is important to insist that they are complementary approaches. Ideally they are united as moral political science or rational political philosophy.

PROBLEMS OF DEMARCATING IDEOLOGY AND PHILOSOPHY

Any attempt to demarcate political ideology and political philosophy is likely to be challenged by a number of arguments including, first, that all sets of political ideas are ideological and so there can be only an arbitrary and dogmatic distinction between ideology and philosophy as modes of political thought; second, that ideology is not (or not merely) an epistemological category and so cannot properly be distinguished from philosophy and characterised as falsity, distortion or illusion; and third, that a strict demarcation of ideology and philosophy denies the possibility that philosophy may function as ideology and that ideology may have some philosophical content.

1. Restrictive and Inclusive Conceptions of Ideology

The problem of demarcating political ideology and political philosophy is the problem of maintaining a negative and restrictive conception of ideology. Martin Seliger agues against the restrictive conception of ideology, which seeks to 'confine the term to specific political belief systems', and for the inclusive conception, which accepts 'the applicability of the term "ideology" to all political belief systems'. Seliger notes that according to both conceptions political ideology 'denotes sets of ideas not primarily conceived for cognitive purposes'. The inclusive conception is distinguished by its stress on the action-related nature of ideology, by means of which people 'posit, explain and justify ends and means of organised social action, and specifically political action'.[1] All political belief systems are ideological, Seliger argues, because all conform to a structure of formal content, whatever their specific content.[2]

Although he maintains an inclusive conception of ideology, Seliger does not deny that one can distinguish political ideology, political philosophy and political science. However, his distinctions are inadequate and betray mistaken conceptions of the modes of political thought. For Seliger, normative political philosophy is detached and does 'not serve political action directly'.[3] Political ideology is two-dimensional, being concerned with both fundamental principles and the operationalisation of these, whereas political philosophy is one-dimensional, being concerned in a detached way with fundamentals only.[4] I argue below that authentic political philosophy must maintain some detachment from political action, but to argue as Seliger does is to deny political philosophy its practical nature and to reduce it to an analysis of political concepts. As for political science, Seliger assumes it is a value-free discipline.[5] Seliger's distinctions between action-related political ideology, detached and inactive political philosophy, and value-free political science are similar to those made by linguistic analysis between normative political ideology, analytic political philosophy and empirical political science. These are inadequate ways to demarcate political philosophy and political ideology for they fail to maintain the integrity of authentic normative political philosophy. Political philosophy, properly understood, cannot be detached from questions about the correctness of both fundamental principles and their enactment in policy.

Seliger is prepared to grant a formal distinction between political philosophy and political ideology, but he denies that an absolute distinction can be maintained. It is 'almost unavoidable' that political philosophy will become directly involved in political action and so become ideology.[6] All action-related political belief systems are ideological and so

Seliger favours the inclusive conception of ideology. The restrictive conception is, he argues, dogmatic and incoherent. It may, as Seliger argues, be dogmatic of Marx to assume that his thought is scientific while all other thought is merely ideological, and dogmatic of the end-of-ideology theorists to assume that only certain sorts of extremist political belief systems are ideological.[7] But such dogmatism arises from failure to supply good reasons for distinguishing ideological and non-ideological ideas. If good reasons could be furnished for the distinction, the restrictive conception of ideology would not be dogmatic. I consider the possibility of such good reasons below. The argument that any attempt to demarcate ideological and non-ideological political belief systems is dogmatic holds only if one denies, in dogmatic fashion, that there are rational criteria for such a demarcation. Seliger's claim that all political belief systems are ideological because all conform to a structure of formal content neglects the possibility of distinguishing political ideology and political philosophy in terms of specific content. Seliger thinks the restrictive conception of ideology is incoherent because it proposes that which can never be: non-ideological politics. Seliger argues: 'ideology is linked to all politics no less than all politics are linked to ideology. Ideology requires politics as its mode of implementation while political decisions are always, at one stage or another, related to moral principles.'[8] Seliger's argument holds only if one assumes that practical normative principles are always ideological and that there cannot be non-ideological moral and political principles. Such an assumption, on Seliger's part, is dogmatic because unproved (and unprovable). Seliger is correct in insisting that politics cannot be conducted without some principles, but his ideological characterisation of politics suffers from relativism and offers no means of establishing which principles are valid and preferable. It is doubtful if coherence in politics can be established by any and all ideological principles, regardless of their objective validity. Seliger, rather than those who uphold the restrictive conception of ideology, may render politics incoherent by failing to allow for a coherent choice and application of appropriate political principles.

The inclusive conception of ideology may be dogmatic

and incoherent. It is certainly indiscriminate and so likely to prove unhelpful in political analysis. As David McLellan says, Seliger's 'ecumenical concept of ideology . . . robs the concept of any critical edge'.[9] If the term 'ideology' refers to all political belief systems then it means nothing more than the term 'political belief system', and so is a pleonasm. The term 'ideology' is useful in political analysis only if it can be referred to a mode of political thought which can be distinguished from other modes such as philosophy and science.

2. Epistemological and Political Dimensions of Ideology

It would seem that any distinction between philosophy and science on the one hand, and ideology on the other, suggests that the latter is properly characterised as poor thought, and in particular bad epistemology, because of its distortion and falsity. I would not wish to deny this suggestion. Some theorists, though, wish to argue that such a categorisation of ideology is misleading and prohibits a proper understanding of the concept. Anthony Giddens states: 'I want to *reject* any definition of ideology as falsity, as non-science or as poor science – the concept of ideology should not be formulated by comparing or contrasting it with the achievements of science.'[10] Giddens seems to believe that there can be no successful and convincing demarcation of ideology from science or philosophy in terms of intellectual content. Indeed he says: 'I want also to reject the idea that ideology can be defined in terms of any specific *content* at all.' He proceeds to argue that 'the concept of ideology should be reformulated in relation to a theory of *power* and *domination* – to the modes in which systems of signification enter into the existence of sectional forms of domination'.[11] Giddens seeks to move beyond the views of language as a medium of describing the world, and of ideology as the content of propositional belief systems. Rather, language is to be seen as 'the modes in which signification is incorporated as part and parcel of daily life' and ideology is defined as 'the mode in which forms of signification are incorporated within systems of domination so as to sanction their continuance'.[12]

Writing from a Marxist perspective, Joe McCarney also argues that 'ideology is not an epistemological category' and that 'the role of ideas in the class struggle constitutes the substance of Marx's conception of ideology'.[13] Accordingly, McCarney concludes that 'the question, "what is the nature of the distinction between science and ideology?" generates no fruitful lines of inquiry in Marxist theory'.[14] McCarney's interpretation of Marx faces many problems in terms of the evidence of Marx's writings. In particular, McCarney has to deal with Marx's references in *The German Ideology* to 'ideological deception', 'ideological distortion', 'the illusions of the ideologists' and the famous passage in which Marx says 'in all ideology men and their circumstances appear upside down as in a camera obscura'.[15] McCarney's attempt to deal with such references, which seem to characterise ideology as epistemologically false, involves a re-translation of Marx's original German. McCarney notes that 'in der ganzen Ideologie' is usually translated as 'in all ideology',[16] but is more naturally translated as 'in the whole ideology'. If the latter translation is accepted, then, according to McCarney, Marx's references to the whole ideology can only mean, in the general context, the German or Hegelian ideology. Thus, for McCarney, when Marx does occasionally refer to ideology as distorted or inverted consciousness, he refers not to ideology in general but to a specific (Hegelian) ideology.

Such an interpretation of Marx is questionable. It neglects references in Marx's earlier and later works, which support an interpretation of ideology as falsity or illusion and as something different from science. As I noted in Chapter 2, in his early *A Contribution to the Critique of Hegel's Philosophy of Right: Introduction,* Marx refers to religion, an ideology presumably, though not identical with Hegelianism, as 'inverted consciousness' and as 'illusory', and in his later *Capital* he comments that 'all science would be superfluous if the outward appearances and the essence of things coincided'. This comment, which, significantly, is neglected by McCarney, seems to suggest that for Marx science is the corrective of false appearances and unmasker of essences, and that there is a fruitful distinction between science and ideology. Moreover, McCarney should note that in the famous 'ruling ideas' passage in *The German Ideology,* again noted above in Chapter

2, Marx explicitly links the epistemological and political dimensions of ideology.

Both Giddens and McCarney are correct in stressing the political dimension of ideology, in so far as ideology is concerned with the exercise of power and domination and with political struggle. Giddens is also correct in noting that language plays an important part in political domination and struggle. However, this political dimension is not necessarily neglected nor denied in advancing the epistemological dimension of ideology. The distinction between political philosophy and political ideology involves a distinction between the philosophical truth-value and political use-value of ideas and beliefs. This distinction suggests that ideology is necessarily both an epistemological and a political category. The two dimensions of ideology, far from being exclusive, are related.

3. Fusion and Confusion of Ideology and Philosophy

It must be conceded that philosophy and ideology can be, and often are, fused, and so confused. Political ideology may seek to imitate political philosophy, if only to enhance its appearance; political ideology may borrow heavily from philosophy and so have significant philosophical content; and political philosophy may be used for ideological purposes and become contaminated by ideology. I noted in Chapter 2 that for Marx the partial bourgeois ideology will be presented as rational and universally valid. Yves Simon argues that ideology seeks to imitate philosophy, and 'in order to fulfil its utilitarian, social and historical function, an ideology must have the appearance of a philosophy and express itself in terms of universal truth'.[17]

Although all the sciences are open to ideological distortion it does seem likely that the problem increases as one moves from the physical sciences through the life sciences to the human and social sciences. Brian Midgley notes this and is 'inclined to the opinion that there are quasi-permanent', as distinct from temporary and accidental, 'reasons why the avoidance of ideological deformations in the social sciences is commonly more difficult than the avoidance of such deformations in the physical sciences'. He speculates that 'it may, perhaps, be the case that, other things being equal, those empirical studies which deal with subject matter higher in the scale of created being will be more vulnerable to ideological distortion'.[18] The ideological distortion of human thought results, in part, from the intrusion of human interests, such that the use value of beliefs serving human interests takes precedence over their truth value. It is because political science and political philosophy are primarily concerned with human values and interests that they are likely to be most vulnerable to ideological distortion.

It is unlikely that in any particular case one may distinguish pure political philosophy and pure political ideology. Simon claims that a 'philosophy unaffected by any ideological feature would involve a degree of perfection that human affairs do not admit of'.[19] It may be necessary to agree with Richard Ashcraft's observation that for those who seek to defend the tradition of political theory, '"ideology" is like original sin'.[20] All political philosophy may be tainted to some degree with ideological distortion. But redemption of fallen thought is always possible. The chronic confusion of philosophy and ideology presents a problem for their demarcation, but not a good reason for not attempting it.

FIVE ARGUMENTS FOR THE DEMARCATION OF IDEOLOGY AND PHILOSOPHY

The demarcation of political philosophy and political ideology does seem to require certain presuppositions: it is necessary that there be an objective political reality, and that there be human reason capable of knowing the truth of the nature of political things and the good political order. If such reality, rationality and objectivity are denied, then no demarcation is likely to be sustained. A refusal to grant such presuppositions may be seen as the starting point of ideology. The demarcation of ideology and philosophy is not entirely a matter of presupposition, however. It can be supported by the five closely related arguments offered below.

1. Political Philosophy Strives for a Universal, Objective, and Rational Understanding of Political Reality; Political Ideology is Socially Mediated Thought which Promotes Partial Group Interests

Leo Strauss argues that '[p]olitical philosophy is the attempt truly to know both the nature of political things and the right, or the good, political order'.[21] Thus, political philosophy, as a rational enquiry into the nature of politics, seeks to offer propositions which may be judged according to their objective truth, or their correspondence with political reality. Political philosophy seeks to conform to political reality rather than seeks to reconstruct politics according to abstract ideals.[22] This is not to deny that political philosophy, as a normative discipline, may be critical of political practice. To offer a proper criticism of politics, to make a proper distinction between, say, just and unjust practice, political philosophy must have an appreciation of the objective good political order. Also, political philosophy claims to offer propositions which are of universal applicability.

Simon offers a characterisation of ideology which distinguishes it from political philosophy.

> According to the familiar use of the word, an ideology is a system of propositions which, though indistinguishable so far as expression goes from statements about facts and essences, actually refer not so much to any real state of affairs as to the *aspirations* of a *society* at a certain *time* in its evolution. These are the three components which taken together, distinguish ideology from philosophy.[23]

Political ideology is not a rational enquiry into objective political reality, but, rather, socially mediated thought which is determined or influenced by certain partial, subjective interests or pressures. Ideology does not so much conform to reality as seek to reconstruct reality according to the ideals, or aspirations, of particular social groups. Ideology does not offer propositions of universal applicability, but represents the interests of limited groups, firmly located within specific times and places. Thus ideological thought is relative.

Frederick Copleston notes that, in so far as it serves the

interests of restricted and exclusive groups, ideology is divisive. By contrast, philosophy 'tends, by its nature to unite human beings, inasmuch as it aims at objective and universal truth and tries to convince by rational argument, which, in principle at any rate, is accessible to all minds'. Of course philosophy may also divide, as is evident from the various schools of philosophy. However, as ideology is always concerned with particular group interests and so is 'historically conditioned . . . there cannot be any one permanent ideology'.[24] In principle, at least, there can be one permanent rational philosophy. Political ideology, precisely because it is limited to particular group interests, cannot hope to be truly applicable to all of humanity. In so far as political philosophy is rational, its arguments are open to the scrutiny of all rational human beings, and it can hope to engage the whole of rational humanity in a common discourse.

The socially mediated nature, and social utility, of ideology can be contrasted with the rational enquiry of philosophy. Lewis Feuer goes so far as to distinguish philosophy and ideology in terms of individual thought and social thought. He argues:

> a philosophy is only recognised as such when it is conceived as the genuine, un-counterfeit, un-imitative expression of the person's experience in relation to the universe; a philosophy is the fullest self-discovery of an individual and what he stands for. . . . A philosophy is the fullest expression of an individual temperament and experience. It is precisely that aspect of intellectual reality which cannot be subsumed under general laws of sociological fashion. . . . An ideology, on the other hand, is the outcome of social circumpressures; it takes philosophy, and reduces it to the lowest common social denominator.[25]

An obvious, though mistaken, criticism of such a distinction is offered by Barbara Goodwin, who claims that 'the conception of an individual as a free and rational being, who chooses objectively between political doctrines on the basis of their manifest truth and rightness' is no more than an ideological, and particularly liberal, conception.[26] It certainly would be wrong to attempt to demarcate ideology and philosophy on the basis only of an ideological concept, for this would permit only 'escape from one ideology into another'.[27] However, it is not clear that the conception of the individual as a free-thinking and rational being is only ideological. If political philosophy is to be a rational discipline, then it must be the product of human reason. Human reason is a faculty possessed only by individual human beings. Social groups cannot be said to think or reason as groups; they can be said to do so only in so far as individuals think for them. Theories of collective consciousness are really only theories of individual reason and thought, with an emphasis on the social mediation of human thought. It may be appropriate to characterise collective human action as being rational or irrational, but again such action cannot be held to be anything more than the action of so many rational or irrational individuals. It may be the case that individual thought and reason are influenced, constrained and even determined by social conditions and pressures, but such mediation or distortion of human thought and reason is a feature of ideology, and not of philosophy.

2. Political Philosophy has Primarily a Truth-Value; Political Ideology has Primarily a Use-Value

As noted in the previous point, political philosophy seeks to offer propositions which conform to, or correspond with, objective political reality. Thus, the value of political philosophy lies in its truthful account of the nature of political things and the good political order. The notion of truth in political philosophy is objective. Because ideology is socially mediated thought which serves particular interests, Simon says the 'notion of truth which an ideology embodies is utilitarian, sociological and evolutionistic'.[28] I deal later with the time-bound and evolutionistic notion of truth in ideology. The utilitarian and sociological notion of truth in ideology is something quite distinct from scientific or philosophical truth. Simon first distinguishes the scientific or philosophical weight from the psychological weight of a proposition. This distinction corresponds to that between the intrinsic truth of a proposition and the reasons why an individual might accept it as being true. The further distinction between scientific or philosophical weight and sociological weight corresponds to that between the intrinsic truth of a proposition and widespread social acceptance of it as being true. It may be that the objective scientific or philosophical weight of a proposition coincides with its psychological or sociological weight, but this need not be so, and for ideology, as distinct from philosophy, the sociological weight is of greater importance. In other words, ideology has primarily a use-value rather than a truth-value.

Simon expresses the threat to truth that this primacy of use-value over truth-value, in ideology, poses.

> An ideology, precisely considered as such, is a system of propositions which carry a heavy sociological weight. Without an appearance of objectivity these propositions would have no weight at all; but their objective weight may be light or, in spite of appearances, nil, without their ideological function being impaired; *it may also be heavy.* Ideological propositions are not necessarily deceitful, although any truth entrusted to an ideology is exposed to all sorts of dangers.[29]

I noted in Chapter 2 that ideology emerges when traditional rationality is attacked. When human reason is concerned not so much with reflection on the nature of the world and the quest for knowledge of the world, but more with serving human passions and interests, then the propositions of human thought are more significantly useful than truthful. Thus, political ideology, which may be characterised as serving the interests or aspirations of a distinct social group, puts human reason to a partial, limited use, and so jeopardises the understanding of truth, which is the proper task of reason. William Oliver Martin observes that when metaphysics, or philosophy, lacks its own formal object, philosophical truth, and hence ceases to be autonomous, 'it does not become nothing. Rather, it becomes a formal system to be used as a means for some human purpose. The inversion carries over even with respect to truth. Instead of a system proving satisfactory because it is true, it becomes 'true' because of its usefulness as a means of serving some human purpose. . . . A metaphysics becomes an ideology.'[30] This ideological inversion of philosophical enquiry after truth is noted also by Feuer, who says: 'When ideas are used as weapons, they are finally evaluated for their fire power in psychological warfare, not for their truth.'[31]

In arguing that political philosophy is concerned with the truth of political reality, whereas political ideology is concerned with the usefulness of ideas in serving sectional political purposes, I do not wish to deny that political philosophy is a useful and practical discipline. Political philosophy seeks to know the nature of politics and the good political order, and so is concerned with the direction of human action to the good end of politics. Political philosophy thus involves the use of practical reason, which is concerned both to know, and to order knowledge to a good end. In this sense, political philosophy is eminently useful, and has a use-value. What, then, of the distinction between political philosophy and political ideology in terms of truth-value and use-value? The distinction between political philosophy, which orders knowledge to an end, and political ideology, which serves some human desire or interest, rests on the distinction between proper and improper ends. Practical reasoning differs from ideological thinking in that the latter may serve any human purpose, whereas the former can distinguish proper and improper human desires and interests. Political ideology has a use-value, being unable to determine the truth of the good political order and so being more or less useful in serving any desire or interest. Political philosophy seeks to determine the truth of the good political order, and in ordering knowledge to such an end it assumes a use-value. Further consideration of practical reason is offered in the next chapter.

3. Political Philosophy Maintains an Attitude of Openness and Self-Criticism in the Search for Knowledge of the Truth of Politics; Political Ideology Tends to Neglect this Search, to Rest on Unquestioned Assumptions, and to Close Off the Path of Enquiry

Strauss says that political philosophy, as the attempt to know the nature of politics, would not be necessary if such knowledge was immediately available. In the absence of knowledge human beings will have thoughts about politics. Thus, Strauss says, 'philosophy is necessarily preceded by opinions. . . . It is, therefore, the attempt to replace opinions . . . by knowledge'.[32] I noted in Chapter 7 that Michael Walzer sees truth as just another opinion, and philosophers as just opinion-makers, and that Richard Rorty denies the distinction between knowledge and opinion. Precisely because they deny the distinction between philosophy and opinion, they fail to distinguish philosophy and ideology. Political philosophy challenges political opinion; refuses to rest on unquestioned assumptions; and offers rational discourse on political reality open to the scrutiny of all rational human beings.

Ideology emerges from the attack on traditional political philosophy, and in particular from the subordination of reason to human passion or interest, and the social and historical mediation of human thought. As socially mediated thought, which has a use-value rather than a truth-value, and which serves the interests of particular social groups, political ideology will not readily conduct an open, rational and self-critical enquiry into the truth of political matters. Rather, in serving its social function, political ideology will tend to neglect questions of truth for more immediate concerns; allow particular interests to close off enquiry; operate upon some unquestioned assumptions; and assert points dogmatically.

Feuer argues that because political ideology is the outcome of certain social pressures and serves certain social interests, it cannot be concerned with philosophical investigation. Rather, an 'ideology is an "ism", that is, a philosophical tenet which has been dissociated from the process of investigation and search, and has been affirmed as the maxim for a political group'.[33] The dissociation of ideology from philosophical investigation makes the ideological affirmation of any set of political ideas dogmatic. Ideology closes the door not only to search but also to doubt and criticism. Copleston argues:

> Radical criticism puts the critic outside ideology, whereas radical criticism of philosophy need not put the critic outside philosophy. The reason for this state of affairs is that if ideological language is the language of adherence and commitment, ideology cannot accommodate radical criticism of itself, whereas philosophy, being not only

> constructive but also an activity of radical criticism, can, and indeed does, clear a place for self-criticism.[34]

The need for political philosophy to avoid dogmatism, and to maintain an open and self-critical approach, is stressed by Germino, who argues that 'authentic political theory is never closed within itself, never pretends to be complete, all-inclusive, finished for all time' and this because in its search for truth the 'finite human mind is experienced as incapable of grasping ultimate, transcendent reality and holding it in its conceptual nets'.[35] A political ideology, which seeks to remake the world in the light of some human passion or interest, is likely to be tempted into false claims of omniscience.

The precise nature of the openness of philosophical investigation is expressed by Martin.

> No system in any experiential, rational science can be complete in its truth. In this sense – but not just in this sense – the whole truth is not something to be had at any one time, but something to be asymtotically approached. This recognition of incompleteness is expressed by saying that a system must be 'open' and not 'closed'. It should be added, as a word of caution, that a system, just as a human mind, should be open only at one end, not both ends. Otherwise, as in some interpretations of 'open-mindedness', there are no principles, no system – in fact, no knowledge at all.[36]

Were the human mind and philosophical investigation to be open at both ends, allowing a free flow of information and ideas, the notion of truth would be made vulnerable to a radical relativism, which recognised only fleeting, transient propositions, quickly replaced by other, different and perhaps contradictory ones. As I noted in Chapter 7, even Richard Rorty, who advocates a liberal openness, warns against being so open-minded that one's brains fall out. But if the human mind is closed at one end, it must soon accumulate a mass of different and perhaps incompatible propositions. Thus, the human mind and philosophical enquiry must remain critical and self-critical, and so able to sort and evaluate all information and propositions so as to accumulate truth and abandon error.

The claim that political philosophy maintains an open enquiry into the nature of politics does not entail, and does not allow for, the conclusion that the truth which political philosophy embodies is evolutionistic, in the way that, for Simon, the notion of truth embodied in an ideology is. That is, the truth of the nature of politics does not itself change in time. This is not to deny that political practice changes, nor to deny that the attainment of certain political ends may be possible only in time and in certain favourable circumstances, but, rather, to claim that the basic nature of political things and the good political order remain unchanged. Martin argues that metaphysics or philosophy is distinguished from ideology in terms of, among other things, the criterion of continuity. That is, given that full truth may not be available once and for all, but may have to be approached by open enquiry, it is important that there be a possible continuity and so development of human thought and knowledge. Whereas the being of truth itself does not change, the becoming of truth in human knowledge does, as thinking beings make discoveries and make and correct errors. Continuity in the becoming of truth in human knowledge is possible only if there is an objective truth towards which to move, and according to which the truth of all claims to knowledge can be measured and all changes in belief can be ordered. In ideology, the being of truth, and not just the becoming of truth in knowledge, may change as the use to which concepts and propositions are put changes. Thus, in ideology there can be no continuity of knowledge, but only a history of belief in various ideas.[37] Philosophy, as distinct from ideology, displays the criterion of system. That is, the various propositions of philosophy form a system of truth, which is open (and so open to continuity), coherent, and allows for a distinction between essential and non-essential propositions.[38] Also, philosophy is distinguished from ideology in terms of the criterion of adequacy. This involves philosophy being adequate in accounting for other kinds of knowledge; in accounting for itself as knowledge; and in accounting for the development of knowledge. The openness, continuity and systematic nature of philosophy requires the possible development of knowledge, according to which newly acquired knowledge must be in accord and continuous with previously acquired knowledge, and all present knowledge must allow for the addition of future knowledge.[39] It is the notion of truth as objective, and not as evolutionistic, which allows philosophy, as the quest for truth, to be systematic, continuous and adequate.

Philosophy is open and self-critical, whereas ideology tends to be closed and not self-critical. Some writers go so far as to argue that political philosophy is conducted with honesty and integrity, whereas political ideology involves, in some way, philosophical dishonesty. As noted in an earlier point, Feuer characterises philosophy as genuine and un-counterfeit thought, and ideology as thought subordinated to some political purpose. Germino notes that the authentic political theorist 'is particularly concerned with rooting out self-deception, cant, and the ignoring of inconvenient or uncomfortable realities'.[40] It is true that political philosophy should be conducted with honesty and integrity, acknowledging all evidence and treating all arguments fairly, but it is not clear that political ideology is easily recognised as being bereft of these qualities. Ideology often imitates and claims to possess the characteristics of philosophy, but ideology need not be deceitful. As Simon argues, an ideology may be held and offered with some sincerity. He says: 'Sincerity is a thing which admits of many degrees, and if the adherents to an ideology did not believe with some sort of sincerity that they were adhering to incontrovertible facts and essential necessities, the ideology would not work.'[41] Sincerity can be no adequate substitute for intellectual rigour and integrity in the conduct of political thought. But lack of sincerity does not define ideology. In the attempt to identify an ideology, a scrutiny of the content and use of a body of thought is more important than a scrutiny of a thinker's sincerity.

4. Political Philosophy Maintains a Critical Detachment from the Everyday Political Struggle; Political Ideology is Enmeshed in, and Driven by, Political Struggle

I noted in Chapter 7 the problems of relativism and critical impotence that arise for Michael Walzer given his argument that the political philosopher or social critic cannot be more than marginally detached from his or her community. Earlier in the present chapter I noted that Seliger's demarcation of political philosophy and political ideology involves detaching the former from political activity, thus rendering it purely theoretical and seemingly politically impotent and irrelevant. Thus, to avoid being merely political ideology, political philosophy must maintain a certain detachment from the pressures and competing interests of politics; but to be the rational corrective of ideology political philosophy must remain relevant to the practical problems of political life.

Political philosophy, if it is to pursue its quest for knowledge of the nature of politics and the good political order must seek to avoid being trapped within, or driven by, the pressures of the current political struggle. In particular, political philosophy must avoid becoming the representative of the partial interests of one party to the political struggle. Germino says authentic political theory (what I refer to as political philosophy) must seek 'to transcend the confines of the contemporaneous political struggle, with its immediate issues and relevances, to discover – or rediscover – other issues and relevances'.[42] For Germino:

> The weight of the theorist's analysis falls on . . . universal, perennial questions rather than on the immediate, pressing, time-bound controversies of the day. Whereas the publicist is concerned with derivative, or second order problems, taking the larger questions regarding the end of human life in society for granted or treating them only cursorily in relation to the pursuit of some immediate, practical objective, the theorist is above all preoccupied with elucidating the principles of right order valid for men as men.[43]

For political philosophy to succumb to the transient pressures and partial interests of the political struggle would be for it to collapse into political ideology. This is not to argue that philosophy does not, nor should not, become involved in the issues of its time. Copleston argues that 'although philosophic thought has expressed or precipitated itself in successive philosophies, each of which has been historically conditioned in specific ways, it, nonetheless, aspires to universality, to what is true at all times and for all, whereas an ideology expresses the outlook and goal of a restricted group'.[44]

Andrew Hacker has termed the search of political philosophy for knowledge of the good political order a 'disinterested' one.[45] This term is useful if it is taken to indicate the absence from political philosophy of the distorting influence of the partial and transient interests inherent in political struggle. However, political philosophy is not disinterested in respect to the truth, which is unlikely to be constituted by, and is quite likely to be jeopardised by, such limited interests. Moreover, political philosophy is not uninterested in the political activity of the day. Indeed, it is the task of political philosophy to engage in appraisal and evaluation of the conduct of politics at all times. Political philosophy is a practical discipline. Precisely because political philosophy must engage in critical appraisal of politics, it must retain what Germino calls a 'critical distance' from its subject matter.[46]

Just as disinterested political philosophy is not uninterested in politics, so the critical distance which political philosophy maintains from its subject matter is not to be misunderstood as complete detachment. Richard Ashcraft is wrong when he says that defenders of political philosophy against political ideology, such as Germino and Strauss, deny the relevance both of everyday political struggle for political philosophy, and of political philosophy for practical political concerns.[47] In a critical response to Ashcraft, Bruce Douglass and Gary Marfin clarify the involvement of political philosophy in politics.

> The difference between political philosophy and ideology with respect to political action is not a matter of withdrawal vs. involvement, but rather of two different modes of involvement. Ideology, because it is designed specifically to address the current struggle for power, can have an immediate practical effect. Political philosophy rarely does. But this does not mean that political philosophy is without political effect altogether. In the long run, it may well have a profound effect on political life. What political philosophy addresses is the foundations of political order, the principles and presuppositions of the world view on which political life is based. Whole societies do not change quickly at this level, and popular thinking is not

> often influenced immediately by what is said in truly philosophical books.[48]

It is not the case that political philosophy is not concerned with the immediate, day-to-day issues of politics. Rather, political philosophy is concerned with mundane, occasional issues, but is not anchored in them nor driven by them. It is primarily concerned with universal and perennial issues, and reflects on these so as better to deal with more transient issues. Strauss says that it is 'only when the Here and Now ceases to be the centre of reference that a philosophic or scientific approach to politics can emerge'.[49]

If the political philosopher is to retain a critical distance from political activity, then political philosophy and politics may coexist, but in a state of tension. Political philosophy must be prepared to offer criticism and evaluation of political practice. By criticising any given political order, political philosophy seeks not to undermine politics, but rather to offer support for good politics. This critical attitude of political philosophy may bring it into conflict with political authority. However, this tension can be exaggerated, as is evident in the work of Strauss. As noted above, Strauss holds that political philosophy seeks to replace opinion about politics with knowledge of politics. According to Strauss there is 'a necessary conflict between philosophy and politics if the element of society necessarily is opinion, i.e. assent to opinion'. For Strauss, philosophy may be 'the attempt to dissolve the element in which society breathes'.[50] Strauss concludes that political philosophers must present their writings in an esoteric or hidden form in order to protect both themselves, from persecution by political authority, and society, from the truths which would disrupt cohesive opinion. Thus, political philosophers must conceal their truth from all but a wise few, and be prepared to perpetrate 'noble lies' for consumption by the vulgar mass.[51] Political philosophers will know that truth differs from socially useful opinion, but they will 'respect the opinions on which society rests. To respect opinions is something entirely different from accepting them as true'.[52] Strauss's position is clearly elitist, inequalitarian and illiberal.[53] More disturbing, Strauss's position brings political philosophy dangerously close to ideology.

I argued in Chapter 2 that Plato's notion of the noble lie is an early example of the use-value of a proposition overriding its truth-value, and so an early example of ideological thought.

Strauss does, of course, wish to distinguish political philosophy and political ideology, but his distinction still involves an exaggerated tension between philosophy and authority. He says: 'By submitting to authority, philosophy, in particular political philosophy, would lose its character; it would degenerate into ideology, i.e., apologetics for a given or emerging social order'.[54] Strauss identifies the original distinction between nature and convention, in ancient Greece, as the starting point of political philosophy, in that human reason, which knows nature, is able to measure all claims to authority by the standard of nature, and to judge what is good by nature as distinct from convention. However, in his desire to free reason and philosophy from the ties of any given authority, and to free political philosophy from the danger of collapsing into ideology, Strauss seems to seek to free reason from all authority, including the authority of nature. He says: 'By calling nature the highest authority, one would blur the distinction by which philosophy stands or falls, the distinction between reason and authority'.[55] If political philosophy is not to be obedient or submissive to the truth of the nature of political things and the good political order, then there is a danger that political philosophy will not be anchored in any objective reality, and so a danger that it will not be distinguished from ideology. Brian Midgley comments: 'In denying that any intellection must be an obedience of the mind to the truth of things, Strauss is taking a position which is subversive of our knowledge of truth'.[56]

5. Political Philosophy, Although an Eminently Practical Discipline, Does Not Attempt to Impose its Findings on Political Reality; Political Ideology Tends to Offer Itself as a Programme of Action for Immediate Implementation

Political philosophy seeks knowledge of the good political order, recognising that all such knowledge may not be available and so maintaining an open enquiry. Political philosophy uses the knowledge it has as the basis of a criticism of politics, but does not seek to impose its knowledge in any thorough and immediate reconstruction of society. Political ideology, on the other hand, is motivated by some human interest or desire and is tempted to reconstruct society so as to promote the satisfaction of such interests and desires.

Germino characterises authentic political theory by its 'theoretical intention', in that the 'political theorist is not out to make reality conform to his will but to form his concepts so that they are adequate to the reality which he observes and in which he participates'. The ideologist, on the other hand, accepts on principle the various human desires and interests and 'seeks to re-create the human condition in his own image'.[57] Germino goes on to distinguish what he terms the 'realism' of political theory from the 'utopianism' of political ideology. 'The political theorist is vividly aware of the inappropriateness of seeking to impose his model of the good society directly upon a concrete historical situation.' He employs 'a paradigm for critical analysis, not a utopian blueprint to be implemented by an intrepid band of social engineers' and he 'knows what utopian thinkers . . . never learned: that human nature cannot be changed by the black magic of institutional tinkering . . . and that institutions must be adapted to the particular environment'.[58] Copleston argues that 'the essential feature of ideological thinking is its orientation to realization of a goal other than simply understanding of how things are, a goal which cannot be realized merely by thinking but only by concerted human action'.[59] Douglass and Marfin, on the basis of their distinction between the intended immediate effect of political ideology and the possible long-term effect of political philosophy, conclude: 'The ideologist deals with themes that lend themselves to an explicit programme of action. The political philosopher does not. Short of totalitarian control, there really is no programme for the transformation of culture.'[60]

If political philosophy does not seek to implement its findings by transforming political life, then to what extent is it a practical discipline and how is it related to political practice? Political philosophy, like all practical philosophy, deals with contingent and not necessary things. That is, it deals with human conduct, based on deliberation and choice, where the necessity linking ends and means is moral rather than physical. For this reason, political philosophy should not attempt to prescribe a comprehensive course of human conduct and to enforce it politically by all the available means of coercion, law and opinion. To attempt to constrain and enforce human conduct in such a way would be to deny the moral choice and responsibility of the individual, and to deny that there may be a variety of legitimate ways for humans to fulfil themselves and realise the good life. Of course, in all societies certain forms of behaviour will not be tolerated and will be outlawed in order to maintain certain standards of decency and public order. But to make illegal all human conduct considered to be immoral would be to choke society with legal proceedings. The task of political philosophy, then, is to enquire into the nature of the good political order, to evaluate current political practice, and to encourage citizens to reflect thoughtfully on such matters. This conclusion may seem to coincide with some form of liberalism, which encourages free thought for its own sake and tolerates diverse views in an open society. There is, though, one crucial difference between my position and such liberalism. My conclusion rests on the assumption that there is some objective standard of human and political conduct, of which it is the task of political philosophy to seek knowledge. Liberalism, in some contemporary forms at least, rests on the assumption that it is precisely because there is no objective standard of human conduct, and only an insoluble dispute about human ends, that one should maintain an openness in society, tolerating all manner of belief and behaviour because there is no good reason to reject and criticise it. Such liberalism is unable, I believe, to defend itself against the challenge of ideology, which may serve any and all human interests and desires, no matter how improper.

Such a conclusion may be thought to be naive in that it may seem to posit the rationality and freedom of the individual thinker and to disregard the ways in which human thought is constrained by existing ideologies and intellectual fashions, or by overbearing personal or social pressures. Far from the conclusion being naive, it offers political philosophy as the strongest possible criticism of all that impinges on the proper exercise of human thought, deliberation and choice. Political philosophy, which encourages proper human conduct, does so without coercion and without closing off enquiry.

The preceding set of distinctions between political philosophy and political ideology are unlikely to establish clearly and unambiguously the demarcation of the two modes of political thought. As noted above it may in practice be very difficult, if not impossible, to demarcate the two. But the attempt must be made, and the possibility of success must be granted in principle, if the problem of ideology is to be resolved.

10 Rational Political Philosophy

INTRODUCTION

The solution of the problem of ideology is rational political philosophy, which can avoid the problem of relativism by giving an objective justification of political values and making an objective distinction between proper and improper values. The nature of rational political philosophy, or moral political science, as it might also properly be termed, is the concern of this final chapter. Rational political philosophy, as a normative discipline, is the study of objective moral and political reality. Chapter 5 considered Roy Bhaskar's scientific realism, which holds that there is a scientific reality which is both independent of and accessible to human thought. This stress on objective reality is to be welcomed as an antidote to the relativism of both the post-positivist natural science of Popper, Lakatos, Kuhn and Feyerabend, and the interpretivist social science of Winch and Taylor. However, Bhaskar's normative thought is not adequate. I now propose to argue for a more adequate moral and political realism, as the only antidote to the problem of moral relativism, which is the problem of political ideology. Moral realism holds that there exists an objective moral order, independent of belief, according to which some human acts are morally right and others are wrong, and some moral judgements are true and others are false. Moral realists believe that in making moral judgements humans attempt to identify what is in keeping with moral reality, or is morally right, rather than merely state personal or social preferences. Just as scientific reality is not to be reduced to empirical observations of nature, so moral and political reality is not to be reduced to an account of how humans do actually behave. Rather, moral and political reality is an objective standard of human moral and political life according to which human behaviour is measured.

Moral and political reality is properly rooted in the objective needs of human nature, and the forms of life necessary for the full development of human needs. Thus, the foundation of rational political philosophy is the reality of human nature. Human reason, which is the defining characteristic of humanity, is capable of knowing human nature, and the objective reality of morals and politics. Moral and political realism is evident in the long tradition of natural law theory, which has its roots in ancient Greek and Roman philosophy, is fully developed in the late medieval period, and remains, subject to varying fortune, in the modern period.[1] There is, of course, great diversity of thought in the long tradition of natural law, but it is possible to offer a general characterisation of the theory. Natural law, as law, acts as a rule or measure of human behaviour and offers a guide to action. The binding force of natural law is moral rather than physical. Human beings may choose to break the natural law, but not with moral justification. Natural law has the force of law, according to many theorists, because it is a dictate of reason. Natural law may be said to be natural for a number of reasons. It is not artificial or conventional, but exists by nature. It applies to human nature, and is concerned with right action in accord with human nature, and with the fulfilment of human nature. Because natural law applies to human nature it applies universally and for all time, as human nature is the same everywhere and endures unchanged. Also, natural law is known naturally, by natural human reason's knowledge of human nature and the place of human nature in nature generally.

The argument that rational political philosophy may be founded on a theory of human nature is likely to meet certain fundamental criticisms. First, it might be argued that conceptions of human nature are ideological rather than philosophical. Second, it might be held that in so far as there is a human nature this is not absolute and universal, but variable and relative. Third, it might be held that even if there is such a thing as human nature, there is no moral purpose in this, and it is not possible to derive from the facts of this nature any human values. Responses to these three criticisms are offered below under the headings of human nature and practical reason. A fourth criticism can be dealt with immediately. It might be thought that the evidence of moral diversity and moral disagreement undermines moral realism and natural law. However, the fact that people behave in morally different ways is compatible with the existence of an objective moral reality, for, as noted above, moral laws, unlike physical laws, can be disregarded and broken. Also, the fact that people disagree with one another when making moral judgements indicates not that there is no objective moral reality, but, rather, that people presuppose such a reality and seek to correct the errors of others about it. Chapter 6 noted Leo Strauss's argument that the variety of notions of justice can be understood as the variety of errors, and that this variety does not contradict, but presupposes, the existence of one truth about justice.

HUMAN NATURE

Criticism of human nature as the foundation of rational political philosophy includes the claim that conceptions of human nature may be ideological rather than philosophical. For example, C.B. Macpherson argues that 'it can be seen that Hobbes's analysis of human nature, from which his whole political theory is derived, is really an analysis of bourgeois man; that the assumptions, explicit and implicit, upon which his psychological conclusions depend are assumptions peculiarly valid for bourgeois society'. According to Macpherson, 'Hobbes accepted and regarded as natural a pattern of social relationships and human behaviour which we know as one aspect of bourgeois society.'[2] Macpherson does not claim that all conceptions of human nature are necessarily ideological. He seeks, rather, to expose the ideological character of Hobbes's account of human nature by means of historical and philosophical analysis. I comment below on the adequacy of Macpherson's own account of human nature. At this point it may be noted that to distinguish between ideological and philosophical accounts of human nature it is useful to recall the demarcation of political philosophy and political ideology discussed in the previous chapter.

A second criticism of human nature as the foundation of rational political philosophy is the claim that human nature is not fixed and given, but, rather, variable and relative. In response to criticisms of this sort, Len Doyal and Ian Gough show that for social and political theorists it is not possible both to deny the concept of objective, universal human need and to avoid critically debilitating relativism.[3] They demonstrate the inconsistency of those perspectives which attempt 'both to denounce universal standards of evaluation with one hand only to employ them to endorse some favoured view of the world with the other'.[4] For example, orthodox economics reduces human needs to subjective individual preferences, but, given the limits of information and sales pressure experienced by consumers, cannot deal adequately with want satisfaction and consumer choice without some more objective measure of welfare. New Right theorists criticise actual and potential authoritarian governments which claim to be able to identify and meet the real needs of citizens, but themselves assume some concept of objective need, when they argue that free market capitalism best serves the interests of individuals in the long run. Marxists, who argue that human needs are historically determined, require some concept of fixed human need in order to substantiate their criticism of capitalism and show why human beings will be better off in the post-revolutionary society. Critics of cultural imperialism argue that needs are culturally relative, and yet imply some non-relative notion of human good when they distinguish and side with oppressed cultures against oppressive cultures. Radical democrats argue for a plurality of group interests, but standards external to the group must exist in order to evaluate what is tolerable within the group. Phenomenologists argue that human needs are relative social constructs, and yet betray some concept of real human need in their concern about, and study of, say, poverty or deprivation. In short, Doyal and Gough show that theorists who wish to maintain a critical perspective on social and political reality cannot dispense with a concept of objective and universal human nature.

C.B. Macpherson argues that political theory must be based on some concept of human nature but undermines his own position by acknowledging that the concept may be relative. Macpherson argues that political theory is, among other things, normative. Normative political theory, which seeks either to show why certain political arrangements are justified or to prescribe better arrangements, must be grounded in the 'supposed essential nature of man' and the 'supposed essentially human purposes and capacities'.[5] Political theory must provide an explanation of human nature and of the nature of the state which is 'most congruous with the nature of man, most in conformity with man's needs and capacities.'[6] For Macpherson, in short, 'the adequacy of a political theory is to be assessed by the penetration of its analysis of human nature'.[7]

Macpherson takes human nature to consist of a number of distinct but compatible capacities which can and should be developed. The details of these capacities will be considered below. He employs his notion of human nature in his critique of capitalism and the market. He criticises capitalism for denying some humans free access to the means of production as a means to develop their capacities, and so permitting others to develop at their expense. He also criticises capitalism for manipulating human needs, and the capitalist market for failing to measure and meet real needs.[8] These arguments can be sustained only on the basis of a concept of human nature that permits the distinction between real and false needs. Macpherson fails to offer such a concept.

The inadequacy of Macpherson's concept of human nature becomes apparent when he states that the postulates about the human essence, precisely because they are value postulates, can be discarded when they are at odds with new value judgements about human goals.[9] Macpherson sees human nature not as a fixed essence, but as something subject to change, and he considers an adequate theory of human needs to be 'both ontological and historical', and to make 'no use of the natural/artificial distinction'. He notes, with seeming approval, that Marx held the free and 'creative transformation of nature and of oneself and one's relations with one's fellows' to be '*the* truly human *need*'.[10] Macpherson seems to understand the development of human nature as a process of making and remaking rather than one of realisation and fulfilment. He expresses his antipathy to the notion of a fixed human nature thus: 'If you start from the assumption that there is a permanent unchanging nature of man, then you are forced to subsume all changes, such as increase of desires, under his innate nature'.[11] But this does not follow. Human nature may be fixed and yet have all sorts of false desires attached to it as the result of socialisation and advertising. Indeed, it is only if one can refer to the true conception of fixed human nature that one can identify failures of development and the addition of false needs. If Macpherson has no concept of objective and unchanging human nature, one wonders how he feels able to criticise what he takes to be the erroneous conceptions of others. If Macpherson's argument is, as it seems to be, that he offers a historically adequate account of human nature against historically irrelevant ones, then he places himself in a paradox of relativism: his conception may be historically different from others, but may in time come to be criticised as irrelevant and inadequate, and so is ultimately no better, or worse, than any other conception.

If, as Macpherson holds, human beings are to be free to create and recreate their own needs, it seems they would be able to do this in free exchange with others, that is, in a market. It is not clear how Macpherson can substantiate the distinction between the free creation of needs and market manipulation of needs. Moreover, if human needs are freely created and recreated in a market, it is impossible to argue that markets do not measure and meet real needs. Only if one can refer to the true conception of a given human nature can one demonstrate that needs have been manipulated or neglected by the market. Thus, Macpherson could sustain his criticism of capitalism only on the basis of a concept of human nature according to which one can distinguish true and false needs, and judge the correct development of basic human capacities.

To refer, as natural law theorists do, to the development, fulfilment or flourishing of human nature is not to deny that human nature is a given, fixed essence, or to imply that it is variable and relative. Reference to the development, fulfilment, or flourishing of human nature presupposes a given human nature that can flourish or be developed or fulfilled. Human beings are not without essence, such that they can create and recreate themselves so as to become whatever they choose. Germain Grisez indicates the only sense in which human nature can be said to change when he says 'human nature changes in the sense that the possible human fulfilment which can be realized in and through human action develops in the course of history as humankind unfolds its potentialities'.[12]

What then is human nature? Human nature can be understood in terms of real human needs. Doyal and Gough identify two basic human needs which are 'the preconditions for any individual action in any culture'. These basic human needs are, first, survival and physical health, and second, autonomy, which depends on understanding, mental health, and opportunity (which in turn includes freedom of agency and political freedom).[13] There can be little doubt that physical health and autonomy are basic human goods, but these two items constitute a minimal list. The obvious advantage of such a minimal list is that it is likely to be fairly uncontroversial and might attract widespread endorsement. On the other hand, widespread agreement on very little is likely to be of minimum advantage. It is a merit of Doyal and Gough's list that it includes autonomy as a basic human need, for this indicates that human beings are not merely passive survivors but active doers and developers. However, Doyal and Gough fail to specify how, and for what ends, human autonomy is to be used properly. They thus fail to substantiate their theory of human needs and goods.

Macpherson lists what he takes to be the natural capacities that constitute the human essence: 'the capacity for rational understanding, for moral judgement and action, for aesthetic creation or contemplation, for the emotional activities of friendship and love, and, sometimes, for religious experience'. To this list Macpherson adds the capacity for transforming what is given by Nature, the capacity for wonder and curiosity, the capacity for laughter, and the capacity for controlled physical/mental/aesthetic activity as in making music and playing games.[14] These capacities are developed as ends in themselves. To this empirical list of recognisably human characteristics Macpherson adds the assumption that the development of human nature is harmonious: all essentially human characteristics may be developed fully without hindrance to others; and the full development of one human being does not hinder the development of others.[15]

Macpherson correctly identifies a list of genuine human needs or capacities. However, Macpherson offers only an empirical list, and makes little effort to build an integrated theory of human nature. More importantly, Macpherson concedes that human needs and capacities may not be fixed but historical, and this, as I noted above, renders him vulnerable to the charge of relativism.

A full and integrated theory of human nature is available in the theory of natural law. St. Thomas Aquinas, whose thirteenth-century philosophical-theological synthesis supports perhaps the greatest theory of natural law, argues that 'to the natural law belongs everything to which a man is inclined according to his nature. Now each thing is inclined naturally to an operation that is suitable to it according to its form.'[16] He explains that by 'human nature we . . . mean either that which is proper to man . . . or . . . that nature which is common to man and other animals'.[17] As I will explain below, Aquinas argues that those things to which humans are naturally inclined, and for which they have an appetite, are human goods. 'Since . . . good has the nature of an end . . . hence it is that all those things to which man has a natural inclination are naturally apprehended by reason as being good. . . . Therefore, the order of the precepts of the natural law is according to the order of natural inclinations.' Thus, in common with all things, humans have an inclination to preserve their being. In common with all animals, humans have an inclination to sexual intercourse, the education of their offspring, and so forth. In accord with the rational nature of humans, which is distinct and proper to humans, there is an inclination to know God, and to live in society.[18] Natural inclinations are given rather than chosen, but they do not imply physical necessity in human action, nor do they deny moral choice. It is because humans can pursue their natural inclinations and ends well or badly that they can form moral precepts about them.[19]

Working within the tradition of natural law, although acknowledging that their 'theory's adequacy is not its correspondence with the views of any previous thinker', (including Aquinas), Germain Grisez, Joseph Boyle and John Finnis offer a more elaborate account of human goods, which entails and corresponds to a theory of human nature.[20] They argue that there are seven categories of basic human goods. First, as animals humans have the good of life, including the maintenance of this through health and safety, and the transmission of this through reproduction. Second, as rational beings it is good for humans to have knowledge of reality and aesthetic appreciation of beauty. Third, as rational animals humans can express their meanings and serve their purposes by transforming their world, and so they have the goods of excellence in work and play. Fourth, there is the good of harmony among individuals and groups, which includes peace, friendship and neighbourliness. Fifth, within each individual there is the good of harmony, or inner peace, between one's judgements and choices. Sixth, for individuals there is also the harmony, or peace of conscience, between one's judgements and choices and one's behaviour. Seventh, there is for humans the good of harmony between themselves and the wider reality of the more-than-human source of meaning and value, including God. The first three goods are termed substantive, in that humans can and do engage in them prior to deliberating on them. The last four goods are termed reflexive, in that humans can, through deliberation and choice, strive to avoid personal and interpersonal conflict.

This account of human needs might seem not to contradict anything in Aquinas, and indeed may be taken to clarify and fulfil Aquinas's account. However, there are a number of important differences between Aquinas on the one hand, and Grisez, Boyle and Finnis on the other, one of which can be noted now. Aquinas says there is an order of human inclinations, which moves from that which humans share with all other creatures, to that which they share with only some other creatures, to that which is distinctly and properly human. Aquinas says: 'since the rational soul is the proper form of man, there is in every man a natural inclination to act according to reason'.[21] Ralph McInerny notes the hierarchy of human inclinations and draws the implications of this: 'It is by coming under the guidance of reason that goods which are not peculiar to man come to be constituents of the human good'.[22] Finnis, however, argues that each of the basic human goods is equally self-evidently good; that none can be reduced to being merely instrumental in the pursuit of others; and that each can reasonably be regarded as being most important. 'Hence there is no objective hierarchy amongst them.'[23] Finnis believes that his denial of any hierarchy of human goods permits him to argue that there is not just one way to flourish as a human being, that is, rational contemplation, and that humans are free to make choices between the diversity of equally rationally appealing human goods as they structure their life plans.[24] McInerny responds correctly that the development and perfection of the rational capacity must be the pre-eminent, though not exclusive, human good. The hierarchical ordering of human goods does not entail the reduction of some goods to merely instrumental status, and it certainly does not permit acting contrary to some basic good. Nor does the hierarchy of goods entail only one proper way of life, or one mode of human flourishing. According to McInerny, the 'human good remains complex and irreducible to the well-performing of any single type of rational activity', and the 'moral ideal, whatever the objective ranking of its constituent goods, is open to an infinity of realisations'.[25]

PRACTICAL REASON

Even granted an objective human nature, if it is to be the foundation of rational political philosophy there remains the problem of the derivation of normative propositions from factual statements about it. The denial that one can legitimately derive a value from a fact, or an ought from an is, is characteristic of the positivist critique of normative political philosophy considered in Chapter 1. As modern positivists would acknowledge, the so-called is–ought or fact–value distinction is recognised by David Hume in the eighteenth century. Kai Nielsen says of natural law that 'the whole theory rests on a confusion between *what ought to be* and *what is.* As Hume made us realise. . . . From factual statements alone, including statements of fact about human nature, we cannot deduce or derive any 'ought' statement whatever.'[26] Hume's famous statement on the relationship of facts and values is as follows.

> In every system of morality, which I have hitherto met with, I have always remark'd, that the author proceeds for some time in the ordinary way of reasoning, and establishes the being of a God, or makes observations concerning human affairs; when of a sudden I am surpriz'd to find, that instead of the usual copulations of propositions, *is*, and *is not*, I meet with no proposition that is not coupled with an *ought*, or *ought not*. This change is imperceptible; but is, however, of the last consequence. For as this *ought*, or *ought not*, expresses some new relation or affirmation, 'tis necessary that it should be observ'd and explain'd; and at the same time that a reason should be given, for what seems altogether conceivable, how this new relation can be a deduction from others, which are entirely different from it.[27]

There is much scholarly comment and debate on what Hume means in and by the is–ought passage.[28] I believe the paragraph is best interpreted in the light and terms of the arguments of the whole section of which it is a conclusion. Hume is concerned to advance the general point which is the title of the section: 'Moral Distinctions not deriv'd from Reason'. He offers first a general argument about the role of reason in morality: 'Morals excite passions, and produce or prevent actions. Reason of itself is utterly impotent in this particular. The rules of morality, therefore, are not conclusions of our reason.'[29] That reason is impotent in practical matters, whereas the passions are not, is a point which chimes with another point made earlier by Hume: 'Reason is, and ought only to be the slave of the passions.'[30] Hume reminds his readers that what reason can do is calculate matters of fact, which lie behind sense impressions, and demonstrate relations of ideas. He then argues that morality 'consists not in any relations, that are the objects of science' or 'in any *matter of fact*, which can be discover'd by the understanding'.[31] Morality is, for Hume, a matter of feeling, involving the passions, rather than a matter of reasoning. In the is–ought passage Hume may be taken to be making the following points: first, that there is a logical gulf between facts and values that cannot be bridged by reason; and second, that there is a radical gulf between speculative reason and active, practical passions. This second point can be taken to mean that reason cannot be practical.

The first of Hume's two points, that values cannot be derived from facts, would, if correct, pose a significant challenge to natural law. Henry Veatch asks: 'how can the enterprise of a natural law ethics be anything other than a search for some basis for morals and ethics in nature itself, and in the facts of nature?' Veatch concludes that natural law is possible because 'the very "is" of human nature already has its "ought" contained within it'.[32] Hume's radical separation of facts and values may be challenged by criticising his empiricism. Vernon Burke responds to Nielsen's Humean criticism of natural law by saying: 'In good part due to the influence of Hume (it seems to me), reality has been reduced to a sort of atomic theory of unrelated events. In such a theory, what is given is a collection of sense 'facts' that have no real interconnections. If that is the character of the *is*, then I should say that no oughtness arises from it.'[33] This is reminiscent of Roy Bhaskar's realist critique of positivism and the epistemic fallacy noted in Chapter 5. According to the epistemic fallacy, ontology is reduced to epistemology, or, to put it another way, objective reality is reduced to a matter of human knowledge. Empiricism in general, and positivism in particular, fails to comprehend objective reality because it is limited to human experience of surface impressions. Empiricism thus fails to comprehend moral reality. A proper understanding of human nature involves not merely an account of what humans look like and what they actually do, but an appreciation of essential human needs, inclinations and capacities; of how these may be developed or fulfilled; and so of the goals and goods of human nature. Reference to the fulfilment of human nature implies that the facts of human nature are the foundation of the values of human life.

As noted above, Aquinas argues that as a matter of fact human beings have natural inclinations, and that the ends to which these inclinations are ordered are good for humans. This argument may now be considered in more detail. Aquinas argues that every agent acts for an end, understood either as the action itself or that which is made or achieved by the action.[34] This end is said to be good for the agent for a number of related reasons: it is befitting the agent; it is the object of the appetite of the agent; and it is the perfection of the agent.[35] Aquinas follows Aristotle in holding that good is the object of desire, and explains that something is properly desirable only if it is perfect. Perfection is understood as the fulfilment or development of a thing, and the end for which the thing moves. This line of argument is followed by Leo Strauss who, as noted in Chapter 6, says that in politics humans always act to preserve something good or to make things better. Aquinas's theory of natural law links the facts and values of human nature: human nature is known by its natural inclinations; by following their natural inclinations, humans act for ends which are fitted to, and fulfil their nature; these natural ends, being fitting, perfect and desirable are good. Aquinas offers a clear account of the intimate relationship of facts and values, of what is and what ought to be, when he says:

> Goodness and being are really the same, and differ only in idea. . . . The essence of goodness consists in this, that it is in some way desirable. . . . Now it is clear that a thing is desirable only in so far as it is perfect, for all desire their own perfection. But everything is perfect so far as it is actual. Therefore it is clear that a thing is perfect so far as it is being; for being is the actuality of everything. . . . Hence it is clear that goodness and being are the same really.[36]

To argue for a link between facts and values is to respond only to the first of Hume's two points. To respond to the second, and to clarify and consolidate the response to the first, it is necessary to show how reason can be practical, or active in morals. The notion of practical reason, which is central to Aquinas's doctrine of natural law, is understood in distinction to speculative, or theoretical, reason. These are not two distinct powers, but, rather, the single power of reason distinguished in terms of its end and operation. Aquinas explains that 'the speculative intellect . . . directs what it apprehends, not to operation, but to the sole consideration of truth; while the practical intellect is that which directs what it apprehends to operation'.[37] Both speculative and practical reason know truth, but practical reason orders this knowledge to an end. Whereas speculative reason is concerned with truth alone, and with 'necessary things, which cannot be otherwise than they are', practical reason is concerned with 'contingent' things, which can be operated or ordered by human beings.[38] In particular, practical reason is concerned to know the end or good of human beings and to direct human conduct to this good end. That practical and speculative reason are not distinct powers, but, rather, the single power of reason distinguished by its end, should be clear from the argument of Aquinas, noted above, that being, which is the end of speculative reason, and good, which is the end of practical reason, are really the same, and differ only in the way they are understood. As speculative and practical reason are distinguished in terms of their end, so too they are distinguished in terms of truth. For the speculative intellect, truth 'depends on the conformity of the intellect to the thing', whereas 'the truth of the practical intellect depends on conformity with right appetite'.[39] As noted above, human good is what humans properly desire, or have an appetite for, and practical reason orders human action to this desired and proper end. Both will, as the appetitive power, and reason are involved in moral judgement and conduct. However, reason is the higher power, for the will is moved only by its object, the apprehended good, and it is for reason to know that things are good.[40]

Both speculative and practical reason start from first principles which are self-evident or indemonstrable, that is, principles in which the 'predicate is contained in the notion of the subject'. If one understands the terms of a self-evident proposition, one knows, without need of further information, that the proposition is true. Speculative reason is concerned with the truth of being, or with what is and is not the case, and so its first self-evident principle is that 'the same thing cannot be affirmed and denied at the same time'. This is the principle of non-contradiction. Practical reason is concerned with good and the direction of human conduct to the good, and so its self-evident first principle is that 'good is to be done and promoted, and evil is to be avoided'.[41] Critics of natural law dismiss the self-evident first principle of practical reason as 'vacuous' and an 'empty tautology'.[42] For Russell Hittinger, though, the first principle of practical reason 'is an imperative, not a tautology'.[43] The principle does not specify what is good, but it commands that good be done. Practical reason knows the actual goods of human nature by knowing the natural inclinations of humanity. Thus, from its self-evident first principle, and from its knowledge of human goods, practical reason can formulate the precepts of natural law. From the general principles of natural law, practical reason can deduce or determine what particular things ought to be done.

However, not all natural law theorists accept that natural law requires the derivation of values from facts, and that such derivation is possible. Grisez, Boyle and Finnis argue that 'the moral *ought* cannot be derived from the *is* of theoretical truth – for example, of metaphysics and/or philosophical anthropology'.[44] Rather, the first principles of practical reason are self-evident and as such are 'not conclusions from theoretical knowledge about human persons'.[45] This would seem to separate natural law from any foundation in human nature, and Lloyd Weinreb has characterised such a theory as 'natural law without nature'.[46] However, Grisez, Boyle and Finnis argue that they do not deny the relevance, for practical reason, of theoretical knowledge of the facts of human nature, for 'theoretical reflection deepens understanding of the basic goods, and knowledge about facts bearing on their instantiation is necessary to pursue them effectively'.[47] Nor do they 'mean that morality is cut off from its roots in human nature'.[48] The appropriate relation between human nature and morality is not, according to Finnis, that of premise and deduced conclusion. Finnis says: 'a statement of the basic human goods entails an account of human nature. But it does not presuppose such an account. It is not an attempt to deduce reasons for action from some preexisting theoretical conception of human nature. Such an attempt would vainly defy the logical truth . . . that "ought" cannot be deduced from "is".'[49]

Finnis and Grisez clearly, and correctly, wish to stress that the principles of natural law are principles of practical reason, and they clearly, and correctly, wish to avoid any erroneous derivation of these principles. In particular, Grisez states correctly that 'the addition of will to theoretical knowledge cannot make it practical. This point is precisely what Hume saw when he denied the possibility of deriving ought from is.'[50] The serious problem with their work is that they seem to concede the fact/value distinction as maintained by the positivists, and, consequently, they seem to concede too great a distinction between practical and speculative reason.[51] In their attempt to defend the natural law against its critics and misinterpreters, Grisez and Finnis may accept too readily some key assumptions of the opposition case.

POLITICAL JUDGEMENT AND PRUDENCE

Rational political philosophy has its foundation in natural law, which is concerned with the objective needs of human nature. Upon this foundation political philosophy must develop so as to be commensurate with all the requirements of political life. According to Aquinas, natural law by itself is not sufficient for social and political life. Human law, that is positive law written and enacted by human authorities, is necessary for a couple of reasons. First, humans will not always apply right reason when following their inclinations, and those who do not always comply with natural law must be restrained and trained by human law.[52] Second, the general principles of natural law must be applied to the variety of particular cases that arise in social and political life.[53] Aquinas argues that 'every human law has just so much of the nature of law as it is derived from the law of nature', and that 'something may be derived from the natural law in two ways: first, as a conclusion from principles; secondly, by way of a determination of certain notions'.[54] Aquinas offers the following examples. From the general principle that one should do no harm to anyone, it follows as a conclusion that one should not kill. It is a general principle of the natural law that evil-doers should be punished, but the specific form of punishment is a particular determination of the natural law. Rational political philosophy is concerned not only with general normative principles, but also with the, perhaps more difficult, determination of general principles for particular cases. McInerny says: 'There has been much talk of universalizability in recent ethics, but the real moral problem is particularizability, that is, the application of these principles in the fluctuating circumstances in which we find ourselves, tailoring them to the here and now. This is the realm of the judgements and commands of prudence.'[55] The role of judgement and prudence in political philosophy may now be considered.

Ronald Beiner recognises the need for political judgement, and he correctly locates judgement somewhere between the operation of explicit methodological rules and arbitrary subjectivism.[56] However, he misrepresents the grounds of its necessity. He says:

> Concern with the idea of political judgement . . . arises out of the common intuition that there is a natural and unbridgeable gap between theory and practice. . . . If theoretical understanding could offer unlimited guidance for its own application, judgement would be superfluous. But, in fact, there is an inescapable need for wisdom and discrimination in confronting a veritable infinity of concrete particulars, and happily, practice has its own independent integrity and its own cognitive resources on which to draw.[57]

Beiner is wrong in suggesting that the need for judgement arises from an unbridgeable gap between theory and practice. Theoretical or speculative reason neither needs to be, nor can be, supplemented by judgement to make it practical. As noted above, practical reason is not just speculative or theoretical reason with something – for example, will or judgement – added to it, but, rather, the single power of reason concerned with applying its knowledge to an operation.

Beiner is correct in noting that judgement is required when dealing with particular things, but he is wrong when he argues that '"natural law" doctrines . . . in general, allow no room for the free exercise of judgement. . . . Natural law rests upon the supposition that a universal can be discerned for the (in principle) unproblematic subsumption of particulars.'[58] Natural law theorists do, generally, suppose that universal principles are relevant to particular cases, but not that all particular cases can be dealt with by means of the unproblematic application of universal principles. Natural law involves practical reason, and, as noted above, one of the distinctions between speculative and practical reason is that the former is concerned with necessary things, and the latter with contingent things. A further distinction, also noted above, is that the truth of speculative reason depends on its conformity to its object, and that of practical reason on its conformity with right appetite. As a consequence of these distinctions, according to Aquinas, there is a further important distinction. For speculative reason, concerned with things that cannot be other than they are, truth will be the same everywhere, for both principles and conclusions, although not every human being will appreciate the inherent truth of all conclusions. For practical reason, concerned with human actions, 'there is necessity in the common principles' but 'the more we descend towards the particular, the more frequently we encounter defects'. Thus, 'in matters of action, truth or practical rectitude is not the same for all as to what is particular, but only as to common principles'.[59] In particular practical matters people may differ in their beliefs, and different beliefs may be appropriate in different cases. When practical reason deduces conclusions from general principles of natural law, or makes particular determinations of natural law, accuracy and certainty cannot always be expected.[60] I noted above the problem of the particular determination of the general principle of punishment. To this one could add the problems of the particular determination of, say, the education of children and the care of the mentally ill. As an example of the problem of deducing conclusions from general principles, Aquinas offers the following case. From the principle that all should act in accord with reason, it follows, as a conclusion, that goods entrusted to another should be restored to their owner. However, in particular cases it might be unreasonable to restore goods, if, for example, they were reclaimed for the pursuit of injurious purposes.[61]

Thus, in applying the natural law, by means of deduction or determination, to the particular cases of human life, practical reason requires the help of sound judgement. To make a sound judgement, as distinct from an arbitrary choice, one needs not only practical experience of politics, but also some objective foundation on which to base one's judgement, and some general principle to guide one's judgement. This is in accord with the point, made in the previous chapter, that political philosophy may inform and evaluate political practice, but, unlike ideology, is not a programme of action for immediate implementation. Political philosophy can be applied well in practice only by those with practical experience of politics. Without the guiding light of political philosophy, practical politicians may be misled by ideology into making arbitrary decisions. Michael Oakeshott, as noted in Chapter 3, argues for practical wisdom in politics as against ideological rationalism, or rationalist ideology. The problem with Oakeshott's position is that political judgement can rest on nothing but practical experience, and has no objective philosophical principles to guide it. Oakeshott's position is relativistic, and what he can offer as political judgement is no more than what Beiner refers to as arbitrary subjectivism, albeit the subjectivism of various traditions of politics.

In applying general normative principles to particular cases, practical reason will require not only the help of political judgement but also the advantage of prudence. Prudence is, for Aquinas, a virtue, which is 'a quality making its possessor good and rendering good what he does'. Prudence is, though, a special virtue, in that it is both intellectual and moral, concerned both with right reason and right appetite.[62] Prudence is the application of right reason to human conduct.[63] As the virtue which is in practical reason, prudence is concerned with the application of general principles to particular cases of human conduct. Prudence does not determine the right ends of human conduct, for this is the role of natural practical reason itself, but it arranges the appropriate means to ends.[64] Possession of prudence renders one habitually disposed to choosing the appropriate means to an end. Prudence, like other virtues, is not natural but, rather, learned, or produced by teaching and experience.[65]

Given the importance of prudence, and indeed the other virtues, for human conduct, there is a need for political philosophy to inform and support a culture in which the virtues can thrive. Political philosophy has an educative role. This role needs to be distinguished from the process of indoctrination, with which ideology might be associated. It is useful to recall, from the previous chapter, the distinction between ideology, which does not question its assumptions, and political philosophy, which offers rational arguments in public, and invites rational investigation of them.

CONCLUSION

The solution of the problem of non-rational, dogmatic, partial, distorting political ideology is rational political philosophy (or moral political science), which is capable of knowing the nature of politics and the good political order, and so capable of distinguishing proper and improper political values. Rational political philosophy must have an objective foundation, and this must be human nature and its objective needs. Political philosophy requires practical reason, which both knows the needs and goods of human nature, and can order this knowledge to ends and action. Practical reason requires both political judgement and prudence for the application of general normative principles to particular cases. A political philosophy which is founded on objective human nature, and which employs practical reason, political judgement and prudence, is sustained by the tradition of natural law theory. Moral realism, as found in the natural law tradition, is the solution of the moral relativism that is the main problem of political ideology.

Notes

1 THE STATE OF POLITICAL THEORY AND THE PROBLEM OF IDEOLOGY

1. P. Laslett (ed.), *Philosophy, Politics and Society*, First Series (Oxford, Blackwell, 1956), p. vii.
2. Ibid., p. ix.
3. Ibid., p. x.
4. A. Cobban, 'The Decline of Political Theory', *Political Science Quarterly*, 1953, vol. 63, no. 3. Cobban anticipates, with regret, the break with the long tradition of practical, normative political theory. D. Easton, *The Political System*, second edition (New York, Alfred Knopf, 1971) expresses concern about the difficulty of conducting constructive work in value theory on the basis of modern thought.
5. L. Strauss, *What is Political Philosophy?* (Chicago, University of Chicago Press, reprint 1988), p. 17. (The Hebrew version of the essay 'What is Political Philosophy?' was published in *Iyyun, Hebrew Philosophical Quarterly*, 1955, vol. 6, no. 2.)
6. Laslett, *Philosophy, Politics and Society*, First Series, pp. ix and x.
7. A.J. Ayer, *Language, Truth and Logic*, second edition (Harmondsworth, Penguin, 1971), p. 41.
8. Ibid., p. 148.
9. A.J. Ayer, 'The Vienna Circle', in A.J. Ayer *et al.*, *The Revolution in Philosophy* (London, Macmillan, 1956), p. 79.
10. A. Quinton (ed.), *Political Philosophy* (Oxford, Oxford University Press, 1967), p. 1.
11. Ibid., p. 3.
12. Ibid., p. 2.
13. T.D. Weldon, *The Vocabulary of Politics* (Harmondsworth, Penguin, 1953), p. 192.
14. Ibid., p. 19. A further example of the early application of linguistic analysis in political thought is provided by Margaret Macdonald, 'The Language of Political Theory', in A. Flew (ed.), *Logic and Language*, First Series (Oxford, Blackwell, 1951).
15. Strauss, *What is Political Philosophy?*, p. 26. Alfred Cobban argues that history has a 'fatal effect' on the ethical content of political theory because the 'historian naturally sees all ideas and ways of behaviour as historically conditioned and transient.' Cobban, 'The Decline of Political Theory', p. 333.
16. Strauss, *What is Political Philosophy?*, p. 26.
17. Ibid., pp. 25 and 26.
18. Ibid., p. 72.
19. Ibid., p. 66.
20. Easton, *The Political System*, pp. 236–7.

21. Ibid., p. 221.
22. Ibid., p. 220.
23. B. Magee (ed.), *Men of Ideas* (Oxford, Oxford University Press, 1982), p. 107.
24. Ibid., p. 107.
25. E. Gellner, *Words and Things* (Harmondsworth, Penguin, 1968), p. 249.
26. E. Kirkpatrick, 'From Past to Present', in D. Freeman (ed.), *Foundation of Political Science* (New York, The Free Press, 1977), p. 24.
27. R. Dahl, 'The Behavioural Approach in Political Science: Epitaph for a Monument to a Successful Protest', *American Political Science Review,* 1961, vol. 55, no. 4.
28. D. Kavanagh, *Political Science and Political Behaviour* (London, George Allen and Unwin, 1983), pp. 2–5.
29. Easton, *The Political System,* pp. 66–78.
30. See D. Easton, 'The Current Meaning of Behaviouralism', in J.C. Charlesworth (ed.), *Contemporary Political Analysis* (New York, Free Press, 1967), pp. 16–17, and Kirkpatrick, 'From Past to Present', pp. 22–3, for alternative but similar characterisations.
31. Smith says: 'Science is the geat antidote to the poison of enthusiasm and superstition.' A. Smith, *An Inquiry into the Nature and Causes of the Wealth of Nations,* ed. E. Cannan (New York, Random House, 1937), p. 748.
32. Easton, *The Political System,* pp. 323–48.
33. For an account of what he terms the 'belated impact of Marxism' on the study of British politics, see R. Berki, 'The Belated Impact of Marxism', in J. Hayward and P. Norton (eds), *The Political Science of British Politics* (Brighton, Wheatsheaf, 1986).
34. E. Shils, 'End of Ideology', in C. Waxman (ed.), *The End of Ideology Debate* (New York, Simon and Schuster, 1968).
35. D. Bell, *The End of Ideology,* revised edition (New York, The Free Press, 1961); S.M. Lipset, *Political Man* (London, Heinemann, 1960).
36. Bell, *The End of Ideology,* pp. 402–3; Lipset, *Political Man,* pp. 404–6.
37. Lipset, *Political Man,* p. 406.
38. Bell, *The End of Ideology,* pp. 400 and 402.
39. Ibid., p. 402.
40. Lipset, *Political Man,* p. 408.
41. Ibid., p. 403.
42. Bell, *The End of Ideology,* p. 403; Lipset, *Political Man,* pp. 415–17.
43. Lipset, *Political Man,* p. 417.
44. Ibid., p. 403.
45. Ibid., p. 415.
46. Bell, *The End of Ideology,* p. 405.
47. B. Goodwin, *Using Political Ideas,* third edition (Chichester, John Wiley, 1992), p. 26.
48. In Britain the consensus of the 1950s was termed 'Butskellism', thus indicating agreement between leading members of the two main political parties on main points of economic policy and the operation of the mixed economy and the welfare state. The term was coined during the period of the Conservative government of 1951–55 to

refer to the similar economic policies of the Conservative Chancellor of the Exchequer, R.A. Butler, and the previous Labour Chancellor, Hugh Gaitskell.

49. C.W. Mills, 'Letter to the New Left', Waxman (ed.), *The End of Ideology Debate*, p. 128.
50. Mills, 'Letter to the New Left', pp. 129 and 131.
51. A. MacIntyre, *Against the Self-Images of the Age* (London, Duckworth, 1971), p. 5.
52. Ibid., p. 10.
53. See K. Coates and R. Silburn, *Poverty: The Forgotten Englishmen* (Harmondsworth, Penguin, 1973). In Chapter 1, 'The Rediscovery of Poverty', Coates and Silburn note that even in the early 1950s Peter Townsend challenged the myth of affluence.
54. S.M. Lipset, *Political Man*, updated and expanded edition (London, Heinemann, 1983); D. Bell, 'The End of Ideology Revisited', parts 1 and 2, *Government and Opposition*, 1988, vol. 23, nos. 2 and 3.
55. F. Fukuyama, 'The End of History?', *The National Interest*, 1989, no. 16, p. 4. Fukuyama elaborates his thesis in *The End of History and the Last Man* (London, Hamish Hamilton, 1992).
56. Fukuyama, 'The End of History?', p. 3.
57. Ibid., p. 15.
58. Ibid., p. 18.
59. See the six 'Responses to Fukuyama', *The National Interest*, 1989, no. 16, pp. 19–35; various reviews of *The End of History and the Last Man* in *New Left Review*, 1992, no. 193; I. Adams, 'Can History Be Finished?', *Politics*, 1991, vol. 11, no. 2; T. Burns (ed.), *After History: Francis Fukuyama and his Critics* (Rowman and Littlefield, Lanham, Maryfield, 1994); J. McCarney, 'Reflections of Fukuyama', *New Left Review*, 1994, no. 202; and A. Ryan (ed.), *After the End of History* (London, Collins and Brown, 1992).
60. P. Laslett and W.G. Runciman (eds), *Philosophy, Politics and Society*, Second Series (Oxford, Blackwell, 1962), Introduction.
61. P. Laslett and W.G. Runciman (eds), *Philosophy, Politics and Society*, Third Series (Oxford, Blackwell, 1967), p. 3.
62. Ibid., p. 3.
63. J. Rawls, *A Theory of Justice* (Cambridge, Massachusetts, Harvard University Press, 1991).
64. J. Maritain, *Man and the State* (Chicago, University of Chicago Press, 1951); L. Strauss, *Natural Right and History* (Chicago, University of Chicago Press, 1953); E. Voegelin, *Order and History* (Baton Rouge, Louisiana State University Press, from 1956); B. Jouvenel, *Sovereignty*, trans. J. Huntingdon (Cambridge, Cambridge University Press, 1957); H. Arendt, *The Human Condition* (Chicago, University of Chicago Press, 1959); F. Hayek, *The Constitution of Liberty* (London, Routledge and Kegan Paul, 1960); M. Oakeshott, *Rationalism in Politics* (London, Methuen, 1962); H. Marcuse, *One Dimensional Man* (London, Routledge and Kegan Paul, 1964); and C.B. Macpherson, *Democratic Theory: Essays in Retrieval* (Oxford, Clarendon Press, 1973).

65. J. Rawls, 'Justice as Fairness', *The Philosophical Review,* 1958, vol. 57.
66. R. Nozick, *Anarchy, State and Utopia* (Oxford, Blackwell, 1974); R. Dworkin, *Taking Rights Seriously* (London, Duckworth, 1977); B. Ackerman, *Social Justice in the Liberal State* (New Haven, Yale University Press, 1980); and M. Walzer, *Spheres of Justice* (Oxford, Blackwell, 1985).
67. A. Ryan, 'The Ideologist of American Liberalism', *The Times Higher Education Supplement,* 8 October 1982, p. 18.
68. B. Parekh, *Contemporary Political Thinkers* (Oxford, Martin Robinson, 1982), p. 174.
69. Ibid., p. 186.
70. Ibid., p. 188.
71. Ibid., pp. 189 and 176. A similar criticism of the liberal ideological assumptions of Rawls is offered by Steven Lukes, 'Relativism: Cognitive and Moral', *The Aristotelian Society, Supplementary Volume,* 48, 1974, pp. 183–4. In *Political Liberalism* (New York, Columbia University Press, 1993) Rawls confirms that his theory of justice is now 'political and not metaphysical' (p. 10), and applicable to 'a modern constitutional democracy' (p. 11).

2 CONCEPTIONS OF IDEOLOGY: THE MARXIST TRADITION

1. The Macmillan series Key Concepts in Political Science, edited by Leonard Schapiro, and the more recent Open University series, Concepts in the Social Sciences, edited by Frank Parkin, contain the title *Ideology,* by John Plamenatz (London, 1970) and David McLellan (Milton Keynes, 1986), respectively. McLellan starts his book with the bold claim: 'Ideology is the most elusive concept in the whole of social science' (p. 1). Jorge Larrain starts his more comprehensive survey of the concept of ideology with the claim: 'Ideology is perhaps the most equivocal and elusive concept we can find in the social sciences.' See Jorge Larrain, *The Concept of Ideology* (London, Hutchinson, 1979), p. 13.
2. For more extensive accounts of conceptions of ideology see Larrain, *The Concept of Ideology*; Hans Barth, *Truth and Ideology* (Los Angeles, University of California Press, 1977); McLellan, *Ideology*; Plamenatz, *Ideology*; and T. Eagleton, *Ideology: An Introduction* (London, Verso, 1991).
3. R. Cox (ed.), *Ideology, Politics and Political Theory* (Belmont, California, Wandsworth Publishing, 1969), p.13.
4. Quoted in H. Drucker, *The Political Uses of Ideology* (London, Macmillan, 1974), p. 13. Drucker gives the date of Tracy's proposal as 23 May 1797. Emmet Kennedy gives the date as 20 June 1796. See E. Kennedy,'"Ideology" from Destutt de Tracy to Marx', *Journal of the History of Ideas,* 1979, vol. XL, no. 3, p. 354.
5. G. Lichtheim, 'The Concept of Ideology', *History and Theory,* 1965, vol. IV, no. 2, pp. 165–6.

6. Quoted in Cox (ed.), *Ideology, Politics and Political Theory*, pp.12–13.
7. F. Bacon, *Novum Organum*, Book 1, sections 38–44, in F. Bacon, *Essays Civil and Moral, Advancement of Learning, and Novum Organum*, ed. G. Bettany (London, Ward, Lock and Bowden, 1894).
8. Plato, *Republic*, III, 414–15. Trans. P. Shorley, in Plato, *Collected Dialogues*, ed. E. Hamilton and H. Cairns, (Princeton, Princeton University Press, 1980).
9. Plato, *Republic*, Book III, 414.
10. Plato, *Republic*, Book II, 382.
11. In a speech in Prussia in 1808 Napoleon says: '[The *Idéologues*] are dreamers and dangerous dreamers: they are all disguised materialists and not too disguised. Gentlemen, philosophers torment themselves to create systems; they will search in vain for a better one than Christianity, which in reconciling man with himself assures both public order and the peace of states. Your *idéologues* destroy all illusions, and the age of illusions is for individuals as for peoples the age of happiness.' Quoted in Kennedy, '"Ideology' from Destutt de Tracy to Marx', p. 359. In a later speech to the Council of State, made in 1812 on his return to France after defeat in the Russian campaign, Napoleon says: 'We must lay the blame for the ills that our fair France has suffered on ideology, that shadowy metaphysics which subtly searches for first causes on which to base the legislation of peoples, rather than making use of laws known to the human heart and of the lessons of history. These errors must inevitably and did in fact lead to the rule of bloodthirsty men. Indeed, who was it that proclaimed the principle of insurrection to be a duty? Who adulated the people and attributed to it a sovereignty which it was incapable of exercising? Who destroyed respect for and sanctity of laws by describing them, not as sacred principles of justice, but only as the will of an assembly of men ignorant of civil, criminal, administrative, political and military law?' Quoted in Kennedy, '"Ideology" from Destutt de Tracy to Marx', p. 360.
12. B. Parekh, 'Social and Political Thought and the Problem of Ideology', in R. Benewick *et al.* (eds), *Knowledge and Belief in Politics* (London, George Allen and Unwin, 1973), pp. 60–1.
13. Ibid., p. 57.
14. Ibid., p. 58.
15. Ibid., pp. 58–9.
16. Ibid., p. 58.
17. W.O. Martin, *Metaphysics and Ideology* (Milwaukee, Marquette University Press, 1959), pp. 57–8.
18. Parekh, 'Social and Political Thought', p. 59.
19. Ibid., p. 60.
20. Ibid., p. 60. In his account of the genesis of Marx's conception of ideology Parekh acknowledges his debt to Lichtheim, 'The Concept of Ideology'.
21. K. Mannheim, *Ideology and Utopia*, trans. E. Shils (London, Routledge and Kegan Paul, 1979), p. 66.
22. Ibid., p. 59.

23. Ibid., p. 60.
24. Marx, Preface to *A Contribution to the Critique of Political Economy,* in Karl Marx, *Early Writings,* ed. L. Colletti (Harmondsworth, Penguin, 1992 reprint), p. 425. This thesis is expressed in very similar terms in the earlier work, *The German Ideology*: 'It is not consciousness that determines life, but life that determines consciousness.' See Karl Marx, *Early Political Writings,* ed. J. O'Malley (Cambridge, Cambridge University Press, 1994), p. 125.
25. Marx, Preface to *A Contribution to a Critique of Political Economy,* p. 426.
26. Marx, *Theses on Feuerbach,* especially theses 1 and 3, in Marx, *Early Political Writings,* ed. O'Malley, pp. 116–17.
27. Engels, letter to J. Bloch, 21 September, 1890, in *Marx/Engels Selected Correspondence,* ed. S. Ryazanskaya, third revised edition (Moscow, Progress Publishers, 1975), pp. 394–5.
28. Marx, *A Contribution to the Critique of Hegel's Philosophy of Right: Introduction,* in Marx, *Early Political Writings,* ed. O'Malley, p. 57.
29. Marx and Engels, *The German Ideology,* pp. 124–5.
30. Engels, letter to Franz Mehring, 14 July 1893, in *Marx/Engels, Selected Correspondence,* p. 434. The translation here offers 'the wrong kind of consciousness' and not 'false consciousness', which is favoured by others. Elsewhere Engels refers to the 'ideological method' as the '*a priori* method, which consists in ascertaining the properties of an object not from the object itself but a logical deduction from the concept of the object'. F. Engels, *Anti-Duhring* (Peking, Foreign Languages Press, 1976), p. 120.
31. Marx, *Capital,* vol. III, trans. D. Fernbach (Harmondsworth, Penguin, 1981), p. 311.
32. Marx, *Capital,* vol. I, trans. and ed. D. Torr (London, George Allen and Unwin, 1957), chapter 29, p. 547.
33. See Marx, *Capital,* vol. I, chapter 1, section 4. For a clear account of the crucial role of commodity fetishism in Marx's theory of ideology, see John Mepham, 'The Theory of Ideology in *Capital*', in J. Mepham and D.-H. Ruben (eds), *Issues in Marxist Philosophy,* vol. 3 (Brighton, Harvester, 1974).
34. Marx, *Capital,* vol. I, chapter 1, section 4, p. 43.
35. J. Larrain, *Marxism and Ideology* (London, Macmillan, 1983), chapters 1 and 4; and Larrain, *The Concept of Ideology,* chapter 2.
36. Marx, *Capital,* vol. I, chapter 19, pp. 550–1. For an ironic account of the appearances of capitalist social relations see *Capital,* vol. I, chapter 6, penultimate paragraph, p. 155.
37. Ibid., vol. I, chapter 1, section 4, p. 46.
38. Marx and Engels, *The German Ideology,* p. 145.
39. Ibid., p. 146.
40. Marx, *Capital,* vol. III, chapter 48, p. 956.
41. Marx, *A Contribution to the Critique of Hegel's Philosophy of Right: Introduction,* p. 58, and Marx and Engels, *The German Ideology,* p. 137.
42. Marx, *Theses on Feuerbach,* 2, p. 116.
43. Larrain, *The Concept of Ideology,* pp. 13–14. A similar distinction be-

tween negative and positive or neutral conceptions of ideology appears earlier in E.H. Carr, *What is History?* (London, Macmillan, 1961) p. 133.

44. M. Seliger, *Ideology and Politics* (London, George Allen and Unwin, 1976), p. 14.
45. N. Abercrombie, *Class, Structure and Knowledge* (Oxford, Blackwell, 1980), p. 27.
46. Larrain, *Marxism and Ideology*, p. 64.
47. Lenin, *What is to be Done?*, ed. S. Utechin (Oxford, Clarendon Press, 1963), p. 71.
48. Ibid., p. 60.
49. Ibid., p. 63.
50. G. Lukács, *History and Class Consciousness*, trans. R. Livingstone (London, Merlin, 1971), p. 88.
51. Ibid., p. 103.
52. Ibid., pp. 98–9.
53. Ibid., p. xx, in a Preface prepared for a German edition of the work in 1967.
54. Ibid., p. 7. A similar notion of science as bourgeois ideology is developed later by Herbert Marcuse, who argues that modern science is necessarily involved in the exploitation and domination of humans. Modern science is structured for the domination and exploitation of nature and as such is employed in economic production. In modern industrial societies the dominant class manipulates the interests of the dominated, producing class, and then satisfies these by the provision of wanted, though not necessarily needed, goods. Their manipulated, false desires being thus satisfied (by the effort of their own labour, no less), the proletariat is fully assimilated to capitalism. Potential opposition is defused. Science's role in the exploitation of nature for the manufacture of goods which secure the unopposed exploitation of the proletariat makes it no more than ideology. See H. Marcuse, *One Dimensional Man* (London, Routledge and Kegan Paul, 1964).
55. Lukács, *History and Class Consciousness*, p. 64; see also pp. 27–8 and pp. 66–7.
56. Marx, *A Contribution to the Critique of Hegel's Philosophy of Right: Introduction*, p. 69.
57. Lukács, *History and Class Consciousness*, p. 149.
58. Ibid., p. 20.
59. Ibid., p. 41.
60. Ibid., p. xviii.
61. Ibid., pp. 50–1.
62. Marcuse offers a distinction between true and false consciousness, corresponding to his distinction between true and false needs and interests. See Marcuse, *One Dimensional Man*, Introduction and chapter 1.
63. See G.S. Jones, 'The Marxism of the Early Lukács', in New Left Review eds, *Western Marxism* (London, Verso, 1978), and R. McDonough, 'Ideology as False Consciousness: Lukács', in Centre for Contemporary Cultural Studies eds, *On Ideology* (London, Hutchinson, 1978).

64. Lukács, *History and Class Consciousness*, p. 21.
65. McDonough, 'Ideology as False Consciousness: Lukács', p. 43.
66. L. Kolakowski, *Main Currents of Marxism*, vol. 3 (Oxford, Oxford University Press, 1978), p. 282.
67. For a discussion of structure and superstructure, social formation, and complex structured whole, see particularly the essays 'Contradiction and Overdetermination' and 'On the Marxist Dialectic', in L. Althusser, *For Marx*, trans. B. Brewster (London, Verso, 1982). These topics are also dealt with by Althusser in his parts of *Reading Capital* (with Etienne Balibar), trans. Ben Brewster (London, Verso, 1983). A further practice, technical practice, is mentioned by Althusser, but need not be considered in this context; see Althusser, *Reading Capital*, p. 58.
68. Althusser, *For Marx*, p. 166.
69. Ibid., p. 167.
70. Althusser, *Lenin and Philosophy*, trans. B. Brewster (New York, Monthly Review Press, 1971), p. 171; Althusser, *For Marx*, p. 167.
71. Althusser, *For Marx*, pp. 167–8.
72. Ibid., p. 200; Althusser, *Reading Capital*, p. 58.
73. Althusser, *For Marx*, p. 113.
74. Althusser, *Reading Capital*, p. 97.
75. Ibid., p. 319: Althusser's addition to a glossary prepared by his translator Ben Brewster. These glossaries are particularly useful guides to Althusser's often opaque prose.
76. Althusser's treatment of overdetermination and uneven development is set out in the essays 'Contradiction and Overdetermination' and 'On the Marxist Dialectic', in *For Marx*.
77. See Althusser, 'Ideology and Ideological State Apparatuses', in *Lenin and Philosophy*, from which most of the following paragraph is drawn.
78. Althusser, *Lenin and Philosophy*, p. 173.
79. See Althusser, *For Marx*, p. 232.
80. Marx seems to argue that ideology exists in capitalist society because of the inverted nature of that society and the fetishism consequent on commodity production. In communist society, presumably, there will be neither inversion of society nor inversion of consciousness. It is not surprising that Althusser does not follow Marx in this, for Althusser holds the theory of fetishism to be ideological. See Althusser, *Essays in Self Criticism*, trans. G. Lock (London, New Left Books, 1976), p. 126.
81. Althusser, *Lenin and Philosophy*, p. 165.
82. Althusser, *For Marx*, p. 233.
83. Ibid., p. 231.
84. Ibid., p. 233.
85. Althusser, *Lenin and Philosophy*, p. 166.
86. Ibid., p. 171.
87. See Althusser, 'Introduction: Today', in *For Marx*.
88. See Althusser, *Reading Capital*, p. 141; Althusser seems to support Lenin's thesis against voluntarism.
89. Ibid., p. 133.

90. Ibid., p. 59.
91. N. Geras, *Literature of Revolution* (London, Verso, 1986), pp. 123 and 122.
92. Ibid., pp. 126–7.
93. Althusser, *Essays in Self Criticism*, pp. 119–20.
94. Ibid. p. 121.

3 CONCEPTIONS OF IDEOLOGY: THE NON-MARXIST TRADITION

1. The account of social facts given in this paragraph is drawn from E. Durkheim, *The Rules of Sociological Method*, trans. by W. Halls, ed. S. Lukes (London, Macmillan, 1982), chapter 1.
2. E. Durkheim, *Suicide*, trans. J. Spalding, ed. G. Simpson (London, Routledge and Kegan Paul, 1952).
3. The account of ideology given in this paragraph is drawn from Durkheim, *The Rules of Sociological Method*, chapter 2.
4. Durkheim, *The Rules of Sociological Method*, p. 60. At this point Durkheim's definition of ideology is similar to that of Engels who, as I noted in the previous chapter, equates the ideological method with the *a priori* method.
5. Durkheim, *The Rules of Sociological Method*, p. 162.
6. Ibid., p. 60 (my emphasis).
7. Ibid., p. 60.
8. E. Durkheim, *The Elementary Forms of Religious Life*, trans. J. Swain (London, Allen and Unwin, 1976), pp. 410 and 416.
9. Ibid., pp. 2–3.
10. Ibid., p. 10. Durkheim's argument that the categories of the understanding are social is not, I think, convincing and the example which he offers first for consideration, time, is particularly inappropriate. It is true, as Durkheim insists, that the concept and measure of time cannot be purely individual and subjective, and must be shared by all in society. It is true also that the 'divisions into days, weeks, months, years etc., correspond to the periodic recurrence of rites, feasts and public ceremonies'. (Ibid., p. 10.) But the standard divisions of time noted by Durkheim are not social in origin: they are natural. Nature sets the measure and division of time and societies follow this.
11. Ibid., p. 424.
12. Ibid., p. 427.
13. On this and other similarities between Durkheim and Althusser see S. Strawbridge, 'Althusser's Theory of Ideology and Durkheim's Account of Religion: An Examination of Some Striking Parallels', *Sociological Review*, 1982, vol. 30, no. 1.
14. Durkheim, *The Elementary Forms of Religious Life*, pp. 445 and 438.
15. V. Pareto, *Sociological Writings*, trans. D. Mirfin, ed. S. Finer (Oxford, Blackwell, 1976), p. 184.

16. Ibid., p. 185.
17. Ibid., p. 185.
18. Ibid., p. 196.
19. Pareto distinguishes economics as a 'general science of interests' which has progressed further than other social sciences because 'its concern is with logical actions'. Ibid., p. 196.
20. Ibid., p. 210 and pp. 216–17.
21. Ibid., p. 222.
22. Finer in Pareto, *Sociological Writings*, p. 84; J. Plamenatz, *Ideology* (London, Macmillan, 1971), pp. 24 and 124; J. Hallowell, *Main Currents in Modern Political Thought* (New York, University Press of America, reprint, 1984), p. 539; P. Winch, *The Idea of a Social Science and its Relation to Philosophy*, second edition (London, Routledge, 1990), p. 104.
23. Pareto, *Sociological Writings*, pp. 174, 194, 206–7, 216, 300.
24. Ibid., pp. 216 and 150.
25. Ibid., p. 194.
26. Ibid., pp. 169–72.
27. Ibid., p. 173.
28. Ibid., p. 181.
29. Ibid., p. 172.
30. Ibid., p. 201.
31. Hallowell, *Main Currents in Modern Political Thought*, p. 542.
32. K. Mannheim, *Ideology and Utopia*, trans. E. Shils (London, Routledge and Kegan Paul, reprint 1979), p. 87.
33. Ibid., p. 36.
34. Ibid., p. 36.
35. Ibid., pp. 50–1.
36. Ibid., p. 51.
37. Ibid., p. 51.
38. Ibid., p. 66.
39. Ibid., pp. 68–9.
40. Ibid., p. 69.
41. Ibid., p. 69.
42. Ibid., pp. 38–9 and 261.
43. Ibid., pp. 241–2; for further treatment of these two themes see the essays collected in K. Mannheim, *Essays on the Sociology of Knowledge*, ed. P. Kecskemeti (London, Routledge and Kegan Paul, 1972).
44. Mannheim, *Ideology and Utopia*, pp. 70 and 254.
45. Ibid., pp. 253–5.
46. Ibid., p. 134.
47. Ibid., p. 135.
48. Ibid., p. 137.
49. Ibid., p. 143.
50. A. Arblaster, 'Ideology and Intellectuals', in R. Benewick *et al.* (eds), *Knowledge and Belief in Politics* (London, George Allen and Unwin, 1973).
51. I. Mészáros, *Philosophy, Ideology and Social Science* (Brighton, Wheatsheaf, 1986), p. 36 (Mészáros's emphasis).

52. M. Oakeshott, *Rationalism in Politics* (London, Methuen, reprint 1981), p. 114.
53. Ibid., p. 115.
54. Ibid., p. 114.
55. Ibid., p. 115.
56. Ibid., p. 116.
57. Ibid.: see the essay 'Rationalism in Politics'.
58. Ibid., pp. 7–8.
59. Ibid., pp. 118–19.
60. Ibid., p. 125.
61. Ibid., p. 118.
62. Ibid., pp. 125 and 123.
63. Ibid., p. 125.
64. Ibid., p. 122.
65. Ibid., p. 121.
66. Ibid., p. 122.
67. Ibid., pp. 122 and 125.
68. Ibid., p. 125.
69. Ibid., p. 123 and 124. In his more recent and most substantial work of political philosophy, *On Human Conduct* (Oxford, Clarendon Press, 1975), Oakeshott introduces a new vocabulary and new categories, but the general thrust of his thought remains substantially unchanged. Human conduct is now structured within 'practices' rather than 'traditions'; practices are sets of, among other things, manners, uses, customs, standards, principles, and rules (p. 55); practices may be moral, concerned with human excellence or the human good, or prudential, concerned with some common, extrinsic purpose (pp. 60–2); moral rules are abridgements of moral practices (pp. 66–7); 'political activity' is now referred to as 'civil association', which is a moral practice (p. 122) and so distinct from the prudential practice of an enterprise association, which is a relationship in terms of the pursuit of a common, extrinsic purpose (p. 114); the authority of a civil association consists of the common recognition by its members of the rules which constitute 'respublica' (p. 149); politics is now narrowly defined as the consideration or exploration of the desirability of the conditions prescribed by respublica (pp. 163–4).
70. M. Oakeshott, *Experience and Its Modes* (Cambridge, Cambridge University Press, reprint 1985), pp. 49 and 27.
71. Ibid., p. 8.
72. Ibid., p. 50.
73. Ibid., p. 58.
74. Ibid., p. 27.
75. Ibid., p. 81.
76. Ibid., pp. 331 and 84. In a later essay, 'The Voice of Poetry in the Conversation of Mankind', reprinted in *Rationalism in Politics,* Oakeshott deals with what may be termed artistic or aesthetic experience.
77. Oakeshott, *Experience and Its Modes,* pp. 2 and 347.
78. Ibid., p. 82.
79. Ibid., pp. 83 and 3–4.

80. Ibid., p. 85.
81. Ibid., p. 79.
82. Ibid., p. 75.
83. Ibid., p. 316.
84. Ibid., p. 354.
85. Ibid., pp. 274–88.
86. Ibid., p. 278.
87. Ibid., p. 196.
88. Ibid., p. 350.
89. Ibid., p. 320.
90. Ibid., pp. 334–5.
91. Ibid., p. 344.
92. Oakeshott, *Rationalism in Politics,* pp. 132–3.
93. Oakeshott, *On Human Conduct,* p. 106.
94. Ibid., p. 176, and Oakeshott, *Rationalism in Politics,* p. 134.
95. Oakeshott, *Experience and its Modes,* p. 274.
96. Oakeshott, *Rationalism in Politics,* p. 128.
97. That Oakeshott's political philosophy entails conservatism is made explicit in his essay 'On Being Conservative', reprinted in *Rationalism in Politics.*

4 NATURALIST POLITICAL SCIENCE AND POLITICAL IDEOLOGY

1. For Popper's sustained critique of Marxism, see *The Open Society and its Enemies,* vol. 2, fifth edition (London, Routledge and Kegan Paul, 1966). See also his *The Poverty of Historicism,* second edition (London, Routledge and Kegan Paul, 1961), and *Unended Quest,* new edition with Postscript (London, Routledge, 1992), chapter 8.
2. Popper's account of falsification is set out in the opening chapers of the following books: *The Logic of Scientific Discovery* (London, Hutchinson, reprint 1980); *Conjectures and Refutations,* fourth edition (London, Routledge and Kegan Paul, reprint 1983) and *Objective Knowledge,* revised edition (Oxford, Clarendon Press, 1979).
3. Popper, *The Open Society and its Enemies,* vol. 2, p. 375.
4. Ibid., vol. 2, p. 369.
5. Ibid., vol. 2, p. 375.
6. Popper has always believed this, it seems, but the position is most fully articulated in *Objective Knowledge.*
7. Popper, *Objective Knowledge,* p. 74.
8. Ibid., p. 47.
9. Popper, *Unended Quest,* p. 116.
10. Popper, *The Open Society and its Enemies,* vol. 1, fourth edition (London, Routledge and Kegan Paul, 1962), p. 61.
11. Popper, *Unended Quest,* p. 194.
12. Popper, *The Open Society and its Enemies,* vol. 2, p. 386.
13. K. Popper, *Conjectures and Refutations,* p. vii.
14. Popper, *Unended Quest,* p. 87.

15. K. Popper, 'On Reason and the Open Society', *Encounter*, May 1972, p. 18. See also his *Conjectures and Refutations*, p. 357.
16. Popper, *The Open Society and its Enemies*, vol. 2, p. 381.
17. I. Lakatos, *The Methodology of Scientific Research Programmes, Philosophical Papers*, vol. 1, ed. J. Worrall and G. Curie (Cambridge, Cambridge University Press, 1978), p. 1.
18. Ibid., p. 1 and p. 7.
19. Ibid., pp. 5–6 and p. 8.
20. What follows in the next six paragraphs is largely a summary of Lakatos, *The Methodology*, pp. 10–52.
21. Ibid., p. 28.
22. Ibid., p. 29.
23. Lakatos fails to make clear where he feels he leaves Popper behind in order to break new ground, if, indeed, the latter is left behind.
24. Lakatos, *The Methodology*, p. 48; see also p. 110.
25. Ibid., p. 88.
26. Ibid., p. 86 (Lakatos's emphasis).
27. Ibid., p. 113.
28. Ibid., p. 76 and 113.
29. P. Feyerabend, 'Consolations for the Specialist', in I. Lakatos and A. Musgrave (eds), *Criticism and the Growth of Knowledge* (Cambridge, Cambridge University Press, 1970), p. 215.
30. T. Kuhn, 'Logic of Discovery or Psychology of Research', in Lakatos and Musgrave (eds), *Criticism and the Growth of Knowledge*, p. 1.
31. Feyerabend, 'Consolations for the Specialist', p. 198.
32. What follows in the next four chapters is largely a summary of T. Kuhn, *The Structure of Scientific Revolutions*, second edition (Chicago, University of Chicago Press, 1970), Chapters 2–9.
33. One of Kuhn's critics, Margaret Masterman, counts at least 21 different senses of the term in his *The Structure of Scientific Revolutions*; see M. Masterman, 'The Nature of a Paradigm', in Lakatos and Musgrave (eds), *Criticism and the Growth of Knowledge*, pp. 61–5.
34. Kuhn, *The Structure of Scientific Revolutions*, p. 92.
35. Ibid., p. 103.
36. Ibid., p. 94.
37. Ibid., p. 200.
38. E. Burke, *Reflections on the Revolution in France*, ed. C. O'Brien, (Harmondsworth, Penguin, 1968), p. 183.
39. T. Kuhn, 'Objectivity, Value Judgement and Theory Choice', in *The Essential Tension* (Chicago, University of Chicago Press, 1977). Kuhn seems convinced that criticism of him is based on misunderstanding.
40. Kuhn, 'Objectivity, Value Judgement and Theory Choice', p. 322. In 'Reflections on my Critics', in Lakatos and Musgrave (eds), *Criticism and the Growth of Knowledge*, p. 261, Kuhn refers to standard reasons for theory choice: 'accuracy, scope, simplicity, fruitfulness, and the like'.
41. Kuhn, 'Reflections on my Critics', p. 262.
42. Kuhn, 'Objectivity, Value Judgement and Theory Choice', p. 325.
43. Ibid., p. 335.

44. I. Lakatos, 'Falsification and the Methododology of Scientific Research Programmes', in Lakatos and Musgrave (eds), *Criticism and the Growth of Knowledge*, p. 178.
45. K. Popper, 'Replies to my Critics', in P. Schlipp (ed.), *The Philosophy of Karl Popper* (La Salle, Illinois, Open Court, 1974), p. 1111.
46. Kuhn, *The Structure of Scientific Revolutions*, p. 206. It would be wrong, however, to interpret Kuhn as a non-realist idealist. In 'Reflections on my Critics', p. 263, Kuhn states: 'no part of the argument here or in my book [*The Structure of Scientific Revolutions*] implies that scientists may choose any theory they like so long as they agree in their choice and therefore enforce it. Most of the puzzles of normal science are directly presented by nature and all involve nature indirectly.' Also, the notion of 'anomalies' makes sense only if they are thrown up by something other than the ruling paradigm.
47. For Kuhn, the explanation of scientific progress, in terms of paradigm shifts, 'must, in the final analysis, be psychological and sociological. It must, that is, be a description of a value system, an ideology, together with an analysis of the institutions through which that system is transmitted and enforced.' See Kuhn, 'Logic of Discovery or Psychology of Research', p. 21.
48. A. Ryan, '"Normal" Science or Political Ideology', in P. Laslett *et al.* (eds), *Philosophy, Politics and Society*, Fourth Series (Oxford, Basil Blackwell, 1972), p. 91. Ryan does not believe Kuhn's picture of science to be correct and does believe that social science can be distinguished from ideology. I agree with Ryan's conclusions, but not always with his arguments.
49. P. Feyerabend, *Science in a Free Society* (London, New Left Books, 1978), p. 106.
50. P. Feyerabend, *Against Method* (London, Verso, 1975), p. 295.
51. Feyerabend, *Science in a Free Society*, p. 7.
52. Ibid., p. 13.
53. Feyerabend, *Against Method*, title page and p. 28.
54. P. Feyerabend, 'How to Defend Society Against Science', *Radical Philosophy*, 1978, no. 11, p. 6.
55. Feyerabend, *Against Method*, p. 29.
56. Ibid., p. 48, note 2.
57. Ibid., p. 55.
58. Ibid., p. 284.
59. Ibid., p. 302.
60. Ibid., p. 284.
61. Ibid., p. 21, note 12.
62. Feyerabend, *Science in a Free Society*, p. 83.
63. Ibid., p. 79.
64. K. Popper, *The Poverty of Historicism*, pp. 131 and 130.
65. T. Kuhn, *The Structure of Scientific Revolutions*, p. 208.
66. Popper, *The Open Society and its Enemies*, vol. 2, Addenda, pp. 369–96.

5 NON-NATURALIST AND REALIST POLITICAL SCIENCE AND POLITICAL IDEOLOGY

1. Such arguments are offered by K. Popper, *The Poverty of Historicism*, second edition (London, Routledge and Kegan Paul, 1961), pp. 137–8; T. Abel, 'The Operation Called Verstehen', *American Journal of Sociology*, 1948, vol. 54, pp. 211–18; and C. Hempel, *Aspects of Scientific Explanation and Other Essays in the Philosophy of Science* (New York, The Free Press, 1965), pp. 239–40.
2. A very useful survey of the variety and development of the non-naturalist concepts of interpretation, understanding and *Verstehen* is provided by W. Outhwaite, *Understanding Social Life: The Method Called Verstehen* (London, George Allen and Unwin, 1975). A more difficult work, which covers similar and other material, is J. Habermas, *On the Logic of the Social Sciences*, trans. S. Nicholson and J. Stark (Cambridge, Polity, 1988).
3. P. Winch, *The Idea of a Social Science and its Relation to Philosophy*, second edition (London, Routledge, 1990). The book was first published in 1958.
4. William Outhwaite says: 'Winch's *Idea of a Social Science* has interested philosophers, and social scientists in their more reflective moments, but it has had little practical effect on social research, except perhaps to encourage certain trends in social anthropology which were already well established – in particular, the "indiscriminately charitable" attitude to alien beliefs which Ernest Gellner criticised in his important article, "Concepts and Society".' W. Outhwaite, *Understanding Social Life: The Method Called Verstehen*, p. 108. Gellner's article is reprinted in his *Cause and Meaning in the Social Sciences* (London, Routledge and Kegan Paul, 1973).
5. Winch, *The Idea of a Social Science*, p. 136.
6. Ibid., pp. 45–6.
7. Ibid., p. 52.
8. Ibid., p. 58. The trouble with Winch's claim, as critics have pointed out, is that it does not seem to make much sense to talk of the right or wrong way of doing certain things like going for a walk. See A. MacIntyre, *Against the Self Images of the Age* (London, Duckworth, 1971), p. 218.
9. There are similarities between Oakeshott's contextual analysis of civil association, noted in Chapter 3 above, and Winch's conceptual analysis of meaningful behaviour. Winch notes the coincidence of much of his own and Oakeshott's views on human behaviour, but notes also a crucial difference: for Oakeshott it is the case 'that most human behaviour can be adequately described in terms of the notion of *habit* or *custom* and that neither the notion of a rule nor that of reflectiveness is essential to it'. Winch, *The Idea of a Social Science*, pp. 54–65; quote is from p. 57 (Winch's emphasis).
10. Ibid., p. 116.
11. Ibid., p. 121.
12. Ibid., p. 72; but see also pp. 94 and 95 for similar remarks.

13. Ibid., pp. 8–9.
14. Winch says: 'philosophy, conceived as the study of the nature of man's understanding of reality, may be expected to illuminate the nature of human interrelations in society'. Ibid., p. 40.
15. Ibid., p. 128.
16. Ibid., p. 113.
17. Ibid., p. 92.
18. Ibid., pp. 84–7.
19. Interestingly, Winch, writing in 1958, comments that writers on scientific methodology tend to overlook the importance of this second relationship. Since the publication of Thomas Kuhn's *The Structure of Scientific Revolutions* in 1962, and the subsequent growth of the sociology and history of science, such a comment is out of place.
20. A. Giddens, *New Rules of Sociological Method* (London, Hutchinson, 1976), p. 162.
21. Winch, *The Idea of a Social Science*, p. 87.
22. Ibid., p. 89.
23. Ibid., p. 46.
24. Ibid., p. 110.
25. P. Winch, 'Understanding a Primitive Society', in B. Wilson (ed.), *Rationality* (Oxford, Blackwell, 1970), p. 89.
26. Winch, *The Idea of a Social Science*, p. 108 (Winch's emphasis).
27. For criticism of Winch see: Giddens, *New Rules of Sociological Method*, pp. 44–51; A. Ryan, *The Philosophy of the Social Sciences* (London, Macmillan, 1970), especially chapter 7; A. MacIntyre, 'The Idea of a Social Science' and 'Is Understanding Religion Compatible with Believing?', in Wilson (ed.), *Rationality*; E. Gellner, 'Winch's Idea of a Social Science' and 'The New Idealism – Cause and Meaning in the Social Sciences', in *Cause and Meaning in the Social Sciences*; A.R. Louch, 'The Very Idea of a Social Science', *Inquiry*, 1963, vol. 6, no. 4, pp. 273–86; P. Mattick, *Social Knowledge* (London, Hutchinson, 1986); R. Bhaskar, *The Possibility of Naturalism* (Brighton, Harvester, 1979), pp. 169–95.
28. Bhaskar, *The Possibility of Naturalism*, p. 173, p. 169, p. 2 and p. 3.
29. For a critical discussion of Winch on this matter see MacIntyre, 'The Idea of a Social Science'.
30. Winch, *The Idea of a Social Science*, p. xii.
31. Winch, 'Understanding a Primitive Society', p. 95.
32. MacIntyre, *Against the Self-Images of the Age*, pp. 228–9. MacIntyre acknowledges that if one accepts the more plausible claim that one can go beyond the self-description of a society only after one has understood the concepts embodied therein, then cross-cultural study is possible but difficult.
33. Winch, 'Understanding a Primitive Society', p. 81; Winch's emphasis.
34. Gellner, *Cause and Meaning in the Social Sciences*, p. 58 and p. 69.
35. Winch, *The Idea of a Social Science*, p. 15; Winch, 'Understanding a Primitive Society', p. 82.
36. Winch, *The Idea of a Social Science*, p. 15.
37. Ibid., p. 100; see also p. 126: 'It will seem less strange that social

relations should be like logical relations between propositions once it is seen that logical relations between propositions themselves depend on social relations between men.'

38. P. Winch, 'Nature and Convention', *Proceedings of the Aristotelian Society*, 1959–60, vol. 60, p. 238.
39. Ibid., p. 235; P. Winch, *Trying to Make Sense* (Oxford, Blackwell, 1987), p. 192.
40. Winch, *Trying to Make Sense*, pp. 188–9.
41. Winch, 'Nature and Convention', p. 242.
42. Winch, 'Understanding a Primitive Society', p. 99.
43. Winch, 'Nature and Convention', p. 250; Winch, 'Understanding a Primitive Society', p. 99.
44. C. Taylor, *Philosophy and the Human Sciences: Philosophical Papers*, vol. 2, (Cambridge, Cambridge University Press, 1985), p. 1.
45. Ibid., p. 3.
46. Ibid., p. 8.
47. Ibid., pp. 117–18 and 123.
48. Ibid., p. 118.
49. An argument about the problems of maintaining distinctions between agents' reasons and causally effective reasons, and between false and true consciousness, on the basis of Winch's distinction of understanding and causal explanation is offered by MacIntyre, *Against the Self-Images of the Age*, p. 217.
50. Taylor, *Philosophy and the Human Sciences*, pp. 126 and 131.
51. Ibid. p. 125.
52. Ibid., pp. 125–26.
53. Ibid., p. 131.
54. Ibid., pp. 148–51; quote is from p. 149 (Taylor's emphasis).
55. For a critique of Taylor's relativism, see Hartmut Rosa, 'Goods and Life Forms: Relativism in Charles Taylor's Political Philosophy', *Radical Philosophy*, May/June 1995, no. 71, pp. 20–6.
56. Winch, *The Idea of a Social Science*, p. 102 (Winch's emphasis).
57. R. Bhaskar, *A Realist Theory of Science*, second edition (Hassocks, Harvester, 1978); *The Possibility of Naturalism*; *Scientific Realism and Human Emancipation* (London, Verso, 1986); *Reclaiming Reality* (London, Verso, 1989).
58. Bhaskar, *Scientific Realism and Human Emancipation*, p. 5.
59. Ibid., p. 5.
60. Ibid., p. 6 (Bhaskar's emphasis).
61. Bhaskar, *A Realist Theory of Science*, p. 29.
62. Bhaskar, *Reclaiming Reality*, p. 14; Bhaskar, *A Realist Theory of Science*, p. 10.
63. Bhaskar, *A Realist Theory of Science*, p. 56.
64. Ibid., p. 35 and p. 47.
65. Ibid., p. 59 and p. 57.
66. Ibid., p. 21.
67. Bhaskar, *Reclaiming Reality*, p. 183.
68. Bhaskar, *Scientific Realism and Human Emancipation*, p. 25.
69. Bhaskar, *A Realist Theory of Science*, p. 249. In subsequent writings Bhaskar refers to epistemic relativity.

70. Bhaskar, *Scientific Realism and Human Emancipation*, pp. 51–2.
71. Bhaskar, *A Realist Theory of Science*, p. 249.
72. Bhaskar, *The Possibility of Naturalism*, p. 73; Bhaskar's emphasis.
73. Bhaskar, *Scientific Realism and Human Emancipation*, p. 92.
74. Bhaskar, *A Realist Theory of Science*, pp. 24–5.
75. Ibid., p. 16.
76. Ibid., p. 10.
77. Bhaskar, *Scientific Realism and Human Emancipation*, pp. 56–61.
78. Bhaskar, *A Realist Theory of Science*, p. 25.
79. Bhaskar, *The Possibility of Naturalism*, p. 3.
80. Ted Benton argues that Bhaskar's limits are such that he offers not so much qualified naturalism as anti-naturalism. T. Benton, 'Realism and Social Science: Some Comments on Roy Bhaskar's "The Possibility of Naturalism"', in R. Edgley and R. Osborne (eds), *Radical Philosophy Reader* (London, Verso, 1985), p. 189.
81. Bhaskar, *The Possibility of Naturalism*, pp. 48–9.
82. Ibid., pp. 39–47.
83. Ibid., p. 173 (Bhaskar's emphasis).
84. Ibid., pp. 65–6.
85. Ibid., p. 66.
86. Ibid., pp. 57–8.
87. Ibid., p. 59.
88. Bhaskar, *Scientific Realism and Human Emancipation*, p. 134.
89. Ibid., p. 177.
90. Ibid., p. 178.
91. Bhaskar, *A Realist Theory of Science*, p. 249.
92. R. Trigg, *Understanding Social Science* (Oxford, Blackwell, 1985), p. 109.
93. Bhaskar, *The Possibility of Naturalism*, p. 67.
94. Ibid., pp. 66–7 and 83–91.
95. Ibid., p. 178.
96. Ibid., p. 81.
97. Bhaskar, *Scientific Realism and Human Emancipation*, p. 170 (Bhaskar's emphasis).
98. Ibid., p. 170.
99. Ibid., p. 170.
100. Ibid., p. 170.
101. Ibid., pp. 202 and 171.
102. Ibid., p. 207.
103. Ibid., p. 208.
104. Ibid., p. 187.

6 A CRITIQUE OF VALUE-FREE POLITICAL SCIENCE

1. N. Machiavelli, *The Prince*, trans. G. Bull (Harmondsworth, Penguin, 1961), p. 91.
2. Machiavelli's political ends are discussed by John Plamenatz, *Man and Society*, revised edition (London, Longman, 1992), vol. 1, pp. 78–81.

3. F. Bacon, *The Advancement of Learning,* ed. A. Johnston (Oxford, Clarendon Press, 1974), p. 157.
4. A. Quinton, *Francis Bacon* (Oxford, Oxford University Press, 1980), p. 70.
5. Ibid., p. 49.
6. M. Weber, *From Max Weber,* trans. and ed. H. Gerth and C. Wright Mills (London, Routledge and Kegan Paul, 1948), p. 145.
7. Ibid., p. 146.
8. Ibid., p. 147.
9. Ibid., p. 148.
10. M. Weber, *The Methodology of the Social Sciences,* trans. and ed. E. Shils and H. Finch (New York, The Free Press, 1949), p. 16. Elsewhere Weber refers (in translation at least) to 'two fundamentally differing and irreconcilably opposed maxims': the 'ethic of ultimate ends' and the 'ethic of responsibility'; *From Max Weber,* p. 120.
11. Weber, *The Methodology of the Social Sciences,* p. 21.
12. Ibid., p. 76 (Weber's emphasis).
13. On this final subpoint, it is interesting to note that there seems to be little fear that facts will influence values. It is with reference to such a possibility that Charles Taylor offers his critique of ethical neutrality in political science. Taylor argues that 'a given framework of explanation in political science tends to support an associated value position, secretes its own norms for the assessment of polities and policies'; this because 'in setting out a given framework, a theorist is also setting out the gamut of possible polities and policies. But a *political* framework cannot fail to contain some, even implicit, conception of human needs, wants and purposes. The context of this conception will determine the value-slope of the gamut'; and this because 'that something is conducive to human happiness, or in general to the fulfilment of human needs, wants, and purposes, is a *prima facie* reason for calling it good.' Charles Taylor, *Philosophy and the Human Sciences: Philosophical Papers,* vol. 2 (Cambridge, Cambridge University Press, 1985), pp. 81 and 89 (Taylor's emphasis).
14. For criticism of Strauss, see S. Drury, *The Political Ideas of Leo Strauss* (London, Macmillan, 1988); S. Holmes, *The Anatomy of Antiliberalism* (Cambridge, Mass., Harvard Univeristy Press, 1993), pp. 61–87; E.B.F. Midgley, *The Ideology of Max Weber* (Aldershot, Gower, 1983), chapter 1.
15. L. Strauss, *What is Political Philosophy?* (Chicago, University of Chicago Press, reprint 1988), p. 10.
16. Ibid., p. 12.
17. Machiavelli, *The Prince,* p. 99.
18. Ibid., p. 100.
19. J. Maritain, *The Range of Reason* (London, Geoffrey Bles, 1953), p. 137 (Maritain's emphasis).
20. Ibid., p. 141.
21. Ibid., p. 148.
22. J. Hallowell, 'Politics and Ethics', *American Political Science Review,* 1944, vol. 38, no. 4, p. 644.
23. Weber, *The Methodology of the Social Sciences,* p. 11.

24. Ibid., p. 39.
25. Strauss, *What is Political Philosophy?*, p. 89.
26. Weber, *The Methodology of the Social Sciences*, p. 21.
27. Ibid., p. 22.
28. Ibid., p. 84.
29. L. Strauss, *The Rebirth of Classical Political Rationalism* (Chicago, University of Chicago Press, 1989), p. 19. Strauss is summarising Lukács's argument in *The Destruction of Reason*.
30. R. Dahrendorf, *Essays in the Theory of Society* (London, Routledge and Kegan Paul, 1968), pp. 6. and 7.
31. Ibid., p. 10.
32. Dahrendorf refers his readers to Karl Popper, *The Open Society and its Enemies*, vol. 2, pp. 260–1, where Popper writes of the necessity of selectivity for objectivity. In *The Logic of Scientific Discovery*, eleventh impression, revised (London, Hutchinson, 1983), p. 31, Popper writes: 'the work of the scientist consists in putting forward and testing theories. The initial stage, the act of conceiving or inventing a theory, seems to me neither to call for logical analysis nor to be susceptible to it. . . . As to the task of the logic of knowledge – in contradistinction to the psychology of knowledge – I shall proceed on the assumption that it consists solely in investigating the methods employed in those systematic tests to which every new idea must be subjected.'
33. Dahrendorf, *Essays in the Theory of Society*, p. 6. In Chapter 4, I noted that Popper is unable to establish the rationality and objectivity of science because he is unable to justify the choice of reason as the characteristic of science.
34. Strauss, *What is Political Philosophy?*, p. 22.
35. H. Lasswell and M. Kaplan, *Power and Society* (New Haven, Yale University Press, 1950), p. xiv.
36. St. Augustine, *Concerning The City of God Against the Pagans*, trans. H. Bettenson, ed. D. Knowles (Harmondsworth, Penguin, 1972), p. 139. There is much discussion and disagreement about St Augustine's intended meaning in this famous sentence. It seems that St Augustine, in rejecting Cicero's definition of the state in terms of a common acknowledgement of justice, wishes both to deny that pagan states could practise true justice, which involves giving God his due, and to accept that pagan states are nevertheless states. In this case, states without justice are states and yet no different from bands of robbers, except in terms of size. Immediately after the sentence quoted, St Augustine asks: 'What are criminal gangs but petty kingdoms?' However, St Augustine probably conceives of more or less perfect earthly states, and believes that the greater the justice of a state, the more perfect it is.
37. S. Lukes, *Power: A Radical View* (London, Macmillan, 1974), p. 15 (Lukes's emphasis). Lukes identifies this one-dimensional view of power in such works as R. Dahl, *Who Governs? Democracy and Power in an American City* (New Haven, Yale University Press, 1961), and N. Polsby, *Community Power and Political Theory* (New Haven, Yale University Press, 1963). Lukes notes that the one-dimensional view of power is associated

with pluralist theories of the distribution of power.

38. Lukes, *Power: A Radical View*, pp. 16–20. Lukes identifies the two-dimensional view of power in various pieces by P. Bachrach and M. Baratz: 'The Two Faces of Power', *American Political Science Review*, 1962, vol. 56; 'Decisions and Nondecisions: An Analytic Framework', *American Political Science Review*, 1963, vol. 57; and *Power and Poverty: Theory and Practice* (Oxford, Oxford University Press, 1970). Lukes notes that the two-dimensional view of power is associated with a critique of the pluralist theory of the distribution of power.
39. Lukes, *Power: A Radical View*, pp. 24–5 (Lukes's emphasis).
40. Ibid., p. 9.
41. Hallowell, 'Politics and Ethics', p. 652.
42. Ibid., pp. 652–3.
43. D. Easton, 'The Current Meaning of Behaviouralism', in J. Charlesworth (ed.), *Contemporary Political Analysis* (New York, The Free Press, 1967), p. 16.
44. A. MacIntyre, *Against the Self-Images of the Age* (London, Duckworth, 1971), p. 278.
45. Ibid., p. 278.
46. An argument which makes a similar point, but in a different way, with a greater emphasis on historicism, is presented by Strauss, *What is Political Philosophy?*, pp. 25–6.
47. Ibid., p. 22.
48. L. Strauss, *Natural Right and History*, (Chicago, University of Chicago Press, 1953), pp. 97–8.
49. Weber, *The Methodology of the Social Sciences*, p. 12.
50. Ibid., p. 13.
51. Strauss, *What is Political Philosophy?*, p. 23.
52. Thomas Kuhn offers 'accuracy, consistency, scope, simplicity and fruitfulness' as characteristics of a good theory. T. Kuhn, *The Essential Tension* (Chicago, University of Chicago Press, 1977), p. 332. I argue in Chapter 4 that Kuhn is unable to justify these as objective values: they are, rather, subject to change, much as paradigms are. I note above in the present chapter that Kuhn shares with Weber the notion of science directed by the prevailing values of the age.
53. E. Voegelin, *The New Science of Politics* (Chicago, University of Chicago Press, 1952), p. 21.
54. Hallowell, 'Politics and Ethics', p. 647.
55. D. Easton, *The Political System*, second edition (New York, Alfred Knopf, 1971), p. 359.
56. Weber, *The Methodology of the Social Sciences*, p. 5.
57. Ibid., p. 11.
58. Weber, *From Max Weber*, p. 143. Elsewhere, Weber writes: 'The *objective* validity of all empirical knowledge rests exclusively upon the ordering of the given reality according to categories which are *subjective* in a specific sense, namely in that they present the presuppositions of our knowledge and are based on the presuppositions of the *value* of these *truths* which empirical knowledge alone is able to give us. The means available to our science can offer nothing to

those persons to whom the truth is of no value. It should be remembered that the belief in the value of scientific truth is the product of certain cultures and is not a product of man's original nature.' Weber, *The Methodology of the Social Sciences*, p. 110 (Weber's emphasis).
59. I note in Chapter 4 that for Popper science is based on a value, a human decision, which science cannot justify.
60. Strauss, *What is Political Philosophy?*, p. 19. A similar point is made by Hallowell, 'Politics and Ethics', p. 648.
61. Hallowell, 'Politics and Ethics', p. 654.
62. C.A. McCoy and J. Playford (eds), *Apolitical Politics: A Critique of Behavioralism* (New York, Thomas Y. Crowell, 1967), p. 5.
63. J.S. Mill, *Collected Works*, vol. 10, ed. J.M. Robson (Toronto, University of Toronto Press, 1969), p. 80.
64. L. Strauss, *Liberalism Ancient and Modern* (Ithaca, Cornell University Press, reprint 1989), p. 221.
65. Strauss, *Natural Right and History*, p. 4.
66. Voegelin, *The New Science of Politics*, p. 5.
67. Strauss, *What is Political Philosophy?*, p. 23.
68. Ibid., pp. 24–5.
69. Ibid., p. 14.

7 CONTEMPORARY CONFUSION OF POLITICAL PHILOSOPHY AND POLITICAL IDEOLOGY

1. The most important essays are collected in J. Tully (ed.), *Meaning and Context: Quentin Skinner and His Critics* (Cambridge, Polity, 1988), which also contains a bibliography of Skinner's principal publications on pp. 342–4.
2. Q. Skinner, 'Some Problems in the Analysis of Political Thought and Action', in Tully (ed.), *Meaning and Context*, p. 104.
3. Q. Skinner, 'Meaning and Understanding in the History of Ideas', in Tully (ed.), *Meaning and Context*, p. 32.
4. The remainder of this paragraph summarises the arguments of Skinner, ibid., pp. 32–48.
5. Ibid., p. 50.
6. Ibid., p. 51.
7. Ibid., p. 55.
8. Ibid., p. 64 (Skinner's emphasis).
9. Ibid., p. 65.
10. Ibid., p. 63. The term 'illocutionary force' is that of J.L. Austin. Skinner refers his readers to Austin's *How to Do Things With Words*, ed. J.O. Urmson (Oxford, Oxford University Press, 1962).
11. It is interesting to note, however, that Skinner has been criticised for failing to heed his own methodological advice in the writing of his major work, *The Foundations of Modern Political Thought*, 2 vols (Cambridge, Cambridge University Press, 1978). For a brief summary of such criticism, see Cary Nederman, 'Quentin Skinner's State: Historical Method and Traditions of Discourse', *Canadian Journal of Political*

Science, 1985, vol. XVIII, no. 2, pp. 339–41.
12. Skinner, 'Some Problems in the Analysis of Political Thought and Action', p. 108.
13. Ibid., p. 99.
14. K. Minogue, 'Method in Intellectual History: Quentin Skinner's *Foundations*', in Tully (ed.), *Meaning and Context*, p. 189.
15. Skinner, 'Some Problems in the Analysis of Political Thought and Action', p. 103. Skinner refers his readers to his 'Motives, Intentions and the Interpretation of Texts', in Tully (ed.), *Meaning and Context*, pp. 68–78.
16. See Skinner, '"Social Meaning" and the Explanation of Social Action', in Tully (ed.), *Meaning and Context*, pp. 79–98.
17. Ibid., p. 93.
18. Ibid., p. 94.
19. Skinner, 'Meaning and Understanding in the History of Ideas', p. 66 and 67.
20. The quotation is from R. Ashcraft, 'Political Theory and the Problem of Ideology', *The Journal of Politics*, 1980, vol. 42, no. 3, p. 691. For a bibliography of some of Ashcraft's relevant works, see his 'Rethinking the Nature of Political Theory: A Single Handed Defence of a Dialogue', *The Journal of Politics*, 1982, vol. 44, no. 2, p. 577. To Ashcraft's list I should wish to add his 'On the Problem of Methodology and the Nature of Political Theory', *Political Theory*, 1975, vol. 3, no. 1.
21. Ashcraft, 'On the Problem of Methodology and the Nature of Political Theory', p. 20. The fundamental difference between Ashcraft and Skinner seems to lie with their attitudes to Marxism. Skinner says that 'it is a commonplace – we are all Marxists to this extent – that our own society places unrecognised constraints upon our imaginations'. Skinner, 'Meaning and Understanding in the History of Ideas', p. 67. Such a commonplace is not, of course, distinctly Marxist, and it is clear that Skinner, in investigating the history of ideas, does not employ a distinctly Marxist analysis, which is materialist and dialectical. Rather, Skinner employs, as I have noted, an analysis which borrows most from linguistic analysis. Ashcraft, on the other hand, considers Marxism to be a theoretical paradigm which is adequate at both the 'scientific' and 'political' levels. Ashcraft, 'On the Problem of Methodology and the Nature of Political Theory', p. 15 and p. 24, note 17.
22. Ashcraft, 'Political Theory and the Problem of Ideology', p. 703.
23. Ibid., p. 687.
24. Ibid., p. 690.
25. Ashcraft, 'On the Problem of Methodology and the Nature of Political Theory', p. 6.
26. Ibid., p. 20.
27. R. Ashcraft, 'Whose Problem? Whose Ideology? A Reply to my Critics', *The Journal of Politics*, 1980, vol. 42, no. 3, p. 721.
28. J. Nelson, 'Ashcraft's Problem of Ideology', *The Journal of Politics*, 1980, vol. 42, no. 3, p. 712.

29. Ashcraft, 'Whose Problem? Whose Ideology? A Reply to my Critics'.
30. D. Germino, 'Comment on Ashcraft's "Political Theory and the Problem of Ideology"', *The Journal of Politics*, 1980, vol. 42, no. 3, p. 707.
31. L. Strauss, *What is Political Philosophy?* (Chicago, University of Chicago Press, 1988), p. 56.
32. S. Caney, 'Liberalism and Communitarianism: a Misconceived Debate', *Political Studies*, 1992, vol. 40, no. 2, pp. 273–89. Caney summarises the communitarian claims on pp. 273–4.
33. M. Walzer, *Spheres of Justice* (Oxford, Basil Blackwell, 1985), p. xiv.
34. M. Walzer, *The Company of Critics* (London, Peter Halban, 1988), p. ix.
35. M. Walzer, 'Philosophy and Democracy', *Political Theory*, 1981, vol. 9, no. 3, pp. 394–5.
36. Ibid., p. 397.
37. Walzer, *The Company of Critics*, p. ix.
38. M. Walzer, *Interpretation and Social Criticism* (Cambridge, Mass., Harvard University Press, 1987), p. 20.
39. Ibid., p. 64.
40. Ibid., p. 40 and p. 61.
41. R. Dworkin, *A Matter of Principle* (London, Duckworth, 1985), pp. 17 and 219–20.
42. R. Rorty, *Objectivity, Relativism and Truth; Philosophical Papers, Volume 1* (Cambridge, Cambridge University Press, 1991), p. 197; see also pp. 176–9.
43. Ibid., p. 177; p. 198. The claim that John Rawls is, like Rorty himself, a nonfoundational liberal is controversial because Rawls's *A Theory of Justice* is a main target of contemporary communitarian criticism. However, Rawls's *Political Liberalism* (New York, Columbia University Press, 1993), which brings together much of the work he has done since the publication of *A Theory of Justice*, confirms the substantial concessions he has made to his communitarian critics.
44. Rorty, *Objectivity, Relativism and Truth*, p. 198.
45. S. White, *Political Theory and Postmodernism* (Cambridge, Cambridge University Press, 1991), p. 4.
46. J.-F. Lyotard, *The Postmodern Condition: A Report on Knowledge* (Manchester, Manchester University Press, 1984), p. xxiii.
47. R. Rorty, *Essays on Heidegger and Others: Philosophical Papers, Volume 2* (Cambridge, Cambridge University Press, 1991), p. 1.
48. R. Rorty, *Objectivity, Relativism and Truth*, pp. 207–8; see also R. Rorty, *Contingency, Irony, and Solidarity* (Cambridge, Cambridge University Press, 1989), p. 44. Rorty argues that the idea that liberal culture needs a foundation 'was a result of Enlightenment scientism, which was in turn a survival of the religious need to have human projects underwritten by nonhuman authority'. R. Rorty, *Contingency, Irony, and Solidarity* , p. 52.
49. Rorty, *Objectivity, Relativism and Truth*, pp. 1, 6 and 13.
50. Ibid., p. 13.
51. R. Rorty, 'Human Rights, Rationality and Sentimentality', in S. Shute and S. Hurley (eds), *On Human Rights: The Oxford Amnesty Lectures*

1993 (New York, Basic Books, 1993), p. 118.
52. Rorty, *Objectivity, Relativism and Truth,* p. 1.
53. Ibid., p. 33.
54. Ibid., p. 13.
55. Rorty, *Contingency, Irony and Solidarity,* p. 189, and Rorty, *Objectivity, Relativism and Truth,* p. 208.
56. Rorty, *Objectivity, Relativism and Truth,* p. 30.
57. See for example: Rorty, *Objectivity, Relativism and Truth,* p. 29, and Rorty, *Contingency, Irony and Solidarity,* p. 198.
58. R. Bernstein, *The New Constellation* (Cambridge, Polity, 1991), p. 239.
59. Rorty, *Objectivity, Relativism and Truth,* p. 214; and R. Rorty 'Thugs and Theorists: A Reply to Bernstein', *Political Theory,* 1987, vol. 15, no. 4, p. 565.
60. Rorty, 'Human Rights, Rationality and Sentimentality', p. 117.
61. R. Rorty, 'Feminism and Pragmatism', *Radical Philosophy,* 1991, no. 59, p. 4 (Rorty's emphasis).
62. Rorty, *Objectivity, Relativism and Truth,* p. 198.
63. Rorty, 'Feminism and Pragmatism', p. 12, note 18; Rorty, 'Thugs and Theorists', p. 578, note 23; and Rorty, *Essays on Heidegger,* p. 1.
64. Rorty, *Objectivity, Relativism and Truth,* p. 34, and Rorty, 'Human Rights, Rationality and Sentimentality', p. 118.
65. Rorty, 'Human Rights, Rationality and Sentimentality', p. 116.
66. Rorty, *Objectivity, Relativism and Truth,* p. 2.
67. Ibid., p. 203.
68. Ibid., pp. 14 and 204.
69. Ibid., p. 190.
70. Ibid., p. xiii.
71. Ibid., p. 209.
72. Ibid., p. 192.
73. Ibid., p. 13.
74. Ibid., pp. 23–4 (Rorty's emphasis).
75. Rorty, *Contingency, Irony and Solidarity,* p. 44.
76. Ibid., p. 50.
77. Rorty, *Objectivity, Relativism and Truth,* p. 29. For further concessions of circularity see Rorty, *Contingency, Irony and Solidarity,* pp. 57, 73 and 197.
78. Bernstein, *The New Constellation,* p. 272
79. Ibid., p. 233.
80. L. Strauss, 'The Crisis of Our Time', in H. Spaeth (ed.), *The Predicament of Modern Politics* (Detroit, University of Detroit Press, 1964), p. 41.
81. Ibid., pp. 43 and 44.
82. Ibid., p. 41.
83. Ibid., p. 49.
84. Ibid., p. 47.
85. Ibid., p. 49.
86. Ibid., p. 49.
87. Rorty, 'Feminism and Pragmatism', p. 4. Rorty also recommends dropping 'the distinction between rational judgement and cultural bias'. Rorty, *Objectivity, Relativism and Truth,* pp. 207–8.

88. Rorty, *Contingency, Irony, and Solidarity*, p. 59, note 15.

8 A CRITIQUE OF RELATIVISM IN POLITICAL THOUGHT

1. J. Gunnell, 'Relativism: The Return of the Repressed', *Political Theory*, 1993, vol. 21, no. 4, pp. 565 and 563.
2. W. Newton-Smith, *The Rationality of Science* (London, Routledge and Kegan Paul, 1981), p. 35.
3. B. Barnes and D. Bloor, 'Relativism, Rationalism and the Sociology of Knowledge', in M. Hollis and S. Lukes (eds), *Rationality and Relativism* (Oxford, Blackwell, 1982), pp. 22–3.
4. Barnes and Bloor, 'Relativism, Rationalism and the Sociology of Knowledge', pp. 22–3.
5. Ibid., pp. 23.
6. B. Williams, *Ethics and the Limitis of Philosophy* (London, Collins/Fontana Press, 1985), p. 156. Here Williams revises his earlier claims about the truth of moral relativism contained in 'The Truth in Relativism', *Proceedings of the Aristotelian Society*, 1974–75, new series, vol. LXXV.
7. K. Popper, *The Open Society and its Enemies*, vol. 2, fifth edition, revised (London, Routledge and Kegan Paul, 1977), p. 369.
8. Hollis and Lukes, 'Introduction', *Rationality and Relativism*, pp. 11–12.
9. For a critical account of cultural relativism, see N. Koertge, 'Beyond Cultural Relativism', in G. Currie and A. Musgrave (eds), *Popper and the Human Sciences* (Dordrecht, Martinus Nijhoff, 1985), pp. 121–31.
10. R. Trigg, *Reason and Commitment* (Cambridge, Cambridge University Press, 1973), p. 25.
11. W.J. Stankiewicz, *Aspects of Political Theory: Classical Concepts in an Age of Relativism* (London, Cassell and Collier-Macmillan, 1976), p. 128.
12. See Williams, 'The Truth in Relativism' and his later qualification of the argument in *Ethics and the Limits of Philosophy*, chapter 9; and S. Lukes, 'Relativism: Cognitive and Moral', *Proceedings of the Aristotelian Society*, 1974, supplementary vol. XLVIII.
13. M. Weber, *From Max Weber*, trans. and ed. H. Gerth and C. Wright Mills (London, Routledge and Kegan Paul, reprint 1970), p. 143.
14. Ibid., pp. 150–1. Elsewhere Weber writes: 'the discussion of value-judgements can have only the following functions: a) The elaboration and explication of the ultimate, internally "consistent" value-axioms, from which the divergent attitudes are derived . . . b) The deduction of "implications" (for those accepting certain value-judgements) which follow from certain irreducible value-axioms, when the practical evaluation of factual situations is based on these axioms alone . . . c) The determination of the factual consequences which the realisation of a certain practical evaluation must have: (1) in consequence of being bound to certain indispensable means; (2) in consequence of the inevitability of certain, not directly desired repercussions'. Weber, *The Methodology of the Social Sciences*, trans. and

ed. E. Shils and H. Finch (New York, The Free Press, reprint 1968), pp. 20–1.
15. Weber, *From Max Weber*, p. 151 (Weber's emphasis).
16. L. Strauss, *Natural Right and History* (Chicago, University of Chicago Press, 1953), pp. 3–4.
17. S. Lukes, 'The Critical Theory Trip', *Political Studies*, 1977, vol. 25, no. 3, p. 408.
18. S. Lukes, 'On the Social Determination of Truth', in M. Gibbons (ed.), *Interpreting Politics* (Oxford, Blackwell, 1987), p. 68.
19. D. Davidson, 'On the Very Idea of a Conceptual Scheme', in J. Rajchman and C. West (eds), *Post-Analytic Philosophy* (New York, Columbia University Press, 1985), p. 130.
20. R. Trigg, *Reality at Risk* (Hemel Hempstead, Harvester/Wheatsheaf, 1980), p. 109.
21. K. Mannheim, *Ideology and Utopia*, trans. E. Shils (London, Routledge and Kegan Paul, reprint 1979), p. 256.
22. Lukes, 'On the Social Determination of Truth', p. 69.
23. Barnes and Bloor, 'Relativism, Rationalism and the Sociology of Knowledge', p. 21.
24. See B. Barnes, *Scientific Knowledge and Sociological Theory* (London, Routledge and Kegan Paul, 1974), B. Barnes, *Interests and The Growth of Knowledge* (London, Routledge and Kegan Paul, 1977), and D. Bloor, *Knowledge and Social Imagery* (London, Routledge and Kegan Paul, 1976).
25. Barnes and Bloor, 'Relativism, Rationalism and the Sociology of Knowledge', p. 28.
26. R. Aron, *Main Currents in Sociological Thought*, vol. 2 (Harmondsworth, Penguin, 1970), pp. 105–6 (Aron's emphasis).
27. W. Brandon, "Fact" and "Value" in the Thought of Peter Winch: Linguistic Analysis Broaches Metaphysical Questions', *Political Theory*, 1982, vol. 10, no. 2, p. 235.
28. G. Grisez, *Beyond the New Theism* (Notre Dame, University of Notre Dame Press, 1975), p. 221. Whereas Grisez refers to 'irreducibly diverse and untranscendably limited principles', I refer to contexts or circumstances and the standards or beliefs relative to them.
29. M. Mandelbaum, 'Subjective, Objective and Conceptual Relativisms', in J. Meiland and M. Krausz (eds), *Relativism Cognitive and Moral* (Notre Dame, University of Notre Dame Press, 1982), pp. 34–61, especially pp. 37 and 39.
30. M. Hesse, *Revolutions and Reconstructions in the Philosophy of Science* (Brighton, Harvester, 1980), p. 42.
31. S. Lukes, 'Some Problems about Rationality', in B. Wilson (ed.), *Rationality* (Oxford, Blackwell, 1970); Lukes, 'Relativism: Cognitive and Moral'; S. Lukes, 'Relativism in its Place', in Hollis and Lukes (eds), *Rationality and Relativism*; Lukes, 'On the Social Determination of Truth', M. Hollis, 'The Limits of Irrationality' and 'Reason and Ritual', in Wilson (ed.), *Rationality*; M. Hollis, 'The Social Destruction of Reality', in Hollis and Lukes (eds), *Rationality and Relativism*.

32. Lukes, 'Relativism in its Place', p. 262.
33. This account of Lukes's argument derives from his 'Relativism: Cognitive and Moral'.
34. The first two points are made by Barnes and Bloor, 'Relativism, Rationalism and the Sociology of Knowledge', pp. 36 and 39; the third point is made by M. Hesse, *Revolutions and Reconstructions in the Philosophy of Science,* pp. 38–9.
35. Lukes, 'Relativism in its Place', p. 272.
36. Lukes, 'Relativism: Cognitive and Moral', p. 172.
37. S. Lukes, *Power: A Radical View* (London, Macmillan, 1974), p. 34.
38. Lukes, 'Relativism: Cognitive and Moral', pp. 174–5.
39. Ibid., pp. 178 and 177. Lukes refers his readers to the classic original article on this matter: W. Gallie, 'Essentially Contested Concepts', *Proceedings of the Aristotelian Society,* 1955–56, vol. LVI.
40. Lukes, 'Relativism: Cognitive and Moral', pp. 185–8.
41. H. Kelsen, 'Absolutism and Relativism in Philosophy and Politics', *American Political Science Review,* 1948, vol. 42, p. 911.
42. Popper, *The Open Society and its Enemies,* vol. 2, p. 377.
43. L. Kolakowski, *Main Currents of Marxism,* vol. 3 (Oxford, Oxford University Press, 1978), p. 417.
44. B. Russell, *Philosophy and Politics* (London, National Book League / Cambridge University Press, 1947), pp. 24, 21, and 20.
45. P. Winch, *Trying to Make Sense* (Oxford, Blackwell, 1987), pp. 190–91 (Winch's emphasis).
46. B. Williams, *Morality: An Introduction to Ethics* (Harmondsworth, Penguin, 1973), pp. 34–9; see also Williams, *Ethics and the Limits of Philosophy,* p. 159.
47. K. Popper, *The Open Society and its Enemies,* vol.1, fourth edition, revised (London, Routledge and Kegan Paul, 1962), p. 265.
48. E. Gellner, *Relativism and the Social Sciences* (Cambridge, Cambridge University Press, 1985), p. 84.
49. K. Soper, 'A Theory of Human Need', *New Left Review,* January/February 1993, no. 197, p. 115.
50. F. Oppenheim, 'Relativism, Absolutism, and Democracy', *American Political Science Review,* 1950, vol. 44, p. 953. Oppenheim also notes that there is no logical link between philosophical relativism and democracy. A relativist, *qua* relativist, is free to choose as best any sort of political system; see pp. 954–5.
51. Trigg, *Reason and Commitment,* p. 136.
52. Williams, 'The Truth in Relativism'; see also Williams, *Ethics and the Limits of Philosophy,* chapter 9.
53. Williams, *Ethics and the Limits of Philosophy,* p. 162.
54. Ibid., p. 163.
55. Williams, 'The Truth in Relativism', p. 227.

9 DEMARCATING POLITICAL PHILOSOPHY AND POLITICAL IDEOLOGY

1. M. Seliger, *Ideology and Politics* (London, George Allen & Unwin, 1976), p. 14.
2. Ibid., p. 99. Seliger elaborates this formal structure in chapter 3 of his book.
3. Ibid., p. 115.
4. Ibid., pp. 16 and 112.
5. Ibid., pp. 156–7.
6. Ibid., p. 115.
7. Ibid., pp. 20–1 and p. 44.
8. Ibid., p. 15.
9. D. McLellan, *Ideology* (Milton Keynes, Open University Press, 1986), p. 82.
10. A. Giddens, 'Four Theses on Ideology', *Canadian Journal of Political and Social Theory*, 1983, vol. 7, nos. 1–2, p. 18 (Giddens's emphasis).
11. Ibid., p. 19 (Giddens's emphasis).
12. Ibid., pp. 20 and 19.
13. J. McCarney, *The Real World of Ideology* (Brighton, Harvester, 1980), p. 80.
14. Ibid., p. 99.
15. Cited in ibid., pp. 84 and 85.
16. Ibid., p. 86. McCarney's re-translation may be no more accurate than the usual translation. The use of the definite article in such a phrase in German is ambiguous and so the phrase is open to the alternative translations noted. For this information I am grateful to my colleague Dr Brian Barton.
17. Y. Simon, *The Tradition of Natural Law*, ed. V. Kuic (New York, Fordham University Press, 1965), p. 18.
18. E.B.F. Midgley, *The Natural Law Tradition and the Theory of International Relations* (London, Elek, 1975), pp. 235 and 514, note 15. For an account of the ideological distortion of the life sciences see Z. Medvedev, *The Rise and Fall of T.D. Lysenko* (New York, Doubleday, 1968), and D. Lecourt, *Proletarian Science? The Case of Lysenko* (London, New Left Books, 1977.)
19. Simon, *The Tradition of Natural Law*, p. 22.
20. R. Ashcraft, 'Political Theory and the Problem of Ideology', *The Journal of Politics*, 1980, vol. 42, no. 3, p. 695.
21. L. Strauss, *What is Political Philosophy?* (Chicago, University of Chicago Press, reprint 1988), p. 12.
22. Joseph Owens, in distinguishing true philosophy from ideology, argues: 'From the philosophical viewpoint the basic question centers on whether the human mind in some way provides the content of its ideas, or whether it itself and its concepts have rather the role of instruments for directly knowing things external to itself. The fundamental issue in the confrontation is whether reality or human ideas come first. From the manner in which that underlying metaphysical problem is solved will emerge the respective ways in which ideology

on the one hand, and traditional 'right reason' on the other, are brought to bear upon the organization and direction of human conduct.' 'Ideology and Aquinas', in V. Brezik (ed.), *Thomistic Papers 1* (Houston, Texas, Center for Thomistic Studies, University of St Thomas, 1984), p. 138.

23. Simon, *The Tradition of Natural Law,* p. 17 (Simon's emphasis).
24. F. Copleston, 'Philosophy and Ideology', in A. Parel (ed.), *Ideology, Philosophy and Politics* (Waterloo, Ontario, Wilfrid Laurier University Press, 1983), pp. 29 and 30.
25. L. Feuer, *Ideology and the Ideologists* (Oxford, Blackwell, 1975), pp. 187–8.
26. B. Goodwin, *Using Political Ideas,* third edition (Chichester, John Wiley, 1992), p. 29.
27. Ibid., p. 29.
28. Simon, *The Tradition of Natural Law,* p. 17 (Simon's emphasis).
29. Ibid., p. 20 (Simon's emphasis).
30. W. Oliver Martin, *Metaphysics and Ideology* (Milwaukee, Marquette University Press, 1959), pp. 8–9.
31. Feuer, *Ideology and the Ideologists,* p. 190.
32. Strauss, *What is Political Philosophy?* , p. 11.
33. Feuer, *Ideology and the Ideologists,* p. 188.
34. Copleston, 'Philosophy and Ideology', p. 32.
35. D. Germino, *Beyond Ideology: The Revival of Political Theory* (Chicago, University of Chicago Press, reprint 1976), pp. 42 and 43.
36. Martin, *Metaphysics and Ideology,* p. 28.
37. See ibid., pp. 9–27.
38. See ibid., pp. 27–33.
39. See ibid., pp. 34–43.
40. Germino, *Beyond Ideology,* p. 44.
41. Simon, *The Tradition of Natural Law,* p. 18.
42. Germino, *Beyond Ideology,* p. 37.
43. Ibid., p. 39.
44. Copleston, 'Philosophy and Ideology', p. 20.
45. A. Hacker, *Political Theory: Philosophy, Ideology and Science* (New York, Macmillan, 1961), p. 5.
46. Germino, *Beyond Ideology,* p. 37.
47. Ashcraft, 'Political Theory and the Problem of Ideology', p. 691. Ashcraft's selective quotation of Germino and Strauss presents a misleading picture of their respective views. According to Ashcraft, 'Dante Germino writes, "I am quite deliberately omitting major consideration of ideas directly related to the everyday political struggle" because "the study of political theory and philosophy has other concerns".' Ashcraft, 'Political Theory and the Problem of Ideology', p. 691. Ashcraft refers to D. Germino, *Machiavelli to Marx: Modern Western Political Thought* (Chicago, University of Chicago Press, 1972), p. vii (and not p. vvi as cited by Ashcraft). What Germino also says, but Ashcraft does not quote, is: 'This does not mean, of course, that I attach little importance to the study of public opinion and the popular literature of political life. . . . But the study of political theory

and philosophy has other concerns than the examination of literature conceived in the language and style of any particular political struggle. One of the advantages of studying less popular – because more theoretical and systematic – writings is that they help bring into focus the assumptions and limitations of popular journalism.' Germino, *Machiavelli to Marx,* pp. vii–viii. Thus, Germino makes it clear that political philosophy may be said to transcend political ideology (including journalism) on a theoretical level, but not by removing itself from the concerns of politics, which is the subject matter of the discipline. Ashcraft continues: 'Strauss adheres to this view [the view of political philosophy which Ashcraft mistakenly attributes to Germino], adding that "the teaching of the classics can have no immediate practical effect" in our society.' Ashcraft, 'Political Theory and the Problem of Ideology', p. 691. Ashcraft refers to L. Strauss, 'On a New Interpretation of Plato's Political Philosophy', *Social Research,* 1946, vol. 13, no. 3, p. 332. Again Ashcraft misleads by selective quotation. Elsewhere Strauss makes it very clear that 'it is not self-forgetting and pain-loving antiquarianism nor self-forgetting and intoxicating romanticism which induces us to turn with unqualified willingness to learn, toward the political thought of classical antiquity. We are impelled to do so by the crisis of our time, the crisis of the West.' Strauss continues: 'Only we living today can possibly find a solution to the problem of today. But an adequate understanding of the principles as elaborated by the classics may be the indispensable starting point for an adequate analysis, to be achieved by us, of present day society in its peculiar character, and for the wise application, to be achieved by us, of those principles to our tasks.' L. Strauss, *The City and Man* (Chicago, University of Chicago Press, 1978), pp. 1, 7 and 11.

48. R.B. Douglass and G. Marfin, 'The Political Role of Political Philosophy: A Reply to Richard Ashcraft', *The Journal of Politics,* 1982, vol. 44, no. 2, p. 574.
49. Strauss, *What is Political Philosophy?* , p. 16.
50. Ibid., p. 229 and p. 221.
51. L. Strauss, *Persecution and the Art of Writing* (Glencoe, Illinois, The Free Press, 1952), pp. 34–5. Strauss perhaps demonstrates his own hidden or esoteric style by attributing the notion of tension between political philosophy and politics to earlier, pre-modern writers. Given Strauss's support of the Ancients against the Moderns, it is fairly clear that he accepts the notion of the tension.
52. Strauss, *What is Political Philosophy?,* p. 222.
53. Shadia Drury notes Strauss's elitism and conservatism in *The Political Ideas of Leo Strauss* (London, Macmillan, 1988), p. 16. Stephen Holmes notes Strauss's inequalitarianism and the 'illiberal nature of his elitism' in *The Anatomy of Antiliberalism* (Cambridge, Massachusetts, Harvard University Press, 1993), pp. 70 and 75.
54. L. Strauss, *Natural Right and History* (Chicago, University of Chicago Press, 1953), p. 92.
55. Strauss, *Natural Right and History,* p. 52.

56. E.B.F. Midgley, 'Concerning the Modernist Subversion of Political Philosophy', *The New Scholasticism*, 1979, vol. 53, no. 2, p. 175.
57. Germino, *Beyond Ideology*, p. 38.
58. Ibid., p. 41 and p. 42.
59. Copleston, 'Philosophy and Ideology', p. 25.
60. Douglass and Marfin, 'The Political Role of Political Philosophy', p. 575.

10 RATIONAL POLITICAL PHILOSOPHY

1. John Wild argues that it is moral realism, the thesis that 'certain moral norms are grounded on nature, not merely on human decree . . . that binds together the various strands [of natural law theory] into a single tradition and which radically separates them from the subjectivist schools of modern thought'. J. Wild, *Plato's Modern Enemies and the Theory of Natural Law* (Chicago, University of Chicago Press, 1953), p. 105.
2. C.B. Macpherson, 'Hobbes's Bourgeois Man', in K. Brown (ed.), *Hobbes Studies* (Oxford, Blackwell, 1965), pp. 170 and 180.
3. L. Doyal and I. Gough, *A Theory of Human Need* (London, Macmillan, 1991), chapter 2.
4. Ibid., p. 33.
5. C.B. Macpherson, *The Rise and Fall of Economic Justice* (Oxford, Oxford University Press, 1985), pp. 55–6.
6. C.B. Macpherson, *Democratic Theory: Essays in Retrieval* (Oxford, Clarendon Press, 1973), p. 198.
7. Ibid., p. 202.
8. See ibid., pp. 8–11 and 40–2; p. 182; and 62. For a fuller discussion of Macpherson's critique of capitalism, see D. Morrice, 'C.B. Macpherson's Critique of Liberal Democracy and Capitalism', *Political Studies*, 1994, vol. 42, no. 4, pp. 646–61.
9. Macpherson, *Democratic Theory*, p. 38.
10. C.B. Macpherson, 'Needs and Wants: An Ontological or Historical Problem?', in. R. Fitzgerald (ed.), *Human Needs and Politics* (Rushcutters Bay, NSW, Pergamon, 1977), p. 34 (Macpherson's emphasis).
11. Macpherson, *Democratic Theory*, p. 34.
12. G. Grisez, 'The Structures of Practical Reason', *The Thomist*, 1988, vol. 52, pp. 278–9.
13. Doyal and Gough, *A Theory of Human Need*, Chapter 4. The quotation is from p. 54.
14. Macpherson, *Democratic Theory*, pp. 4 and 54.
15. Ibid., p. 54.
16. St Thomas Aquinas, *Summa Theologiae*, Sub-part I of Part II, question 94, article 3. All subsequent references to the *Summa Theologiae* follow this standard pattern, but in abbreviated notation. Where the reference is not to the body of the article, but to a response to a numbered objection, the abbreviation 'ad' is used. The translation used throughout is that in A. Pegis (ed.), *Basic Writings of Saint Thomas*

Aquinas, 2 vol. (New York, Random House, 1945).
17. Aquinas, *Summa Theologiae*, I-II, q. 94, a. 3, ad 2.
18. Ibid., I-II, q. 94, a. 2.
19. See R. McInerny, 'Ethics', in N. Kretzman and E. Stump (eds), *The Cambridge Companion to Aquinas* (Cambridge, Cambridge University Press, 1993), p. 211.
20. G. Grisez, J. Boyle and J. Finnis, 'Practical Principles, Moral Truth, and Ultimate Ends', *American Journal of Jurisprudence*, 1987, vol. 32, pp. 107–8. Their disclaimer about the adequacy of their theory appears on p. 150. Some clarification of this account of human goods is presented in J. Finnis, 'Natural Law and Legal Reasoning', in R. George (ed.), *Natural Law Theory: Contemporary Essays* (Oxford, Clarendon Press, 1992), p. 135. In a number of publications over the past three decades, Grisez and Finnis, together with others, have advanced an important, if controversial, account of natural law. The seminal article is G. Grisez, 'The First Principle of Practical Reason: A Commentary on the *Summa Theologiae*, 1–2, Question 94, Article 2', *Natural Law Forum*, 1965, vol. 10. Important subsequent publications include J. Finnis, *Natural Law and Natural Rights* (Oxford, Clarendon Press, 1980), and G. Grisez, *The Way of the Lord Jesus*, vol. 1, *Christian Moral Principles* (Chicago, Franciscan Herald Press, 1983). The article by Grisez, Boyle and Finnis, noted above, offers a recent reformulation and summary of the theory, and takes account of criticisms. It contains an annotated bibliography of some of the authors' publications.
21. Aquinas, *Summa Theologiae*, I-II, q. 94, a. 3.
22. R. McInerny, *Ethica Thomistica* (Washington, DC, The Catholic University of America Press, 1982), p. 46.
23. Finnis, *Natural Law and Natural Rights*, p. 92.
24. Finnis, 'Natural Law and Legal Reasoning', pp. 135 and 136.
25. McInerny, *Ethica Thomistica*, pp. 32, 58, 59 and 33.
26. K. Nielsen, 'An Examination of the Thomistic Theory of Natural Moral Law', *Natural Law Forum*, 1959, vol. 4, p. 59 (Nielsen's emphasis). D.J. O'Connor makes a similar case. He asserts: 'Any form of a natural-law theory of morals entails the belief that propositions about man's duties and obligations can be inferred from propositions about his nature.' He continues: 'It is often held by contemporary philosophers that there is a general logical objection to any doctrine of this kind, an objection first clearly formulated by David Hume.' D.J. O'Connor, *Aquinas and Natural Law* (London, Macmillan, 1967), pp. 68 and 69.
27. D. Hume, *A Treatise of Human Nature*, second edition ed. L.A. Selby-Bigge, revised by P.H. Nidditch (Oxford, Oxford University Press, 1978), p. 469.
28. For some of the important contributions to the debate, see W.D. Hudson (ed.), *The Is–Ought Question* (London, Macmillan, 1969).
29. Hume, *A Treatise of Human Nature*, p. 457.
30. Ibid., p. 415.
31. Ibid., p. 468 (Hume's emphasis).

32. H. Veatch, 'Natural Law and the "Is"–"Ought" Question', *The Catholic Lawyer*, 1981, vol. 26, pp. 251 and 258.
33. V. Bourke, 'Natural Law, Thomism – And Professor Nielsen', *Natural Law Forum*, vol. 5, 1960, p. 118.
34. St Thomas Aquinas, *Summa Contra Gentiles*, book 3, chap. 2. The translation used is that in Pegis (ed.), *Basic Writings of St. Thomas Aquinas.*
35. Aquinas, *Summa Contra Gentiles*, book 3, chap. 3.
36. Aquinas, *Summa Theologiae*, I, q. 5, a. 1. See also I, q. 79, a. 11, ad 2., where Aquinas argues that truth and good include one another.
37. Ibid., I, q. 79, a. 11.
38. Ibid., I-II, q. 94, a. 4, and I, q. 14, a. 16.
39. Ibid., I-II, q. 57, a. 5, ad 3.
40. Aquinas, *Summa Contra Gentiles*, book 3, chap. 26; see also, *Summa Theologiae*, I, q. 82, a. 3 and a. 4.
41. Aquinas, *Summa Theologiae*, I-II, q. 94, a. 2.
42. Nielsen, 'An Examination of the Thomistic Theory of Natural Law', p. 54, and O'Connor, *Aquinas and Natural Law*, p. 43.
43. R. Hittinger, 'Varieties of Minimalist Natural law Theory', *American Journal of Jurisprudence*, 1989, vol. 34, p. 159.
44. Grisez, Boyle, and Finnis, 'Practical Principles, Moral Truth, and Ultimate Ends', p. 102.
45. Ibid., p. 111.
46. L. Weinreb, *Natural Law and Justice* (Cambridge, Massachusetts, Harvard University Press, 1987). The phrase quoted is the title of Chapter 4 of Weinreb's book, in which he criticises, among others, Finnis, *Natural Law and Natural Rights.*
47. Grisez, Boyle, and Finnis, 'Practical Principles, Moral Truth, and Ultimate Ends', p. 111.
48. Ibid., p. 127.
49. Finnis, 'Natural Law and Legal Reasoning', p. 135.
50. Grisez, 'The First Principle of Practical Reason', p. 194.
51. Commenting on Grisez's seminal article, 'The First Principle of Practical Reason', Brian Midgley says the author makes a 'deep division between practical and theoretical reason', and 'he seems to accept Hume's position concerning the lack of a relation between "is" and "ought"'. E.B.F. Midgley, *The Natural Law Tradition and the Theory of International Relations* (London, Elek, 1975), pp. 237 and 238. Commenting on the work of Finnis and Grisez, Ralph McInerny says their 'excessive distinction of value from fact . . . renders dubious the interpretation of practical reason'. McInerny, *Ethica Thomistica*, p. 50.
52. Aquinas, *Summa Theologiae*, I-II, q. 95, a. 1.
53. Ibid., I-II, q. 91, a. 3.
54. Ibid., I-II, q. 95, a. 2.
55. McInerny, *Ethica Thomistica*, p. 102.
56. R. Beiner, *Political Judgement* (London, Methuen, 1983), p. 2.
57. R. Beiner, review of P. Steinberger, *The Concept of Political Judgment*, in *Political Theory*, 1994, vol. 22, no. 4, p. 688.
58. Beiner, *Political Judgement*, pp. 110–11.
59. Aquinas, *Summa Theologiae*, I-II, q. 94, a. 4.

60. Ibid., I-II, q. 91, a. 3, ad 3; see also I-II, q. 96, a. 1, ad 3.
61. Ibid., I-II, q. 94, a. 4.
62. Ibid., II-II, q. 47, a. 4.
63. Ibid., II-II, q. 47, a. 2.
64. Ibid., II-II, q. 47, a. 6, and a. 7.
65. Ibid., II-II, q. 47, a. 15.

Bibliography

Abel, T., 'The Operation Called Verstehen', *American Journal of Sociology*, 1948, vol. 54.
Abercrombie, N., *Class, Structure and Knowledge* (Oxford, Blackwell, 1980).
Ackerman, B., *Social Justice in the Liberal State* (New Haven, Yale University Press, 1980).
Adams, I., 'Can History Be Finished?', *Politics*, 1991, vol. 11, no. 2.
Althusser, L., *Essays in Self Criticism*, trans. G. Lock (London, New Left Books, 1976).
Althusser, L., *For Marx*, trans. B. Brewster (London, Verso, 1982).
Althusser, L., *Lenin and Philosophy*, trans. B. Brewster (New York, Monthly Review Press, 1971).
Althusser, L., *Reading Capital* (with Etienne Balibar), trans. B. Brewster, (London, Verso, 1983).
Aquinas, St Thomas, *Summa Contra Gentiles*, in A. Pegis (ed.), *Basic Writings of St. Thomas Aquinas*, 2 vols (New York, Random House, 1945).
Aquinas, St Thomas, *Summa Theologiae*, in A. Pegis (ed.), *Basic Writings of Saint Thomas Aquinas*, 2 vols (New York, Random House, 1945).
Arblaster, A., 'Ideology and Intellectuals', in R. Benewick *et al.* (eds), *Knowledge and Belief in Politics* (London, George Allen and Unwin, 1973).
Arendt, H., *The Human Condition* (Chicago, University of Chicago Press, 1959).
Aron, R., *Main Currents in Sociological Thought*, vol. 2 (Harmondsworth, Penguin, 1970).
Ashcraft, R., 'Political Theory and the Problem of Ideology', *The Journal of Politics*, 1980, vol. 42, no. 3.
Ashcraft, R., 'Whose Problem? Whose Ideology? A Reply to my Critics', *The Journal of Politics*, 1980, vol. 42, no. 3.
Ashcraft, R.,'Rethinking the Nature of Political Theory: A Single Handed Defence of a Dialogue', *The Journal of Politics*, 1982, vol. 44, no. 2.
Ashcraft. R., 'On the Problem of Methodology and the Nature of Political Theory', *Political Theory*, 1975, vol. 3, no. 1.
Augustine, St, *Concerning The City of God Against the Pagans*, trans. H. Bettenson, ed. D. Knowles (Harmondsworth, Penguin, 1972).
Austin, J.L., *How to Do Things With Words*, ed. J.O. Urmson (Oxford, Oxford University Press, 1962).
Ayer, A.J., *Language, Truth and Logic*, second edition (Harmondsworth, Penguin, 1971).
Ayer, A.J., 'The Vienna Circle', in A.J. Ayer *et al.*, *The Revolution in Philosophy* (London, Macmillan, 1956).
Bachrach, P. and Baratz, M., *Power and Poverty: Theory and Practice* (Oxford, Oxford University Press, 1970).
Bachrach, P. and Baratz, M., 'The Two Faces of Power', *American Political Science Review*, 1962, vol. 56.

Bachrach, P. and Baratz, M., 'Decisions and Nondecisions: An Analytic Framework', *American Political Science Review*, 1963, vol. 57.
Bacon, F., *Novum Organum*, in F. Bacon, *Essays Civil and Moral, Advancement of Learning, and Novum Organum*, ed. G. Bettany (London, Ward, Lock and Bowden, 1894).
Bacon, F., *The Advancement of Learning*, ed. A. Johnston (Oxford, Clarendon Press, 1974).
Barnes, B., *Interests and the Growth of Knowledge* (London, Routledge and Kegan Paul, 1977).
Barnes, B., *Scientific Knowledge and Sociological Theory* (London, Routledge and Kegan Paul, 1974).
Barnes, B. and Bloor, D., 'Relativism, Rationalism and the Sociology of Knowledge', in M. Hollis and S. Lukes (eds), *Rationality and Relativism* (Oxford, Blackwell, 1982).
Barth, H., *Truth and Ideology* (Los Angeles, University of California Press, 1977).
Beiner, R., *Political Judgement* (London, Methuen, 1983).
Beiner, R., review of P. Steinberger, *The Concept of Political Judgment*, in *Political Theory*, 1994, vol. 22, no. 4.
Bell, D., 'The End of Ideology Revisited', parts 1 and 2, *Government and Opposition*, 1988, vol. 23, nos 2 and 3.
Bell, D., *The End of Ideology*, revised edition (New York, The Free Press, 1961).
Benton, T., 'Realism and Social Science: Some Comments on Roy Bhaskar's "The Possibility of Naturalism"', in R. Edgley and R. Osborne (eds), *Radical Philosophy Reader* (London, Verso, 1985).
Berki, R., 'The Belated Impact of Marxism', in J. Hayward and P. Norton (eds), *The Political Science of British Politics* (Brighton, Wheatsheaf, 1986).
Bernstein, R., *The New Constellation* (Cambridge, Polity, 1991).
Bhaskar, R., *A Realist Theory of Science*, second edition (Hassocks, Harvester, 1978).
Bhaskar, R., *The Possibility of Naturalism* (Brighton, Harvester, 1979).
Bhaskhar, R., *Reclaiming Reality* (London, Verso, 1989).
Bhaskhar, R., *Scientific Realism and Human Emancipation* (London, Verso, 1986).
Bloor, D., *Knowledge and Social Imagery* (London, Routledge and Kegan Paul, 1976).
Bourke, V., 'Natural Law, Thomism – And Professor Nielsen', *Natural Law Forum*, vol. 5, 1960.
Brandon, W., '"Fact" and "Value" in the Thought of Peter Winch: Linguistic Analysis Broaches Metaphysical Questions', *Political Theory*, 1982, vol. 10, no. 2.
Burke, E., *Reflections on the Revolution in France*, ed. C. O'Brien (Harmondsworth, Penguin, 1968).
Burns, T. (ed.), *After History: Francis Fukuyama and his Critics* (Rowman and Littlefield, Lanham, Maryfield, 1994).
Caney, S., 'Liberalism and Communitarianism: a Misconceived Debate', *Political Studies*, 1992, vol. 40, no. 2.
Carr, E.H., *What is History?* (London, Macmillan, 1961).

Coates, K. and Silburn, R., *Poverty: The Forgotten Englishmen* (Harmondsworth, Penguin, 1973).
Cobban, A., 'The Decline of Political Theory', *Political Science Quarterly*, 1953, vol. 63, no. 3.
Copleston, F., 'Philosophy and Ideology', in A. Parel (ed.), *Ideology, Philosophy and Politics* (Waterloo, Ontario, Wilfrid Laurier University Press, 1983).
Cox, R. ed., *Ideology, Politics and Political Theory* (Belmont, California, Wandsworth Publishing, 1969).
Dahl, R., 'The Behavioural Approach in Political Science: Epitaph for a Monument to a Successful Protest', *American Political Science Review*, 1961, vol. 55, no. 4.
Dahl, R., *Who Governs? Democracy and Power in an American City* (New Haven, Yale University Press, 1961).
Dahrendorf, R., *Essays in the Theory of Society* (London, Routledge and Kegan Paul, 1968).
Davidson, D., 'On the Very Idea of a Conceptual Scheme', in J. Rajchman and C. West (eds), *Post-Analytic Philosophy* (New York, Columbia University Press, 1985).
Douglass, R. B. and Marfin, G., 'The Political Role of Political Philosophy: A Reply to Richard Ashcraft', *The Journal of Politics*, 1982, vol. 44, no. 2.
Doyal, L. and Gough, I., *A Theory of Human Need* (London, Macmillan, 1991).
Drucker, H., *The Political Uses of Ideology* (London, Macmillan, 1974).
Drury, S., *The Political Ideas of Leo Strauss* (London, Macmillan, 1988).
Durkheim, E., *Suicide*, trans. J. Spalding, ed. G. Simpson (London, Routledge and Kegan Paul, 1952).
Durkheim, E., *The Elementary Forms of Religious Life*, trans. J. Swain (London, Allen and Unwin, 1976).
Durkheim, E., *The Rules of Sociological Method*, trans. W. Halls, ed. S. Lukes (London, Macmillan, 1982).
Dworkin, R., *A Matter of Principle* (London, Duckworth, 1985).
Dworkin, R., *Taking Rights Seriously* (London, Duckworth, 1977).
Eagleton, T., *Ideology: An Introduction* (London, Verso, 1991).
Easton, D., 'The Current Meaning of Behaviouralism', in J. Charlesworth (ed.), *Contemporary Political Analysis* (New York, The Free Press, 1967).
Easton, D., *The Political System*, second edition (New York, Alfred Knopf, 1971).
Engels, F., *Anti-Duhring* (Peking, Foreign Languages Press, 1976).
Feuer, L., *Ideology and the Ideologists* (Oxford, Blackwell, 1975).
Feyerabend, P., *Against Method* (London, Verso, 1975).
Feyerabend, P., 'Consolations for the Specialist', in I. Lakatos and A. Musgrave (eds), *Criticism and the Growth of Knowledge* (Cambridge, Cambridge University Press, 1970).
Feyerabend, P., 'How to Defend Society Against Science', *Radical Philosophy*, 1978, no. 11.
Feyerabend, P., *Science in a Free Society* (London, New Left Books, 1978).
Finnis, J., 'Natural Law and Legal Reasoning', in R. George (ed.), *Natural Law Theory: Contemporary Essays* (Oxford, Clarendon Press, 1992).

Finnis, J., *Natural Law and Natural Rights* (Oxford, Clarendon Press, 1980).
Fukuyama, F., *The End of History and the Last Man* (London, Hamish Hamilton, 1992).
Fukuyama, F., 'The End of History?', *The National Interest,* 1989, no. 16.
Gallie, W., 'Essentially Contested Concepts', *Proceedings of the Aristotelian Society,* 1955–56, vol. LVI.
Gellner, E., *Cause and Meaning in the Social Sciences* (London, Routledge and Kegan Paul, 1973).
Gellner, E., *Relativism and the Social Sciences* (Cambridge, Cambridge University Press, 1985).
Gellner, E., *Words and Things* (Harmondsworth, Penguin, 1968).
Geras, N., *Literature of Revolution* (London, Verso, 1986).
Germino, D., *Beyond Ideology: The Revival of Political Theory* (Chicago, University of Chicago Press, reprint 1976).
Germino, D., 'Comment on Ashcraft's "Political Theory and the Problem of Ideology"', *The Journal of Politics,* 1980, vol. 42, no. 3.
Germino, D., *Machiavelli to Marx: Modern Western Political Thought* (Chicago, University of Chicago Press, 1972).
Giddens, A., 'Four Theses on Ideology', *Canadian Journal of Political and Social Theory,* 1983, vol. 7, nos 1–2.
Giddens, A., *New Rules of Sociological Method* (London, Hutchinson, 1976).
Goodwin, B., *Using Political Ideas,* third edition (Chichester, John Wiley, 1992).
Grisez, G., *Beyond the New Theism* (Notre Dame, University of Notre Dame Press, 1975).
Grisez, G., Boyle, J. and Finnis, J., 'Practical Principles, Moral Truth, and Ultimate Ends', *American Journal of Jurisprudence,* 1987, vol. 32.
Grisez, G., 'The First Principle of Practical Reason: A Commentary on the *Summa theologiae,* 1–2, Question 94, Article 2', *Natural Law Forum,* 1965, vol. 10..
Grisez, G., 'The Structures of Practical Reason', *The Thomist,* 1988, vol. 52.
Grisez, G., *The Way of the Lord Jesus,* vol. 1, *Christian Moral Principles* (Chicago, Franciscan Herald Press, 1983).
Gunnell, J., 'Relativism: The Return of the Repressed', *Political Theory,* 1993, vol. 21, no. 4.
Habermas, J., *On the Logic of the Social Sciences,* trans. S. Nicholson and J. Stark (Cambridge, Polity, 1988).
Hacker, A., *Political Theory: Philosophy, Ideology and Science* (New York, Macmillan, 1961).
Hallowell, J., *Main Currents in Modern Political Thought* (New York, University Press of America, reprint, 1984).
Hallowell, J., 'Politics and Ethics', *American Political Science Review,* 1944, vol. 38, no. 4.
Hayek, F., *The Constitution of Liberty* (London, Routledge and Kegan Paul, 1960).
Hempel, C., *Aspects of Scientific Explanation and Other Essays in the Philosophy of Science* (New York, The Free Press, 1965).
Hesse, M., *Revolutions and Reconstructions in the Philosophy of Science* (Brighton, Harvester, 1980).

Hittinger, R., 'Varieties of Minimalist Natural Law Theory', *American Journal of Jurisprudence*, 1989, vol. 34.
Hollis, M., 'The Limits of Irrationality', in B. Wilson (ed.), *Rationality* (Oxford, Blackwell, 1970).
Hollis, M., 'Reason and Ritual', in B. Wilson (ed.), *Rationality* (Oxford, Blackwell, 1970).
Hollis, M., 'The Social Destruction of Reality', in M. Hollis and S. Lukes (eds), *Rationality and Relativism* (Oxford, Blackwell, 1982).
Holmes, S., *The Anatomy of Antiliberalism* (Cambridge, Massachusetts, Harvard University Press, 1993).
Hudson, W.D. (ed.), *The Is–Ought Question* (London, Macmillan, 1969).
Hume, D., *A Treatise of Human Nature*, second edition, ed. L.A. Selby-Bigge, revised by P.H. Nidditch (Oxford, Oxford University Press, 1978).
Jones, G.S., 'The Marxism of the Early Lukács', in New Left Review (eds), *Western Marxism* (London, Verso, 1978).
Jouvenel, B., *Sovereignty*, trans. J. Huntingdon (Cambridge, Cambridge University Press, 1957).
Kavanagh, D., *Political Science and Political Behaviour* (London, George Allen and Unwin, 1983).
Kelsen, H., 'Absolutism and Relativism in Philosophy and Politics,' *American Political Science Review*, 1948, vol. 42.
Kennedy, E., '"Ideology" from Destutt de Tracy to Marx', *Journal of the History of Ideas*, 1979, vol. XL, no. 3.
Kirkpatrick, E., 'From Past to Present', in D. Freeman (ed.), *Foundation of Political Science* (New York, The Free Press, 1977).
Koertge, N., 'Beyond Cultural Relativism', in G. Currie and A. Musgrave (eds), *Popper and the Human Sciences* (Dordrecht, Martinus Nijhoff, 1985).
Kolakowski, L., *Main Currents of Marxism*, vol. 3 (Oxford, Oxford University Press, 1978).
Kuhn, T., 'Logic of Discovery or Psychology of Research', in I. Lakatos and A. Musgrave (eds), *Criticism and the Growth of Knowledge* (Cambridge, Cambridge University Press, 1970).
Kuhn, T., 'Reflections on my Critics', in I. Lakatos and A. Musgrave (eds), *Criticism and the Growth of Knowledge* (Cambridge, Cambridge University Press, 1970).
Kuhn, T., *The Essential Tension* (Chicago, University of Chicago Press, 1977).
Kuhn, T., *The Structure of Scientific Revolutions*, second edition (Chicago, University of Chicago Press, 1970).
Lakatos, I., 'Falsification and the Methododology of Scientific research Programmes', in I. Lakatos and A. Musgrave (eds), *Criticism and the Growth of Knowledge* (Cambridge, Cambridge University Press, 1970).
Lakatos, I., *The Methodology of Scientific Research Programmes, Philosophical Papers*, vol. 1, ed. J. Worrall and G. Curie (Cambridge, Cambridge University Press, 1978).
Larrain, J., *Marxism and Ideology* (London, Macmillan, 1983).
Larrain, J., *The Concept of Ideology* (London, Hutchinson, 1979).
Laslett , P. and Runciman W.G. (eds), *Philosophy, Politics and Society*, Third Series (Oxford, Blackwell, 1967).

Laslett, P. and Runciman, W.G. (eds), *Philosophy, Politics and Society*, Second Series (Oxford, Blackwell, 1962).
Laslett, P. (ed.), *Philosophy, Politics and Society*, First Series (Oxford, Blackwell 1956).
Lasswell, H. and Kaplan, M., *Power and Society* (New Haven, Yale University Press, 1950).
Lecourt, D., *Proletarian Science? The Case of Lysenko* (London, New Left Books, 1977).
Lenin, V.I., *What is to be Done?*, ed. S. Utechin (Oxford, Clarendon Press, 1963).
Lichtheim, G., 'The Concept of Ideology', *History and Theory*, 1965, vol. IV, no. 2.
Lipset, S.M., *Political Man* (1960), updated and expanded edition (London, Heinemann, 1983).
Louch, A.R., 'The Very Idea of a Social Science', *Inquiry*, 1963, vol. 6, no. 4.
Lukács, G., *History and Class Consciousness*, trans. R. Livingstone (London, Merlin, 1971).
Lukes, S., 'On the Social Determination of Truth', in M. Gibbons (ed.), *Interpreting Politics* (Oxford, Blackwell, 1987).
Lukes, S., *Power: A Radical View* (London, Macmillan, 1974).
Lukes, S., 'Relativism in its Place', in M. Hollis and S. Lukes (eds), *Rationality and Relativism* (Oxford, Blackwell, 1982).
Lukes, S., 'Relativism: Cognitive and Moral', *Proceedings of the Aristotelian Society*, 1974, supplementary vol. XLVIII.
Lukes, S., 'Some Problems about Rationality', in B. Wilson (ed.), *Rationality* (Oxford, Blackwell, 1970).
Lukes, S., 'The Critical Theory Trip', *Political Studies*, 1977, vol. 25, no. 3.
Lyotard, J.-F., *The Postmodern Condition: A Report on Knowledge* (Manchester, Manchester University Press, 1984).
Macdonald, M., 'The Language of Political Theory', in A. Flew (ed.), *Logic and Language*, First Series (Oxford, Blackwell, 1951).
Machiavelli, N., *The Prince*, trans. G. Bull (Harmondsworth, Penguin, 1961).
MacIntyre, A., *Against the Self Images of the Age* (London, Duckworth, 1971).
MacIntyre, A., 'Is Understanding Religion Compatible with Believing?', in B. Wilson (ed.), *Rationality* (Oxford, Blackwell, 1970).
MacIntyre, A., 'The Idea of a Social Science', in B. Wilson (ed.), *Rationality* (Oxford, Blackwell, 1970).
Macpherson, C.B., *Democratic Theory: Essays in Retrieval* (Oxford, Clarendon Press, 1973).
Macpherson, C.B., 'Hobbes's Bourgeois Man', in K. Brown (ed.), *Hobbes Studies* (Oxford, Blackwell, 1965).
Macpherson, C.B., 'Needs and Wants: An Ontological or Historical Problem?', in R. Fitzgerald (ed.), *Human Needs and Politics* (Rushcutters Bay, NSW, Pergamon, 1977).
Macpherson, C.B., *The Rise and Fall of Economic Justice* (Oxford, Oxford University Press, 1985).
Magee, B. (ed.), *Men of Ideas* (Oxford, Oxford University Press, 1982).
Mandelbaum, M., 'Subjective, Objective and Conceptual Relativisms', in

J. Meiland and M. Krausz (eds), *Relativism Cognitive and Moral* (Notre Dame, University of Notre Dame Press, 1982).

Mannheim, K., *Essays on the Sociology of Knowledge*, ed. P. Kecskemeti (London, Routledge and Kegan Paul, 1972).

Mannheim, K., *Ideology and Utopia*, trans. E. Shils (London, Routledge and Kegan Paul, reprint 1979).

Marcuse, H., *One Dimensional Man* (London, Routledge and Kegan Paul, 1964).

Maritain, J., *Man and the State* (Chicago, University of Chicago Press, 1951).

Maritain, J., *The Range of Reason* (London, Geoffrey Bles, 1953).

Martin, W.O., *Metaphysics and Ideology* (Milwaukee, Marquette University Press, 1959).

Marx, K. and Engels, F., *Marx/Engels Selected Correspondence*, ed. S. Ryazanskaya, third revised edition (Moscow, Progress Publishers, 1975).

Marx, K. and Engels, F., *The German Ideology*, in K. Marx, *Early Political Writings*, ed. J. O'Malley (Cambridge, Cambridge University Press, 1994).

Marx, K., *A Contribution to the Critique of Hegel's Philosophy of Right: Introduction*, in K. Marx, *Early Political Writings*, ed. J. O'Malley (Cambridge, Cambridge University Press, 1994).

Marx, K., *A Contribution to the Critique of Political Economy*, in Karl Marx, *Early Writings*, ed. L. Colletti (Harmondsworth, Penguin, reprint 1992).

Marx, K., *Capital*, vol. I, trans. and ed. D. Torr (London, George Allen and Unwin, 1957).

Marx, K., *Capital*, vol. III, trans. D. Fernbach (Harmondsworth, Penguin, 1981).

Marx, K., *Theses on Feuerbach*, in K. Marx, *Early Political Writings*, ed. J. O'Malley (Cambridge, Cambridge University Press, 1994).

Masterman, M., 'The Nature of a Paradigm', in I. Lakatos and A. Musgrave (eds), *Criticism and the Growth of Knowledge* (Cambridge, Cambridge University Press, 1970).

Mattick, P., *Social Knowledge* (London, Hutchinson, 1986).

McCarney, J., 'Reflections of Fukuyama', *New Left Review*, 1994, no. 202.

McCarney, J., *The Real World of Ideology* (Brighton, Harvester, 1980).

McCoy, C. and Playford, J. (eds), *Apolitical Politics: A Critique of Behavioralism* (New York, Thomas Y. Crowell, 1967).

McDonough, R., 'Ideology as False Consciousness: Lukács', in Centre for Contemporary Cultural Studies (eds), *On Ideology* (London, Hutchinson, 1978).

McInerny, R., *Ethica Thomistica* (Washington, DC, The Catholic University of America Press, 1982).

McInerny, R., 'Ethics', in N. Kretzman and E. Stump (eds), *The Cambridge Companion to Aquinas* (Cambridge, Cambridge University Press, 1993).

McLellan, D., *Ideology* (Milton Keynes, Open University Press, 1986).

Medvedev, Z., *The Rise and Fall of T.D. Lysenko* (New York, Doubleday, 1968).

Mepham, J. and Ruben, D.-H. (eds), *Issues in Marxist Philosophy*, vol. 3 (Brighton, Harvester, 1974).

Mészáros, I., *Philosophy, Ideology and Social Science* (Brighton, Wheatsheaf, 1986).
Midgley, E.B.F., 'Concerning the Modernist Subversion of Political Philosophy', *The New Scholasticism*, 1979, vol. 53, no. 2.
Midgley, E.B.F., *The Ideology of Max Weber* (Aldershot, Gower, 1983).
Midgley, E.B.F., *The Natural Law Tradition and the Theory of International Relations* (London, Elek, 1975).
Mill, J.S., *Collected Works*, vol. 10, ed. J.M. Robson (Toronto, University of Toronto Press, 1969).
Mills, C.W., 'Letter to the New Left', in C. Waxman (ed.), *The End of Ideology Debate* (New York, Simon and Schuster, 1968).
Minogue, K., 'Method in Intellectual History: Quentin Skinner's *Foundations*', in Tully, J. (ed.), *Meaning and Context* (Cambridge, Polity, 1988).
Morrice, D., 'C.B. Macpherson's Critique of Liberal Democracy and Capitalism', *Political Studies*, 1994, vol. 42, no. 4, pp. 646–61.
Nederman, C., 'Quentin Skinner's State: Historical Method and Traditions of Discourse', *Canadian Journal of Political Science*, 1985, vol. XVIII, no. 2.
Nelson, J., 'Ashcraft's Problem of Ideology', *The Journal of Politics*, 1980, vol. 42, no. 3.
Newton-Smith, W., *The Rationality of Science* (London, Routledge and Kegan Paul, 1981).
Nielsen, K., 'An Examination of the Thomistic Theory of Natural Moral Law', *Natural Law Forum*, 1959, vol. 4.
Nozick, R., *Anarchy, State and Utopia* (Oxford, Blackwell, 1974).
O'Connor, D.J., *Aquinas and Natural Law* (London, Macmillan, 1967).
Oakeshott, M., *Experience and Its Modes* (Cambridge, Cambridge University Press, reprint 1985).
Oakeshott, M., *On Human Conduct* (Oxford, Clarendon Press, 1975).
Oakeshott, M., *Rationalism in Politics* (London, Methuen, reprint 1981).
Oppenheim, F., 'Relativism, Absolutism, and Democracy', *American Political Science Review*, 1950, vol. 44.
Outhwaite, W., *Understanding Social Life: The Method Called Verstehen* (London, George Allen and Unwin, 1975).
Owens, J., 'Ideology and Aquinas', in V. Brezik (ed.), *Thomistic Papers 1* (Houston, Texas, Center for Thomistic Studies, University of St Thomas, 1984).
Parekh, B., *Contemporary Political Thinkers* (Oxford, Martin Robinson, 1982).
Parekh, B., 'Social and Political Thought and the Problem of Ideology', in R. Benewick *et al.* (eds), *Knowledge and Belief in Politics* (London, George Allen and Unwin, 1973).
Pareto, V., *Sociological Writings*, trans. D. Mirfin, ed. S. Finer (Oxford, Blackwell, 1976).
Plamenatz, J., *Ideology* (London, Macmillan, 1970).
Plamenatz, J., *Man and Society*, vol. 1, revised edition (London, Longman, 1992).
Plato, *Republic*, trans. P. Shorley, in Plato, *Collected Dialogues*, ed. E. Hamilton and H. Cairns (Princeton, Princeton University Press, 1980).
Polsby, N., *Community Power and Political Theory* (New Haven, Yale University Press, 1963).

Popper, K., *Conjectures and Refutations*, fourth edition (London, Routledge and Kegan Paul, reprint 1981).
Popper, K., *Objective Knowledge*, revised edition (Oxford, Clarendon Press, 1979).
Popper, K., 'On Reason and the Open Society', *Encounter*, May 1972.
Popper, K., 'Replies to my Critics', in P. Schlipp (ed.), *The Philosophy of Karl Popper* (La Salle, Illinois, Open Court, 1974).
Popper, K., *The Logic of Scientific Discovery*, eleventh impression, revised (London, Hutchinson, 1983).
Popper, K., *The Open Society and its Enemies*, vol. 1, fourth edition (London, Routledge and Kegan Paul, 1962).
Popper, K., *The Open Society and its Enemies*, vol. 2, fifth edition revised (London, Routledge and Kegan Paul, 1977).
Popper, K., *The Poverty of Historicism*, second edition (London, Routledge and Kegan Paul, 1961).
Popper, K., *Unended Quest*, new edition with Postscript (London, Routledge, 1992).
Quinton, A. (ed.), *Political Philosophy* (Oxford, Oxford University Press, 1967).
Quinton, A., *Francis Bacon* (Oxford, Oxford University Press, 1980).
Rawls, J., *A Theory of Justice* (Cambridge, Massachusetts, Harvard University Press, 1971).
Rawls, J., 'Justice as Fairness', *The Philosophical Review*, 1958, vol. 57.
Rawls, J., *Political Liberalism* (New York, Columbia University Press, 1993).
Rorty, R., *Contingency, Irony, and Solidarity* (Cambridge, Cambridge University Press, 1989).
Rorty, R., *Essays on Heidegger and Others, Philosophical Papers, Volume 2* (Cambridge, Cambridge University Press, 1991).
Rorty, R., 'Feminism and Pragmatism', *Radical Philosophy*, 1991, no. 59.
Rorty, R., 'Human Rights, Rationality and Sentimentality', in S. Shute and S. Hurley (eds), *On Human Rights: The Oxford Amnesty Lectures 1993* (New York, Basic Books, 1993).
Rorty, R., *Objectivity, Relativism and Truth, Philosophical Papers Volume 1* (Cambridge, Cambridge University Press, 1991).
Rorty, R., 'Thugs and Theorists: A Reply to Bernstein', *Political Theory*, 1987, vol. 15, no. 4.
Rosa, H., 'Goods and Life Forms: Relativism in Charles Taylor's Political Philosophy', *Radical Philosophy*, May/June 1995, no. 71.
Russell, B., *Philosophy and Politics* (London, National Book League/Cambridge University Press, 1947).
Ryan, A. (ed.), *After the End of History* (London, Collins and Brown, 1992).
Ryan, A., '"Normal" Science or Political Ideology', in P. Laslett *et al.* (eds), *Philosophy, Politics and Society*, Fourth Series (Oxford, Basil Blackwell, 1972).
Ryan, A., 'The Ideologist of American Liberalism', *The Times Higher Education Supplement*, 8 October 1982.
Ryan, A., *The Philosophy of the Social Sciences* (London, Macmillan, 1970).
Seliger, M., *Ideology and Politics* (London, George Allen and Unwin, 1976).
Shils, E., 'End of Ideology', in C. Waxman (ed.), *The End of Ideology Debate* (New York, Simon and Schuster, 1968).

Simon, Y., *The Tradition of Natural Law*, ed. V. Kuic (New York, Fordham University Press, 1965).
Skinner, Q., '"Social Meaning" and the Explanation of Social Action', in J. Tully (ed.), *Meaning and Context* (Cambridge, Polity, 1988).
Skinner, Q., 'Meaning and Understanding in the History of Ideas', in J. Tully (ed.), *Meaning and Context* (Cambridge, Polity, 1988).
Skinner, Q., 'Motives, Intentions and the Interpretation of Texts', in J. Tully (ed.), *Meaning and Context* (Cambridge, Polity, 1988).
Skinner, Q., 'Some Problems in the Analysis of Political Thought and Action', in J. Tully (ed.), *Meaning and Context* (Cambridge, Polity, 1988).
Skinner, Q., *The Foundations of Modern Political Thought*, 2 vols (Cambridge, Cambridge University Press, 1978).
Smith, A., *An Inquiry into the Nature and Causes of the Wealth of Nations*, ed. E. Cannan (New York, Random House, 1937).
Soper, K., 'A Theory of Human Need', *New Left Review*, January/February 1993, no. 197.
Stankiewicz, W.J., *Aspects of Political Theory: Classical Concepts in an Age of Relativism* (London, Cassell and Collier Macmillan, 1976).
Strauss, L., *Liberalism Ancient and Modern* (Ithaca, Cornell University Press, reprint 1989).
Strauss, L., *Natural Right and History* (Chicago, University of Chicago Press, 1953).
Strauss, L., 'On a New Interpretation of Plato's Political Philosophy', *Social Research*, 1946, vol. 13, no. 3.
Strauss, L., *Persecution and the Art of Writing* (Glencoe, Illinois, The Free Press, 1952).
Strauss, L., *The City and Man* (Chicago, University of Chicago Press, 1978).
Strauss, L., 'The Crisis of Our Time', in H. Spaeth (ed.), *The Predicament of Modern Politics* (Detroit, University of Detroit Press, 1964).
Strauss, L., *The Rebirth of Classical Political Rationalism* (Chicago, University of Chicago Press, 1989).
Strauss, L., *What is Political Philosophy?* (Chicago, University of Chicago Press, reprint 1988).
Strawbridge, S., 'Althusser's Theory of Ideology and Durkheim's Account of Religion: An Examination of Some Striking Parallels', *Sociological Review*, 1982, vol. 30, no. 1.
Taylor, C., *Philosophy and the Human Sciences, Philosophical Papers*, vol. 2, (Cambridge, Cambridge University Press, 1985).
Trigg, R., *Reality at Risk* (Hemel Hempstead, Harvester/Wheatsheaf, 1980).
Trigg, R., *Reason and Commitment* (Cambridge, Cambridge University Press, 1973).
Trigg, R., *Understanding Social Science* (Oxford, Blackwell, 1985).
Tully, J. (ed.), *Meaning and Context: Quentin Skinner and His Critics* (Cambridge, Polity, 1988).
Veatch, H., 'Natural Law and the "Is"–"Ought" Question', *The Catholic Lawyer*, 1981, vol. 26.
Voegelin, E., *Order and History* (Baton Rouge, Louisiana State University Press, from 1956).
Voegelin, E., *The New Science of Politics* (Chicago, University of Chicago Press, 1952).

Walzer, M., 'Philosophy and Democracy', *Political Theory*, 1981, vol. 9, no. 3.
Walzer, M., *Interpretation and Social Criticism* (Cambridge, Mass., Harvard University Press, 1987).
Walzer, M., *Spheres of Justice* (Oxford, Basil Blackwell, 1985).
Walzer, M., *The Company of Critics* (London, Peter Halban, 1988).
Weber, M., *From Max Weber*, trans. and ed. H. Gerth and C. Wright Mills (London, Routledge and Kegan Paul, reprint 1970).
Weber, M., *The Methodology of the Social Sciences*, trans. and ed. E. Shils and H. Finch (New York, The Free Press, reprint 1968).
Weinreb, L., *Natural Law and Justice* (Cambridge, Massachusetts, Harvard University Press, 1987).
Weldon, T.D., *The Vocabulary of Politics* (Harmondsworth, Penguin, 1953).
White, S., *Political Theory and Postmodernism* (Cambridge, Cambridge University Press, 1991).
Wild, J., *Plato's Modern Enemies and the Theory of Natural Law* (Chicago, University of Chicago Press, 1953).
Williams, B., *Ethics and the Limits of Philosophy* (London, Collins/Fontana Press, 1985).
Williams, B., *Morality: An Introduction to Ethics* (Harmondsworth, Penguin, 1973).
Williams, B., 'The Truth in Relativism', *Proceedings of the Aristotelian Society*, 1974–75, new series, vol. LXXV.
Winch, P., 'Nature and Convention', *Proceedings of the Aristotelian Society*, 1959–60, vol. 60.
Winch, P., *The Idea of a Social Science and its Relation to Philosophy*, second edition, (London, Routledge, 1990).
Winch, P., *Trying to Make Sense* (Oxford, Blackwell, 1987).
Winch, P., 'Understanding a Primitive Society', in B. Wilson (ed.), *Rationality* (Oxford, Blackwell, 1970).

Index